Property

GLORIA A. ALUISE

Attorney at Law

KEYED TO THE EIGHTH EDITION OF THE DUKEMINIER CASEBOOK

GILBERT

Legalines is a trademark registered in the U.S. Patent and Trademark Office.

Copyright © 2011 by Thomson/West
© 2015 LEG, Inc. d/b/a West Academic
        444 Cedar Street, Suite 700
        St. Paul, MN 55101
        1-877-888-1330

Printed in the United States of America

ISBN: 978-1-62810-686-2

Summary of Contents

Table of Contents

Property

KEYED TO THE EIGHTH EDITION
OF THE DUKEMINIER CASEBOOK

Part I
An Introduction to Some Fundamentals

A. Introduction

1. Acquisition

Property may be acquired in numerous ways, but the most common method is some form of voluntary transfer, such as a gift, a bequest, or a purchase. While each of these is an important subject and is examined in depth at appropriate places later on, the very concept of ownership may be illustrated by the means of acquiring property other than by voluntary transfer. In many cases, ownership is acquired by acquiring possession. The old axiom that possession is nine-tenths of the law has some legal basis. The law protects possessors. Rationales for this include preservation of law and order, rewarding those who possess and maintain property, etc. However, it is important to realize first that possession and ownership are not the same thing.

2. Possession

The legal concept of possession includes not only physical custody of something, for example, holding a pencil in one's hand, but also possession of things not in one's immediate physical custody. An example of this would be a lakeside lot in the mountains that is used by the owner as a weekend retreat. Indeed, people may be in possession of something and not know it, such as a cache of money hidden for years in the walls of a recently purchased old house.

a. Legal Fact vs. Legal Conclusion

"Possession" is often used in one of two contexts. It may refer to a legal fact, such as who was in possession of the automobile at the time of the accident. Or "possession" may refer to a legal conclusion of the court (or other legal body authorized to make legal conclusions), such as whether the owner of Blackacre lost title of the land due to Interloper's adverse possession of the land for seven years. In this last example, if Interloper has not acquired title to the land by adverse possession, Owner is still in possession even though he has not seen the land in 50 years.

b. Ownership Is Not Necessarily Possession

For instance, once a tenant leases an apartment, absent contractual provisions to the contrary, her landlord may not come on the premises without the lessee's permission. Since the lessee has legal possession of the apartment, she could even have her landlord arrested for trespass if the landlord did not leave when asked to do so.

c. The Legal Fiction of Constructive Possession

A person who is not in actual possession of property is in "constructive possession" of property if the law treats him the same as an actual possessor. This is a legal fiction that allows courts to achieve equitable results. For example, if a grantor gives a deed to a third party with instructions not to deliver the deed to the grantee until the grantor's death, depending on the facts (such as whether the third party was in the grantor's control or whether the third party was a neutral party), courts may find that the grantor was still in constructive possession of the deed.

B. First in Time: Acquisition by Discovery, Capture, and Creation

1. Acquisition by Discovery

Property rights exist because they are recognized by the government under whose dominion the rights are asserted. The source of this dominion is frequently overlooked. Ultimately, a property owner's chain of title reaches back to the sovereign. In the United States, dominion is often based on the concept of discovery. In reality, conquest is probably a more realistic concept to explain the basis for property rights.

a. Native American Rights to Property

Johnson v. M'Intosh
21 U.S. (8 Wheat.) 543 (1823).

Facts. M'Intosh (D) owned land in Illinois that he acquired under a grant from the United States. Johnson (P) had purchased the same land from the Piankeshaw Indians. P brought an ejectment action. The district court granted judgment for D and P appeals.

Issue. May the courts of the United States recognize a title to real property obtained under a grant made by an Indian tribe?

Held. No. Judgment affirmed.

♦ When the American continent was discovered by the European nations, each of those nations made claims to the land discovered. The nations agreed that discovery would give title to the discovering nation. The discovering nation also acquired the exclusive rights to regulate its relationship with the Indians. Thus, the Europeans claimed exclusive title, subject only to the right of occupancy in the Indians.

♦ After the revolution, the United States obtained by treaty all the rights to realty that Great Britain previously had. The United States also acquired land from Spain. In these cases, the United States followed the practice of the European nations and claimed the right by discovery.

♦ Discovery gives an exclusive right to extinguish the Indians' right of occupancy either by purchase or by conquest. Normally, title by conquest is limited by humanitarian considerations, so that the conquered people are assimilated into the society of the victorious nation. Because they are fierce savages, the Indians are not susceptible to becoming part of society. The only alternatives are to abandon the land or enforce the claims of the United States by force.

♦ Consequently, the Indians are merely occupants. Their possession may be protected in peace, but they cannot transfer absolute title to others. The courts of the United States cannot recognize title based on a grant by the Indians.

---

2. Acquisition by Capture

At common law, in an age when many people had to hunt to survive (either needing the animals for food or protecting themselves or their crops from the animals), a fairly involved set of rules evolved in determining who had possession of the wild animal. Basically, wild animals (animals *ferae naturae*) were possessed (the old term was "occupied") only when actually captured. For instance, if a trap was involved, the trap door had to be actually shut before the trapper possessed the animal. A similar approach was applied to natural resources.

a. Hunting Wild Animals

Pierson v. Post
2 Am. Dec. 264 (N.Y. 1805).

Facts. Post (P) and his hounds found a fox on a wild, uninhabited stretch of land. As P was hunting and chasing the fox, Pierson (D), knowing that P was pursuing the fox, killed it and carried it off. P brought a suit of trespass on the case against D for taking the fox. P won. D appeals.

Issue. Does the pursuer of a wild animal acquire a right to the animal?

Held. No. Judgment reversed.

♦ A fox is an animal *ferae naturae* and a property right in such an animal is acquired by "occupancy" only.

♦ Authorities agree that mere pursuit of a wild animal does not vest any rights to the animal, even if the animal is wounded by the pursuer (in other words, "occupancy" equals actual corporal possession).

♦ The best approach is to treat pursuit alone as insufficient to constitute occupancy. However, the mortal wounding of a beast, or the trapping of a beast, does give possession to the person who so apprehends the beast.

♦ To allow possession based upon the mere sight or pursuit of wild animals would produce numerous arguments and litigation.

Dissent. The death of foxes is in the public interest. This court's decision should be made with a view to the greatest encouragement of the destruction of these animals. I favor the rationale that wild animals may be acquired without having to touch them, provided the pursuer is within reach, or has a reasonable prospect of taking (such as in tins case). Thus, the trial court should be affirmed.

---

b. No Appropriation by Chance Finder of Dead Whale

Ghen v. Rich
8 F. 159 (Mass. 1881).

Facts. The libellant in Provincetown shot and killed a finback whale, which immediately sank and was carried away by the tide. Ellis found the whale 17 miles from where it was killed and instead of sending word to Provincetown, as was the custom or usage in the trade, he advertised for the whale's sale and sold it to the respondent. The respondent sold the blubber and tried the oil. The libellant heard that the whale had been found and sent a boat to claim it. Neither Ellis nor the respondent knew the whale had been killed by the libellant, but if they had wished, they might have known it had been killed by a bomb-lance, each of which has an identifying mark.

Issue. Did the libellant have title to the whale?

Held. Yes.

♦ The usage on Cape Cod for many years has been that a whale killed and anchored and left with marks of appropriation under the circumstances described above becomes the property of its captors.

♦ Other cases have held that a whale is *ferae naturae* and firm and complete possession by the taker must be established before it becomes property.

♦ The custom in the Arctic that "the iron holds the whale" was held to be valid. It has also been held that "usage for the first iron, whether attached to the boat or not, to hold the whale was fully established," and although local usages should not set aside general maritime law, this objection does not apply to a custom that embraces an industry.

Comment. In admiralty law, a libel is the counterpart to a lawsuit and the libellant the counterpart to a plaintiff.

---

c. Luring Wild Animals to One's Property

Keeble v. Hickeringill
103 Eng. Rep. 1127 (Q.B. 1707).

Facts. Keeble (P) owned land that included a pond. P prepared and installed decoys, nets, and other equipment that he used to lure and catch wildfowl. Hickeringill (D) on three occasions went to P's pond and discharged guns to scare away the wildfowl. D succeeded and P sued for damages. D appeals from a verdict for P.

Issue. Does a landowner have a right to attract wildfowl to his property unimpeded by the direct interference of another aimed solely at keeping the wildfowl away?

Held. Yes. Judgment affirmed.

♦ P's conduct was lawful. As the landowner, he may use the pond for his trade of attracting, catching, and using the wildfowl. One who hinders another in his trade in a violent or malicious manner is liable for damages.

♦ This case is not one where D was setting up a competing pond, in which case P would have no action.

♦ Public policy favors protection of those who use their skill and industry to promote trade.

Comment. The court discussed a similar case in which a schoolmaster set up a new school, attracting students from an older school. The master of the older school had no action. However, if the defendant in that case had used his guns to intimidate the students and keep them from going to school, the schoolmaster would have had a cause of action.

---

3. Acquisition by Creation

a. Creation and Ownership

The notion that the person who creates property also owns it may seem elementary, but the scope of such ownership is not always clear. Apart from statutes that specifically protect creators' rights, such as copyright, trademark, and patent statutes, a creator's ownership rights may be uncertain. For example, an artist's painting or a secret food formula is susceptible to being copied, diminishing the value of the original.

b. Quasi Property

International News Service v. Associated Press
248 U.S. 215 (1918).

Facts. The Associated Press (P) and the International News Service (D) are newsgathering and distributing competitors. Each has member or client newspapers to which it provides news regarding current events. P brought suit to restrain D from pirating P's news by: (i) bribing newspaper employees to provide D with P's news before publication so that D might telegraph or telephone the news to its publications; (ii) providing inducements to P's employees to violate its bylaws and provide P's news to D before publication; and (iii) copying news from P's bulletin boards or early editions and selling it to D's member publications. The district court granted a preliminary injunction against the first two practices, but not the third, choosing to await the outcome of an appeal of this matter of first impression. The appeals court modified and sustained the injunction. The Supreme Court granted certiorari.

Issue. May D lawfully be restrained from appropriating news taken from newspapers or bulletins issued or published by P or its members for the purpose of selling it to D's clients?

Held. Yes. Appeals court affirmed.

♦ The first of the underlying questions in this matter involves whether there is property in news. While D's contention that unless P copyrights its news (which it does not because of the volume of information sent daily and because news is not within the operation of the copyright act), once the news is made public, the property right is lost as to the public is correct, there remains a property right between P and D. Between P and D the news is quasi property. News is the stock in trade of P and D, gathered, distributed, and sold through enterprise, skill, labor, and money as any other merchandise.

♦ While P's publication of the news makes it a common possession as to the public, it does not do the same between P and D. P does not intend to abandon its merchandise to the public for all intents and purposes. D's appropriation of P's news unreasonably interferes with P's right to make merchandise out of the news, to transmit the news for commercial profit. D interferes with P's business at the exact point where P reaps a profit for its labor; furthermore, D has an advantage in that it is not burdened with the expense of gathering the news. This is clearly unfair competition.

♦ Unlike ordinary unfair competition where a party sells its own goods as those of another party, here D is substituting misappropriation in the place of misrepresentation, and selling P's goods as its own.

———————

c. Originality

Feist Publications, Inc. v. Rural Telephone Service Co.

499 U.S. 340 (1991).

Facts. As a public utility, Rural Telephone Service Company, Inc. (P), is subject to a state regulation that requires all telephone companies operating in Kansas to issue annually an updated telephone directory. P's directory contains white and yellow pages, and is distributed free to its customers. P earns revenue by selling yellow pages advertisements. Feist Publications, Inc. (D), publishes area-wide telephone directories which cover a much larger geographical range than P's directory, reducing the need to call directory assistance or consult multiple directories. D's directory at issue here covers 11 different telephone service areas in 15 counties and contains 46,878 white pages listings; P's contains approximately 7,700 listings. Like P's directory, D's is distributed free of charge. Both companies compete for yellow pages advertising. Of the eleven telephone companies operating in northwest Kansas, only P refused D's offer to pay for the right to use its white pages listings. The absence of listings for P's territory would have left a huge omission in D's area-wide directory and made it less attractive to potential advertisers. In a decision that followed the instant case, the District Court determined that this was precisely the reason P refused to license its listings. The refusal was motivated by an unlawful purpose "to extend its monopoly in telephone service to a monopoly in yellow pages advertising." Unable to secure a license for P's white pages listings, D used them without P's consent. D used only the 4,935 listings that were in its covered area; some listings were changed to include street addresses, but 1,309 of the 46,878 listings in D's 1983 directory were identical to listings in P's 1982–1983 white pages. Four of these were fictitious listings that P had inserted into its directory to detect copying. P's suit for copyright infringement resulted in summary judgment in P's favor. The appeals court affirmed. We granted certiorari.

Issue. Does the copyright in P's directory protect the names, towns, and telephone numbers copied by D?

Held. No. Judgment reversed.

♦ Originality is the *sine qua non* of copyright. A work must be original to the author to qualify for copyright. Even a slight amount of creativity will be enough. Originality does not mean novelty; a work may closely resemble other works, yet may be original so long as the similarity is fortuitous, not the result of copying. No one can claim originality as to facts. The issue is between creation and discovery. To discover a fact is not to have created it.

♦ Factual compilations, however, may possess the requisite originality. Choices as to selection and arrangement of data for most effective use, made independently by a compiler of facts and involving a minimal degree of creativity, are sufficiently original to fall under the protection of the copyright laws. As a result, even a directory that contains no protectable written expression, just facts, meets the constitutional minimum for copyright protection if it features an original selection or arrangement.

♦ Copyright in a factual compilation is "thin." Protection may extend to those components of a work that are original to the author, but a later complier may use the facts contained in another person's publication to aid in preparing a competing work, so long as the competing work does not feature the same selection and arrangement.

♦ While most courts understood our decisions regarding originality, some misunderstood the statute, which specifically mentioned factual compilations, and erroneously inferred that directories were copyrightable *per se*. This resulted in the development of a new theory to justify the protection of factual compilations. Based on a notion that copyright was a reward for the hard work that went into the compiling of facts, the "sweat of the brow" or, in the alternative, "industrious collection" theory arose. Because the theory extended copyright protection in a compilation not only to the compiler's original contributions, *i.e.,* selection and arrangement, but to the facts themselves, it had a number of flaws. Independent creation was the only defense to infringement. "A subsequent compiler was 'not entitled to take one word of information previously published,' but rather had to 'independently wor[k] out the matter for himself, so as to arrive at the same result from the same common sources of information.'" The most fundamental axiom of copyright law, that no one may copyright facts or ideas, was abandoned. We made it clear that the statute did not permit the "sweat of the brow" approach in several cases, the best example of which is *International News Service v. Associated Press*, 248 U.S. 215 (1918), where we stated unambiguously that the 1909 Act conferred copyright protection only on those elements of a work that were original to the author.

♦ To establish infringement, two elements must be proven: (1) ownership of a valid copyright, and (2) copying of constituent elements of the work that are original. The first is not at issue here. The question is whether P has proved D copied anything original to P. The raw data is not original. In order to prevail, P has to show it selected, coordinated, or arranged uncopyrightable facts in an original way. We find there is no originality or creativity in P's white pages. P receives data provided by its subscribers and lists it alphabetically by surname, just as other white pages directories do.

♦ Because P's white pages lack the requisite originality, D's use of the listings cannot constitute infringement. This decision should not be construed as demeaning P's efforts in compiling its directory, but rather as making clear that copyright rewards originality, not effort.

---

d. Use of Unpublished Manuscript

Harper & Row Publishers, Inc. v. Nation Enterprises
471 U.S. 539 (1985).

Facts. In February 1977, after leaving the White House, former President Ford contracted with Harper & Row (Harper) and Reader's Digest (the Digest) (Ps), to publish his as yet unwritten memoirs. Never before published material concerning Watergate, the Nixon pardon and Ford's reflection on this period of history and the personalities involved was promised. In addition to the right to publish, Ps were to have the exclusive right to license prepublication excerpts, or "first serial rights." When the book was almost finished, Ps negotiated a prepublication licensing agreement with Time magazine. Time agreed to pay $25,000, $12,500 in advance and an additional $12,500 at publication, in exchange for the right to excerpt 7,500 words from Ford's account of the Nixon pardon. Time's issue was to appear one week before the book was made available to bookstores. Because exclusivity was an important consideration, Harper took action to maintain the confidentiality of the manuscript and Time held the right to renegotiate the second payment if the material was published before Time's release of the excerpts. Two to three weeks before the Time article was scheduled to be released, someone secretly took a copy of the Ford manuscript to Mr. Navasky, the editor of The Nation (D), a political commentary magazine. Navasky knew he was not authorized to have the manuscript and that it had to be returned fast so that his source would be protected. He quickly wrote a news story containing quotes, paraphrases and facts taken exclusively from the manuscript. He did no independent research and refrained from commentary or criticism. He wanted to "make news" by getting his piece out before the book. As a result of the article, Time canceled its article and refused to make its second payment. Ps sued. The district court found for Ps, holding that the manuscript was protected by copyright at the time of D's article. Although parts of the memoirs, such as historical facts and memoranda, were not *per se* copyrightable, the court held that it was "the totality of these facts and memoranda, collected together with Ford's reflections that made them of value to The Nation, [and] this . . . totality . . . is protected by the copyright laws." Ps were awarded actual damages of $12,500. On appeal, the circuit court reversed, holding that D's act was sanctioned as a "fair use" of the copyrighted material. We granted certiorari.

Issue. Was D's use of verbatim excerpts from the unpublished manuscript a fair use?

Held. No. Judgment reversed.

- D has admitted to lifting verbatim quotes of the author's original language totaling between 300 and 400 words which make up about 13% of its article. In using these quotes to lend authenticity to its account of the forthcoming memoirs, D effectively seized for itself the right of first publication, an important marketable subsidiary right.

- The defense of fair use, "a privilege in others than the owner of the copyright to use the copyrighted material in a reasonable manner without his consent," was included in the Copyright Act to codify the common-law doctrine. The statute required a case by case determination of whether a particular use is fair and notes four nonexclusive factors to be considered. The four factors are: (i) the purpose and character of the use; (ii) the nature of the copyrighted work; (iii) the substantiality of the portion used in relation to the copyrighted work as a whole; (iv) the effect on the potential market for or value of the copyrighted work. The codification was intended to restate the judicial doctrine, not to change it in any way.

- The Copyright Act recognized for the first time a distinct statutory right of first publication; this provision gives the copyright owner the right to control the first public distribution of an authorized copy of his work. This right, like the others, is expressly made subject to the fair use provision of the statute, which must always be tailored to the individual case.

- The drafters recognized from the start the importance of preserving the common law protection of undisseminated works until the author chooses to make them available. Only one person can be the first publisher. As Time's contract indicates, the commercial value of the right rests mainly in exclusivity. "Because the potential damage to the author from judicially enforced 'sharing' of the first publication right with unauthorized users of his manuscript is substantial, the balance of equities in evaluating such a claim of fair use inevitably shifts."

- Thus, we find that the unpublished nature of a work is "[a] key, though not necessarily determinative, factor" tending to negate a defense of fair use.

- We are not persuaded by D's argument that because an author has shown no interest in nonpublication, fair use may be made of a soon-to-be-published manuscript. The time surrounding a work's initiation, preparation, refining for dissemination is crucial. The benefit to an author and her audience of assuring authors the unencumbered time to develop ideas free from expropriation outweighs any short term "news value" that comes from premature publication. Not only is creative control involved, but an author's property interest in exploitation of prepublication rights, along with publicity and marketing are valuable.

- Under ordinary circumstances, the author's right to control the first public appearance of his undisseminated expression will outweigh a claim of fair use.

- D argues that the scope of the doctrine is broadened when the information published relates to matters of high public concern. This theory would destroy any expectation of copyright protection in the work of a public figure. Taking away the protection would remove the incentive to create or profit in financing memoirs; in addition, the public would be denied important historical information. We see no need to expand the doctrine of fair use to create a public figure exception.

- The first of the four factors Congress set forth to determine fair use is purpose and character of the use. Here, D's purpose was news reporting, an activity among those set out in the statute as one courts might regard as fair use under individual circumstances. Another factor that weighs against finding fair use is that a publication was commercial rather than nonprofit. D's argument that its purpose was not solely commercial, it misses the point. The issue is not whether the uses material for monetary gain, but whether she stands to profit from the use without paying the customary price.

- D's stated purpose was scooping the book and the Time article. This had not only the effect, but the intended purpose of overriding the copyright holder's commercially valuable right of first publication. The propriety of the defendant's conduct is also relevant to the "character" of the use. Fair use presupposes good faith and fair dealing.

♦ The second factor addresses the nature of the copyrighted work. The book, "A Time to Heal" may be characterized as an unpublished historical narrative or autobiography. The law generally recognizes a greater need to disseminate factual works than works of fiction or fantasy. D used not only isolated phrases like Ford's characterization of the White House tapes as the "smoking gun," but usurped subjective descriptions and portraits of public figures whose power lies in the author's individualized expression and which were the most expressive elements of the work. This exceeds what is necessary to disseminate the facts.

♦ The next consideration is the amount and substantiality of the portion used in relation to the copyrighted work as a whole. Here, while the words quoted were insubstantial, the district court found them to be "the heart of the book." The appeals court erred in overruling the district court's evaluation of the qualitative nature of the taking. Mr. Navasky testified that he used verbatim excerpts because "simply reciting the information could not adequately convey the 'absolute certainty with which [Ford] expressed himself,' . . . or show that 'this comes from President Ford,' . . . or carry the 'definitive quality' of the original . . ." The quoted passages were chosen precisely because they qualitatively embodied Ford's distinctive expression. D's article is set up so that the quoted material become its dramatic focal points. Because these excerpts' expressive value, we cannot agree with the appeals court that D " 'took a meager, indeed an infinitesimal amount of Ford's original language.' "

♦ The final and most important factor addresses the "effect of the use upon the potential market for or value of the copyrighted work." When properly applied, fair use does not materially impair the marketability of the copied work. Here, the trial court found an actual effect on the market. Time cancelled its contract and refused to pay $12,500 as a direct result of the infringement. We disagree with the appeals court's rejection of a causal relation. Rarely is there such clear-cut evidence of actual damage. "Placed in a broader perspective, a fair use doctrine that permits extensive prepublication quotations from an unreleased manuscript without the copyright owner's consent poses substantial potential for damage to the marketability of first serialization rights in general."

---

e. Scope of Patentable Subject Matter

Diamond v. Chakrabarty
447 U.S. 303 (1980).

Facts. In 1972, Chakrabarty (P), a microbiologist, filed a patent application, assigned to the General Electric Co., related to P's invention of a human-made, genetically engineered bacterium capable of breaking down multiple components of crude oil. No naturally occurring bacteria possesses this ability; thus, P's invention is believed to have significant value for the treatment of oil spills. P's patent claims were: first, process claims for the method of producing the bacteria; second, claims for an inoculum comprised of a carrier material floating on water, such as straw, and the new bacteria; and third, claims to the bacteria themselves. The patent examiner rejected the third claim because micro-organisms are "products of nature," and as living things they are not patentable subject matter under 35 U.S.C. 101. The Court of Customs and Patent Appeals reversed, concluding that the fact that micro-organisms are alive is without legal significance for purposes of the patent law. Diamond (D) appealed. We granted certiorari.

Issue. Does P's micro-organism constitute a "manufacture" or "composition of matter" within 35 U.S.C. 101?

Held. Yes. Judgment affirmed.

- The matter before us requires us to interpret 35 U.S.C. 101, which provides: "Whoever invents or discovers any new and useful process, machine, manufacture, or composition of matter, or any new and useful improvement thereof, may obtain a patent therefor, subject to the conditions and requirements of this title."

- We have read both "manufacture" and "composition of matter" in accord with their dictionary definitions. "Manufacture" is defined as "the production of articles for use from raw or prepared materials by giving to these materials new forms, qualities, properties, or combinations, whether by hand-labor or by machinery." "'Composition of matter'" has been construed consistent with its common usage to include 'all compositions of two or more substances and . . . all composite articles, whether they be the results of chemical union, or of mechanical mixture, or whether they be gases, fluids, powders or solids.'" Congress selected these terms to give broad scope to the definitions.

- While the legislative history also supports a broad construction (Congress stated in its Committee Reports accompanying the 1952 Act that it intended statutory subject matter to "'include anything under the sun that is made by man.'"), we do not suggest that the statute has no limits. The laws of nature, physical phenomena, and abstract ideas have been held not patentable; *e.g.*, a newly discovered plant or mineral is not patentable. Einstein's law, E=mc2 is not patentable because it is a "'manifestations of . . . nature, free to all men and reserved exclusively to none.'"

- P's claim, however, is not to a newly discovered natural phenomenon, but to a nonnaturally occurring manufacture or composition of matter—a product of human ingenuity "'having a distinctive name, character [and] use,'" and it is, therefore patentable. P has produced a new bacterium with very different characteristics from any other bacterium found in nature, and one that has the potential to be very useful. His is not a product of nature, but a result of his own handiwork.

- We find neither of D's arguments persuasive. D first contends that because both the 1930 Plant Patent Act, which afforded patent protection to certain asexually reproduced plants, and the 1970 Plant Variety Protection Act, which authorized protection for certain sexually reproduced plants, excluded bacteria from their protection, we are provided with evidence that Congress did not understand the terms "manufacture" or "composition of matter" to include living things. The legislation would not have been necessary if they did, D argues.

- We reject this argument. Before 1930, plants were believed to be products of nature for the purposes of the patent law. Also, plants were not thought to fit in with the "written description" requirement of the patent law. It was thought impossible to describe in writing how one plant might differ from another only in perfume or color. Both of these concerns were addressed in the Plant Patent Act; Congress explained at length that the work of a plant bred "in aid of nature" was patentable invention and relaxed the written requirement to as complete a description as is reasonably possible. No member of Congress expressed the view offered by D that "manufacture" or "composition of matter" exclude living things. Thus, the distinction is between products of nature, whether living or not, and human-made inventions. Here, P's micro-organism is the result of human ingenuity and research.

- Relying on our holding in *Parker v. Flook*, 437 U.S. 584 (1978), and the statement that the judiciary "must proceed cautiously when . . . asked to extend patent rights into areas wholly unforeseen by Congress," D next argues that because genetic technology was not foreseen when the statute was enacted, micro-organisms cannot qualify as patentable until Congress provides express authorization for such protection.

- While it is correct that Congress must define the limits of patentability, it is the province of the judicial department to say what the law is. Here, we have been guided by the legislative history and statutory purpose and can find no ambiguity. In *Flook*, we applied precedents to determine that a claim for an improved method of calculation, even when connected to a specific end use, is unpatentable subject matter. We looked at the claim in *Flook* to decide whether it was precluded from patent protection under the " 'the principles underlying the prohibition against patents for 'ideas' or phenomena of nature.' " We have done the same analysis here. Our decision here is not at odds with *Flook*. We did not announce in *Flook* a new principle that inventions in areas not contemplated by Congress when the patent laws were enacted are unpatentable per *se*. Such a principle would undermine the core concept of the patent law that anticipation undermines patentability.

♦ D also presents the grave risks that come with genetic research, and argues that we should assess those potential hazards in considering whether P's invention is patentable. We do not agree. Our action will not put an end to or encourage genetic research. And the pros and cons of genetic research are beyond our competence.

Dissent. We are not dealing here, as the Court would have it, with "unanticipated inventions." After Congress enacted the Plant Patent Act in 1930, affording patent protection to developers of certain asexually reproduced plants, it enacted the Plant Variety Protection Act in 1970 to extend protection to certain new plant varieties capable of sexual reproduction. The Acts show us that at least since 1930, the statute did not include living organisms. If newly developed living organisms not naturally occurring had been patentable under 101, the plants included in the scope of the 1930 and 1970 Acts could have been patented without new legislation. Those, like the bacteria involved in this case, were new varieties not naturally occurring. In these two Acts Congress has addressed the general problem of patenting animate inventions and has chosen carefully limited language granting protection to some kinds of discoveries, but specifically omitting others. Because Congress thought it had to legislate in order to make agricultural "human-made inventions" patentable and because the legislation Congress enacted is limited, it follows that Congress never meant to make items outside the scope of the legislation patentable. It is the role of Congress, not this Court to extend or limit the reach of the patent laws, especially where, as here, the material sought to be patented uniquely implicates matters of public concern.

---

f.   Property in One's Persona

White v. Samsung Electronics America, Inc.
989 F.2d 1512 (9th Cir. 1992) (denying a rehearing), *cert. denied,* 508 U.S. 951 (1993).

Facts. Vanna White (P) sued Samsung Electronics America, Inc. and David Deutsch Associates, Inc. (Ds), alleging infringement of her intellectual property rights. Ds had run an advertisement that showed a robot, dressed in a manner reminiscent of P, standing in front of the "Wheel of Fortune" game board. The trial court granted summary judgment for Ds on all claims, but the court of appeals reversed in part, holding that issues of material fact precluded summary judgment on P's claim for her common law right of publicity and on her claim for violation of the Lanham Act (concerning false representations in advertising). After the court of appeals denied a petition for rehearing, Judge Kozinski wrote the dissent below.

Issue. Did issues of material fact preclude summary judgment?

Held. Yes.

Dissent (Kozinski, J.).

♦ Although private property, including intellectual property, is essential to our way of life and should be protected, we have to avoid overprotection so as not to stifle creativity. The panel, in its effort to protect P, has created a property right that is too broad. Now advertisers cannot even remind the public of a celebrity or evoke a celebrity's image in the public's mind. This ruling conflicts with the Copyright Act, raises First Amendment issues, and deserves a second look.

- Unlike constitutional rights, intellectual property rights protect only against specific kinds of appropriation. Here, rather than protecting a right, the panel is creating a new one. A celebrity now has an exclusive right to anything that reminds the public of her. Since it is the "Wheel of Fortune" set, not the robot, which evokes P's image, the panel is giving P an exclusive right in what she does for a living.

- Because intellectual property rights are imposed at the expense of future creators and of the public at large, intellectual property law carefully balances what is set aside for the owner and what is left in the public domain. Limitations on protections of intellectual property rights, such as the relatively short life of patents, the finite life of copyrights, and the fair use doctrine, diminish an intellectual property owner's rights and let the public use something created by someone else. They are necessary to maintain a free environment in which creativity can thrive.

- The intellectual property right created by the panel lacks essential limitations. There is no fair use exception, no right to parody. By refusing to recognize a parody exception to the right of publicity, the panel has contradicted the federal Copyright Act. D parodied P appearing in "Wheel of Fortune," a copyrighted television show. Parodies of copyrighted works are governed by federal copyright law, and copyright law specifically gives the public the right to make "fair use" parodies—those that do not borrow too much of the original.

- This decision cannot be squared with the First Amendment. P does not have the right to control our thoughts. Not permitting any means of reminding people of someone is speech restriction unparalleled in First Amendment law.

---

g. Property in One's Person

Moore v. Regents of the University of California
793 P.2d 479 (Cal. 1990), *cert. denied,* 499 U.S. 936 (1991).

Facts. In 1976, Moore (P) sought treatment for hairy-cell leukemia at the Medical Center of U.C.L.A., owned by the Regents (Ds). Ds confirmed the diagnosis after conducting tests and told P his condition was life-threatening and that his spleen should be removed. P was not told that his cells were unique and had scientific and commercial value. After P's splenectomy, Ds retained P's spleen for research purposes, and during seven years of follow-up tests, samples of P's blood, tissue, and other fluids were taken and used for research without his consent. Ds established a cell line from P's cells, obtained a patent for it, and entered into commercial agreements that earned Ds hundreds of thousands of dollars by the mid-1980s. The potential commercial value is estimated in the billions. P sued for wrongful conversion, alleging his blood and bodily substances were his "tangible personal property." The trial court sustained Ds' demurrers for this claim and held that because it was incorporated into other causes of action, all claims were defective. The court of appeal reversed, finding that absent P's consent to Ds' disposition of the tissues, or lawful justification, such as abandonment, the complaint adequately pleads all the elements of a cause of action for conversion. Ds petitioned for certiorari.

Issues.

(i) Has P stated a cause of action for breach of fiduciary duty or lack of informed consent?

(ii) Has P stated a cause of action for conversion?

Held. (i) Yes. (ii) No.

- By failing to disclose the extent of the research and commercial interests in P's cells before obtaining P's consent to the procedures by which P's cells were extracted, Ds invaded a legally protected patient interest.

- The tort of conversion does not give P a cause of action under existing law, and this court is not willing to extend the theory of conversion to include P's claim.

- Under existing law, to establish a conversion, P must establish an actual interference with his ownership or right of possession. Where P neither has title to the property, nor possession thereof, he cannot maintain an action for conversion.

- P did not expect to retain possession of his cells after their removal and he did not retain an ownership interest in them because: (i) no reported judicial decision supports the claim; (ii) state law drastically limits a patient's continuing interest in excised cells; and (iii) Ds' patented materials—the cell line and derivative products—cannot be P's property.

- The nature of genetic materials and research in this case, if properly understood, prevents any analogy to wrongful publicity cases; courts that have addressed the issue of a person's proprietary interest in his likeness have failed to resolve the debate over the proper characterization of this proprietary interest. It is redressible as a tort. The characterization of the right at issue is a necessity as only property can be converted.

- The goal and result of Ds' work is the manufacture of lymphokines; they and the genetic material that produces them have the same molecular structure in every human being; they are not unique to P. The court of appeal erred in forcing the concepts of privacy and dignity into the concept of conversion of personal property. This was not necessary; fiduciary duty and informed consent theories directly protect privacy and dignity by requiring full disclosure.

- California law, in an effort to ensure safe handling of potentially hazardous biological waste materials, severely limits a patient's control over excised cells, restricts their use and requires their eventual destruction, thus limiting many rights ordinarily attached to property. A patient who does not approve of the ultimate use of his excised tissue may withhold consent to treatment by a physician. This right is one protected by the fiduciary duty and informed consent theories.

- P's contention that he owns the patented cell line and its resulting products is not consistent with the patent, which is "an authoritative determination that the cell line is the product of invention."

- It is inappropriate to impose liability for conversion here because: (i) a balancing of the relevant policy considerations, *i.e.*, protection of a patient's right to make autonomous medical decisions, and the protection of innocent parties, such as persons engaged in research, from disabling civil liability, counsels against such an extension of the tort; (ii) resolution of these types of problems is best left to the legislature; and (iii) the tort is not necessary to protect patients' rights.

Concurrence. Whether P's cells should be treated as property is properly determined in the legislature.

Dissent. P's complaint does state a cause of action for conversion. At the time of removal of P's tissue, P at least had the right to do with it whatever Ds did; thus, P could have contracted with Ds to develop its vast commercial potential. The nondisclosure cause of action is illusory: (i) it fails to protect a patient's right to grant consent to commercial use of his tissues; (ii) it fails to reach those potential defendants who are removed from the direct physician-patient relationship; and (iii) proving a causal connection between a patient's injury and a physician's failure to inform, and further proving that had he been fully informed, in the same circumstances *no reasonably prudent person* would have given such consent, are barriers to recovery.

Comment. Although this case deals with a problem that has grown out of sophisticated medical technology, it is laden with ghosts of such early legal concepts as trespass to chattels and the law of capture.

---

h. The Right to Exclude

The right to exclusive possession is protected by both the law of trespass and the law of conversion. Courts have traditionally granted great protection to this right. In *Jacque v. Steenberg Homes, Inc.*, 563 N.W.2d 154 (Wis. 1997), the court granted $100,000 in punitive damages against a man who willfully moved a mobile home across the plaintiff's land over the plaintiff's adamant protests.

i. Limitations on the Right to Exclude

In *State v. Shack*, 277 A.2d 369 (N.J. 1971), the court held that an employer who provides migrant workers with housing in conjunction with their work may not prohibit others from coming onto the land to render governmental services to the migrant workers.

j. Effort to Abandon Fee Simple

Pocono Springs Civic Association, Inc. v. MacKenzie
667 A.2d 233 (Pa. Super. 1995).

Facts. The MacKenzies (Ds) purchased a vacant lot at Pocono Springs Development and later decided to sell it. An offer to purchase was conditioned upon the land being suitable for an on-lot sewage system; an inspection determined it was not and the sale was lost. Ds attempted to abandon the property. The Pocono Springs Civic Association, Inc. (P) sought payment of association fees and D's claimed that because they successfully abandoned their lot, they are relieved from any duty to pay the association fees. The trial court held that Ds' abandonment defense is "not a valid defense," and granted summary judgment in P's favor. Ds appeal.

Issue. Did the trial court err as a matter of law in finding that P's right to summary judgment is clear and free from doubt?

Held. Yes. Judgment affirmed.

♦ Ds attempts to abandon the property consisted of trying to turn it over to P, trying to gift it to P, (both declined by P); stopping payment of real estate taxes, resulting in an offer of the property by the County for sale for delinquent taxes on two occasions, both of which produced no purchasers; allowing the property to be placed on the Tax Bureau's "repository" list; signing a notarized statement, mailed to "all interested parties," expressing their desire to abandon the property; and not accepting mail regarding the property. Ds did not visit the property or use the development's services. Ds claim their conduct shows an intent to abandon and should be a question of fact, not a matter for summary judgment.

♦ We have held that abandoned property is that: " . . . to which an owner has voluntarily relinquished all right, title, claim and possession with the intention of terminating his ownership, but without vesting it in any other person and with the intention of not reclaiming further possession or resuming ownership, possession or enjoyment." Ds have not relinquished their rights, title, claim or possession of their property. They are owners in fee simple, have a recorded deed and "perfect title." Under these circumstances, possession is presumed to be in the party who has recorded title and nothing in our state law allows for abandonment.

♦ Once it is determined that good title exists, abandonment is not possible. Intent is irrelevant. Our law leaves nothing for a jury to decide on this claim.

---

k. Inference of Intent to Abandon One's Property

Hawkins v. Mahoney
990 P.2d 776 (Mt. 1999).

Facts. On the same day Hawkins (P) escaped from prison, July 12, 1997, state prison officials packed up his property, sealed it with security tape, placed his name on each box, took the boxes from his cell and placed them in the prison storage room on July 12, 1997. Two days later, after he was captured and returned to the prison, P was placed in segregation. On July 20, at a disciplinary hearing, he was found guilty of escape, and among the sanctions he received, he was assigned ten days in disciplinary segregation. The hearings officer did not order his personal property destroyed. During the next 30 days, P made several requests for the property. In September 1997, P was escorted to the storage room and allowed to remove his legal papers and materials from his boxes. He was informed that when a prisoner escapes, his personal property is considered abandoned and is destroyed. P was told his property would either be destroyed or sold and it was later destroyed. P's property included a television, stereo, word processor, glasses and books, estimated to be worth $2290. P filed a complaint against several prison officials and the state of Montana (Ds), alleging individual defendants destroyed his property without due process of law. The trial court found P had abandoned the property by his escape and the abandonment was a complete defense to any action brought by P which depended on his ownership of the property. P appeals.

Issue. Did the trial court err by holding P had abandoned his personal property and had no right to request its return and dismissing P's complaint for failure to state a claim upon which relief could be granted?

Held. Yes. Judgment reversed.

♦ The trial court relied on a Missouri case, *Herron v. Whiteside,* 782 S.W.2d 414 (1989) for its finding that P had abandoned his property. In *Herron,* the Court of Appeals held that a prisoner's escape from confinement constitutes, as a matter of law, abandonment of the personal property the prisoner left at the prison. Herron escaped for one day, and during that day, prison employees permitted employees to give away his property and allowed other prisoners to take Herron's property from his cell.

♦ *Herron* is factually distinguishable from this case. The state did not take Herron's property. In the case before us, Ds took P's property from his cell and placed it in storage with his name on it.

♦ Regarding a previous owner's rights to abandoned property, it has been stated that once personal property has been abandoned, it stops being the property of any person, unless and until it is reduced to possession with the intent to acquire title to, or ownership of, it. The property may, therefore, "be appropriated by anyone, *if it has not been reclaimed by the former owner,* and ownership of it vests by operation of law, in the person first lawfully appropriating it and reducing it to possession with the intention to become its owner, provided such taking is fair." 1 C.J.S. *Abandonment* § 12 (1985) (emphasis added).

♦ There is no argument here that P expressed an intent to abandon his property. That intent was inferred when he escaped. Intent is a requisite element of abandonment and without expressed intent, it may be inferred from the owner's acts. The *Herron* court held that a prisoner's escape convincingly infers the intent to abandon property, and that intent is an irrebuttable presumption. We are not persuaded that such a presumption should be conclusive before the time that someone else acquires possession with the intent to acquire ownership.

♦ Here, at no time before P requested the return of his property did Ds reduce P's property to possession with the intent to acquire title to, or ownership of it.

♦ We find that the presumption or inference of intent to abandon one's property, based solely upon the acts of the owner, is a rebuttable presumption. Thus, upon his return to prison and his request for his property before anyone else had claimed it, P effectively rebutted the presumption that he ever intended to abandon it. When he reclaimed his property by asking for it, he regained his status and the owner against all others.

---

l. Razing of Home Against Public Policy

Eyerman et al. v. Mercantile Trust Co.

524 S.W.2d 210 (Mo. Ct. of Appl. 1975).

Facts. Johnston's will directed Mercantile Trust Co. (D), her executor, that upon her death, her home at # 4 Kingsbury Place in the City of St. Louis be razed, the land be sold and the proceeds be transferred to the residue of her estate. Eyerman and other neighborhood property owners (Ps) assert that razing the home will adversely affect their property rights, violate the terms of the subdivision trust indenture for Kingsbury Place, produce an actionable private nuisance and is contrary to public policy. The trust indenture that established Kingsbury Place in 1902 provides that it will be maintained and protected for private residences of the "highest class." It empowers lot owners or trustees to bring suit to enforce its provisions. Now, the subdivision has only one vacant lot and is graced by appealing, large, two and three-story homes. Location, costs, and other features for structures in the subdivision are regulated, as is construction of additional structures. Ps sought an injunction to prevent demolition of Johnston's home. At trial, the temporary restraining order was dissolved and all issues found for D. Ps appeal.

Issue. Did the trial court err in determining that the razing of the property would not violate public policy?

Held. Yes. Judgment reversed.

♦ Involved in this matter is an issue of public policy involving individual property rights and the community at large. Ps have pleaded and proved facts sufficient to show a personal, legally protectible interest. The value of the house and land is $40,000. After demolition and its costs, the estate could earn only $5,000 for the vacant lot, resulting in a loss of $39,350.00 if the unexplained and capricious direction to the executor is effected. Only $650.00 of the $40,000.00 asset would remain.

♦ Because of the nature of Kingsbury Place, an area of high architectural significance, representing excellence in urban space utilization, razing the home will depreciate adjoining property values by an estimated $10,000.00 and result in corresponding losses for other neighborhood homes. To construct a comparable house in the neighborhood would cost $200,000. The significance of the property is underscored by the action of the St. Louis Commission on Landmarks and Urban Design designating Kingsbury Place as a landmark of the City of St. Louis, an action under consideration before the start of this suit. The Landmarks Commission chairman testified that the private place concept promotes higher home maintenance standards and is highly effective methods for stabilizing otherwise deteriorating neighborhoods.

♦ Razing # 4 Kingsbury from the street was compared to having a missing front tooth. The vacant area would allow access to the street from an adjacent alley, potentially subjecting the property to uses detrimental to health and safety. The possibility that a future owner may purchase the property and build an appropriate home does not lend support to sustaining the destruction of the property.

♦ Only the caprice of the testatrix will be served by destruction of the property. No living person, group or community benefits; in fact, all are harmed. No reason has been offered anywhere for the eccentric request. It is against public policy to allow an executor to carry out Johnston's whim.

- The taking of property by inheritance or will is a right created by the state. The state " 'may foreclose the right absolutely, or it may grant the right upon conditions precedent. . . .' " A living person has fewer restraints on the management, use or disposition of her property. Usually, a living person values her property, wants to enjoy it and accumulate it during her lifetime. Here, no such considerations have tempered Johnston's demands; only the court may act as a check Johnston's actions.

- Both early cases, *e.g.*, *Egerton v. Brownlow*, 10 Eng.Rep. 359, 417 (H.L.C. 1853), ("The owner of an estate may himself do many things which he could not (by a condition) compel his successor to do."); and *In re Scott's Will, Board of Commissioners of Rice County v. Scott et al.*, 88 Minn. 386, 93 N.W. 109 (1903), (The court did not permit the executor to carry out the provision in the codicil that all of the money, cash, or evidences of credit belonging to the estate be destroyed.), and the Restatement, Second, Trusts (sect. 124) (Where an attempt is made to confer the power to deal capriciously with property upon a person who is given no other interest in the property, it is against public policy to allow him to exercise the power if the purpose is only capricious.) disallow Johnston's request.

- Our courts have defined acts that are against public policy when the law refuses to recognize or enforce them as those that have "a mischievous tendency, so as to be injurious to the interests of the state, apart from illegality or immorality."

- The waste and destruction at issue here are at odds with a well-ordered society; they are in direct conflict with significant interests of other members of that society.

Dissent. The court assumes Johnston's directive is eccentric. However, there is no indication in the record of Johnston's reasons for her directive. The court proclaims we must prevent land misuse in the City, but the City is not a party; nor are the beneficiaries. The holding is based on vague public policy grounds that were not in evidence. Ps claim they are entitled to an injunction by virtue of language in the trust indenture, because the razing of the property would cause a nuisance, and because of public policy. The first two claims have not been addressed and no grounds exist for the third. By relying on public policy, the majority has violated the limitations of the leading state case on public policy as that doctrine applies to a testator's right to dispose of property. In *In re Rahn's Estate*, 316 Mo. 492, 291 S.W. 120 [1, 2] (banc 1927), cert. den. 274 U.S. 745, 47 S.Ct. 591, 71 L.Ed. 1325, an executor refused to pay a bequest on the ground the beneficiary was an enemy alien, making the bequest against public policy. The court did not agree. It found: "We may say, at the outset, that the policy of the law favors freedom in the testamentary disposition of property and that it is the duty of the courts to give effect to the intention of the testator, as expressed in his will, provided such intention does not contravene an established rule of law." The court added: "it is not the function of the judiciary to create or announce a public policy of its own, but solely to determine and declare what is the public policy of the state or nation as such policy is found to be expressed in the Constitution, statutes, and judicial decisions of the state or nation, . . . not by the varying opinions of laymen, lawyers, or judges as to the demands or the interests of the public."

C. Acquisition by Find

1. Introduction

When an owner loses property, in the eyes of the law she is still the owner. Her title to the lost property is superior to that of everyone else including the finder. The finder of the lost property, as a general rule, has title to the lost property superior to all but the true owner. This legal rule, as do most legal rules, has some notable exceptions.

a. Prior Possessors

The general rule applies to the case of the subsequent possessor. Suppose an owner (O) loses a ring and a finder (F) finds it, only to lose it himself. If someone else (G) later finds it, F has a title to the ring superior to G's. G would be obliged to give it back to F. If O came along, G would then be obliged to give it to O, rather than F, since the true owner's rights are superior to anyone else's. This rule applies even if F steals the ring from O.

b. Finder's Interest

Armory v. Delamirie
1 Strange 505 (K.B. 1722).

Facts. Armory (P), a chimney sweeper's boy, found a jewel and took it to Delamirie's (D's) goldsmith shop. Under the pretext of weighing it, D's apprentice removed the stones. D offered P three half pence for the jewelry, which P refused. When D refused to return the stones, P sued.

Issue. Does the finder of lost property have title to the property superior to all the world except the true owner?

Held. Yes. Judgment for P.

♦   The finder's interest is good as against all the world except the true owner.

♦   D, the master, is responsible for his apprentice's act of removing the stones.

♦   As to the amount of damages, unless D produces the stones, the jury could presume that the removed stones were of the finest quality.

Comment. This case states the general rule that has been applied for over 200 years.

---

c. The Two Elements of Possession

The finder must both acquire actual (physical) possession of the lost property and intend to have dominion over it. Someone may have unconscious possession of lost property if he has possession of the premises where the article is. [*See, e.g.*, Hannah v. Peel, *infra*]

2. Finder vs. "Unconscious" Possessor

Often the finder of lost personal property does not own the land upon which the property is found. In these cases, for O (the landowner) to prevail, he must have actual or constructive possession of the object. Usually, if the property is found in a private residential home of O, O prevails. In other cases different sets of rules have evolved.

a. Servants and Employees

Often, if the servant or employee finds the object while about his master/employer's business, the master/employer prevails.

b. Trespassers

Trespassers always lose.

c. Buried Property

If it is buried property, it belongs to O.

d. Absentee Owner

Hannah v. Peel
[1945] K.B. 509.

Facts. Peel (D) bought a large house in 1938 but never moved in. In 1940 it was requisitioned by the military. While requisitioned, Hannah (P), a soldier, discovered a brooch in a room being used as a sick bay. The brooch was in an obscure place, covered with cobwebs and dirt. P gave it to the police. In 1942, the true owner never having been found, the police gave it to D, who sold it for £66. D never possessed the house himself nor did he have knowledge of the existence of the brooch prior to its discovery by P. P brought a writ seeking the recovery of the brooch or its money's worth.

Issue. Does the finder have a claim to the found property superior to that of the owner of the freehold upon which the property was found (if the freehold owner was never physically in possession of the freehold)?

Held. Yes. Judgment for P.

♦ The law is very unclear as to whether an owner who has never occupied the freehold has a claim to lost property superior to that of the finder.

♦ In *Bridges v. Hawkesworth,* a small parcel was found on the floor of a shop in that portion of the shop frequented by the public. The issue was whether the finder or the shop owner was entitled to the parcel (which contained bank notes). The court there held that the parcel was never in the custody of the shop owner, or within the protection of his house, and that the shop owner had no duty other than to notify the police. Thus, held that court, there were no circumstances warranting an exception to the rule that the finder has a superior claim over anyone but the true owner. There was some dispute among the judges as to whether the place where the parcel was found made any difference.

♦ In *South Staffordshire Water Co. v. Sharman,* a worker, under the landowner's orders, was cleaning a pool of water when he discovered two rings. The issue was whether the finder had a claim to the rings superior to that of the landowner. That court held that if a servant or agent finds something, he finds it for his master. Thus, the finder, an employee, found the rings for the benefit of his employer, the landowner.

♦ In *Elwes v. Brigg Gas Co.,* land was leased to a gas company for 99 years. A prehistoric boat was discovered buried on the leasehold. The court in that case held that the lessor owned the boat and that it made no difference that he did not know it existed prior to its discovery.

♦ It is clear from these authorities that: (i) a person possesses everything attached to or under his land, and (ii) a person does not necessarily possess everything that is unattached on the surface of his land.

♦ Here, it is clear the brooch was lost and that it was not attached to the land. D never physically possessed the premises; the brooch was never his. He had no knowledge of its existence prior to P's discovery of it. In these circumstances P prevails.

Comment. The court noted that:

(i) If Lord Russell is correct in his analysis of *Bridges,* a landowner may possess everything on the land from which he intends to exclude others.

(ii) If Sir Pollock is right (the English view), a landowner may possess those things over which he has de facto control.

e. Public Part/Private Part Distinction

Some courts hold that if the object is found in the private part of a business, such as behind the counter or in the storeroom, then it belongs to the owner. If it is found in the public part of the business—the lobby, waiting room, public hallway—then it belongs to the finder.

1) Lost vs. Mislaid

A distinction evolved at common law between property that was lost and property that was mislaid. Mislaid property was defined as property that the true owner placed somewhere and then forgot. Lost property belonged to the finder; mislaid property to the owner. It was felt that this facilitated the return of the property to the true owner. This required courts to guess whether the true owner had lost or mislaid the property. The lost-mislaid distinction has fallen into disrepute in recent years.

2) Property Voluntarily Placed

McAvoy v. Medina
11 Allen 548 (Mass. 1866).

Facts. D owned a barbershop. A customer (P) found a pocketbook lying on a table in the shop. P told D to keep the money found in the pocketbook until the true owner came for it, otherwise to advertise that the money had been found. Subsequently, since the true owner was never found, P demanded the money and D refused to give it to him. P sued. The judge held that P could not maintain an action. P appeals.

Issue. Does property that was voluntarily placed in a shop by its owner, who then neglects to remove it, belong to the finder?

Held. No. Judgment affirmed.

♦ The finder of lost property has a valid claim to the property against all the world except the true owner, and generally the place in which the property is found makes no difference.

♦ Here, the property was voluntarily placed in the shop by its owner. By merely finding it P did not acquire the right to take it from the shop; rather, it was his duty to use reasonable care for the safekeeping of the property until the true owner claimed it.

♦ *Bridges* (discussed in *Hannah v. Peel, supra*) is distinguishable since the parcel was not voluntarily placed there. There is a distinction between property placed by its owner, who neglects to remove it, and property that is lost.

♦ Here, P acquired no original right to the property and D's acts in receiving and holding the property do not create any rights in P. Thus, D gets the property. The lower court is affirmed.

Comment. This case follows the general rule regarding lost and mislaid property.

---

3. Abandoned Property

Abandoned property belongs to the finder.

4. Statutes

Some legislatures have modified the common law rules on finders. Some have abolished the lost-mislaid distinction, others the distinction between finding property in public vs. private places.

D. Acquisition by Adverse Possession

1. Introduction

The theory of adverse possession is fairly simple. If a person who does not own land possesses it for the period of time specified in the applicable statute of limitations, she acquires title to the land. The prior owner loses his right to the land. Depending on the state, the time period for acquiring title by adverse possession is five to 21 years. Furthermore, the general rule of possessors applies to the adverse possessor before the statute of limitations has run. Thus, if, in a jurisdiction having a seven-year statute of limitations, a third party interferes with the would-be adverse possessor's use and enjoyment of the land, the would-be adverse possessor can go to court and enforce her right to possession. However, until the statutory period has lapsed, she has no rights as against the landowner.

2. Elements of Adverse Possession

a.   Actual entry onto and possession of the land.

b.   The possession must be open and notorious.

c.   The possession must be continuous for the statutory period.

d.   The possession must be adverse.

3. Actual Entry and Possession

The possession must be exclusive and of such a nature that the community would think of the adverse possessor as the true owner.

4. Open and Notorious Possession

This is not very different from the preceding requirement. Constructive possession is never sufficient to satisfy the possessory requirements of adverse possession. Just what is open and notorious depends on the land, its size, condition, and locality. For instance, farming on farmland is clearly "open and notorious."

a.   Statutory Requirements

Some states have codified the requirements of adverse possession. These statutes typically require specific kinds of acts. The next case is a good example of a court applying an adverse possession statute.

b.   Claim of Title

Van Valkenburg v. Lutz
106 N.E.2d 28 (N.Y. 1952).

Facts. Lutz (D) purchased lots 14 and 15 of a subdivision in 1912. In 1937, Van Valkenburg (P) purchased lots 31 and 32. Between P's and D's property was an unsold, irregularly shaped parcel of land composed of lots 19–22. At first D used lots 19–22 only for access to his property. Later D built a shed and a chicken coop on these lots. He also gardened on these lots, selling his produce in the neighborhood. In 1947, P purchased lots 19–22 at a tax sale. P erected thereon a fence across the access way that led to lots 14 and 15 (D's purchased property). D sued P, admitting P owned lots 19–

22 but claiming a right of access across them. D won both at trial and on appeal. P then sued D to have him removed from lots 19–22. D hired a new attorney and asserted that he had acquired, by adverse possession, title to lots 19–22 previous to P's buying the lots at the tax sale. The trial court found for D. The intermediate appellate court reversed, finding that D had not acquired title by adverse possession. D appeals to the court of appeals.

Issue. Must a party occupy another's land "under a claim of title" in order to acquire title by adverse possession?

Held. Yes. Judgment affirmed.

♦   Under the statute, to acquire by adverse possession one must clearly and convincingly show that for at least 15 years there has been "actual" occupation of the land (enclosing the land or cultivating or improving) under a claim of title.

♦   Here, since there was no enclosure, D must show that the land was cultivated or improved sufficiently to satisfy the statute.

D's garden was not shown to be substantial.

D's shed was not much of an improvement.

D's garage encroached on the parcel of land in question only a few inches. This is insubstantial occupation of the land.

D's putting junk (car parts, building materials, etc.) on the land was not a substantial improvement of the property.

♦   D, in a prior lawsuit, voluntarily admitted P owned the land. Thus, D's occupation of the land was not "under a claim of title."

Dissent. There was substantial evidence to indicate that D had a substantial truck farm, cultivating most of the land in question. It is obvious D intended to acquire and use the property as his own. That should be enough to satisfy the statute.

---

c.   Mistaken Claim of Ownership

Mannillo v. Gorski
255 A.2d 258 (N.J. 1969).

Facts. In 1946, Gorski (D) entered land under a contract to purchase. The land was conveyed to D and her husband in 1952. In 1946, D's son made some improvements to D's home, including building concrete steps to replace existing wooden steps. D's steps encroach upon the Mannillos' (Ps') adjacent lot by 15 inches. Ps filed a complaint seeking an injunction against D's alleged trespass. D counterclaimed, seeking a declaratory judgment to determine D had gained title to the disputed premises by adverse possession. The trial court found for Ps. D appealed. Before argument at the appeals court, the supreme court granted D's motion for certification.

Issue. Does an entry and continuance of possession under the mistaken belief that the possessor has title to the land involved exhibit the hostile possession required to obtain title by adverse possession?

Held. Yes. Case remanded for further factual determination.

♦   There are two opposing views on this question. The Maine doctrine, which has been highly criticized, would reward the possessor who entered another's land with a premeditated and predesigned "hostility." The Connecticut doctrine makes no inquiry into the recesses of the adverse claimant's mind. "The very nature of the act (entry and possession) is an assertion of his own title, and denial of the title of all others." We favor the latter view.

- Whether or not the adverse possessor is mistaken, the result is the same—the owner is ousted from possession. If he fails to attempt to recover possession within the requisite time, it is probably the result of lack of knowledge that he is being deprived of lands to which he has title.

- Thus, any entry and possession for the required time that is exclusive, continuous, uninterrupted, visible and notorious, even though under a mistaken claim of title, is sufficient to support a claim of title by adverse possession.

- However, the element of "open and notorious" possession may not be met where the encroachment is of a small area or where the intrusion requires an on-site survey.

- No presumption of knowledge arises from a minor encroachment along a common boundary. Only when the true owner has actual knowledge may it be said that the possession is open and notorious.

Comment. The case was remanded to determine whether the true owners had actual knowledge of the intrusion; and, if there was no knowledge, to determine whether Ps should be obliged to convey the land in dispute to D; and if so, what consideration should be paid.

———————

5. Adverse

To satisfy this requirement the adverse possessor must have a claim to the land adverse to the owner. Thus, if the possessor has the owner's permission, she is not there adversely. Adverse has nothing to do with personal animosity or malice.

a. Majority View

What is "adverse" depends on the actions of the possessor, not her subjective intent. The possessor's acts must look like claims of ownership.

b. Minority View

In these jurisdictions the possessor must have a good faith belief that she has title to the property.

c. Color of Title

A minority of jurisdictions also require that the possessor claim title via a written instrument. The written instrument can be something like a forged deed, a deed from a grantor who did not own the land, etc.

d. Boundary Disputes

In the case of boundary disputes most courts will apply the objective test to determine if one of the parties has acquired title to the disputed strip of land by adverse possession. Thus, by putting up a fence and using the land for the necessary number of years, the one party can acquire title to the land.

6. Continuous Possession

This requirement is met when the possessor maintains possession for the statutorily required period of time. The key here is that the property be used in a customary manner. Thus, if a farmer farms someone else's field for enough years, she may obtain title to the land by adverse possession even though she never lives on the land. The same applies to summer cabins.

a. Tacking

Some, but not all, courts will allow an adverse possessor to tack the time she is in possession onto that of her predecessor in interest's period of adverse possession. In order to tack there must be privity of estate between the two adverse possessors. This usually requires more than mere transfer of physical possession. In most instances this would require a document that gives the successor not only physical possession but also the right to physical possession. Nevertheless, some courts will permit parol transfers (transfers where all that the succeeding adverse possessor gets is physical possession).

b. Parol Transfers

Howard v. Kunto
477 P.2d 210 (Wash. Ct. App. 1970).

Facts. The Howards (Ps) and the Kuntos (Ds) are property holders in a summer resort area where the houses are used primarily for summer occupancy. Ps owned the land that was one lot away from that of Ds. When Ps tried to convey their holdings to a third party, it was found that the title they held was to the lot adjacent to that which they had occupied. In fact, most of the property owners occupied land different from what their deed gave records to. Ps then conveyed their deed to the occupant of the adjacent lot in exchange for his deed, which was for the lot occupied by Ds. Ps next brought action to have title quieted in them to the lot occupied by Ds. The trial court held that since Ds had owned the land for less than a year, and the principle of tacking was not established, the title was quieted in Ps. Ds appeal.

Issue. May a person who receives record title to tract #1 under the mistaken belief that he has title to tract #2, and who subsequently occupies that tract, use the period of possession of tract #2 by his immediate predecessors (who also held record title to the other tract) for the purpose of establishing title to tract #2 by adverse possession?

Held. Yes. Judgment reversed.

♦   The fact that this land was used only in the summer months makes no difference in establishing adverse possession.

♦   This case is unique in its claim for adverse possession. Usually the claimant is claiming more than his record title allows for. However, in this case Ds are asking for an area that is different from what they own. Therefore, the lower court held that because the deed did not describe any of the land that was occupied, the actual transfer of possession did not establish privity (which was needed to tack the estates in order to create the statutorily required time period).

♦   This court has held that the privity requirement is no more than a judicial recognition of the need for some reasonable connection between successive occupants of real property so as to raise their claim of right above the status of the wrongdoer or the trespasser. In this case, there was sufficient connection between estates. Thus, the prior estates could be tacked onto the present defendants' time period to meet the statutorily required time period.

Comment This was a parol transfer since Ps took physical possession of tract #2. The deed to tract #1 was inapplicable to tract #2, and hence Ps' possession of tract #2 was based on the prior owner telling Ps, in effect, "Here are the keys to the house I built. You now own it."

----

7. Adverse Possession of Chattels

The doctrine of adverse possession also applies to chattels.

a. Special Rule

One of the requirements of adverse possession is "open and notorious possession." The old rule applied this requirement strictly to chattels. The modern trend, exemplified in the case that follows, applies the "discovery rule" to adverse possession.

b. Discovery Rule

O'Keeffe v. Snyder
416 A.2d 862 (N.J. 1980).

Facts. O'Keeffe (P) brought a replevin action to recover three of her paintings that were allegedly stolen from an art gallery in 1946. In 1976, P sued Snyder (D), owner of an art gallery, to recover these paintings. (P did not claim that D had actual knowledge of the alleged thefts.) D had received the paintings from Ulrich Frank. Frank claimed his father had had the paintings as early as 1943. D argued that: (i) he was a purchaser for value; (ii) he had title to the pictures by adverse possession; and (iii) the replevin action was barred by a six-year statute of limitations. The trial court granted D summary judgment. The appellate division reversed on the grounds that the pictures were stolen and that the defense of the statute of limitations and title by adverse possession were identical and D had not proved the elements of adverse possession. D appeals.

Issue. Does the "discovery rule" apply to stolen artworks to toll the statute of limitations?

Held. Yes. Judgment reversed and case remanded.

- Whether the paintings were stolen or not is a fact issue for the trial court. The granting of the summary judgment while there was a fact question was, therefore, in error. Thus, the case must be remanded.

- A thief acquires no title and cannot transfer good title to others regardless of their good faith or ignorance of the theft. Hence, if the pictures were stolen, D has no title to them.

- It is possible that either Ulrich Frank or his father, who is alleged to have had the paintings as early as 1943, acquired a voidable title to the paintings and that a subsequent good faith purchaser, such as D alleges he is, obtained good title. This can be determined on remand.

- The key issue remaining, then, is when the six-year statute of limitations began to run.

  > The "discovery rule" holds that a statute of limitations does not begin to run until the injured party discovers (or by reasonable diligence could have discovered) the facts that form the basis of the cause of action. The purpose of dais equitable principle is to mitigate the harsh results of the statute of limitations. We hold this rule applicable to replevin actions brought to recover paintings.

  > At trial the court should consider what reasonable steps P could have taken after the alleged theft to recover the paintings.

- To acquire title to chattels by adverse possession, the possession must be hostile, actual, visible, exclusive, and continuous. It is difficult to apply this doctrine to such things as paintings and jewelry.

- The discovery rule is a much fairer way of handling the problem of stolen artworks than is the doctrine of adverse possession. The "due diligence" required under the discovery rule will vary with the nature, value, and use of the personal property involved.

- This holding does not change the doctrine of adverse possession as applied to real estate.

- The expiration of the six-year replevin period should vest in the possessor title to the property as effectively under the discovery rule as under the doctrine of adverse possession.

- Transfer of the property to others neither tolls nor recommences the statute of limitations. The right of replevin tacks.

- On the limited record, any question of copyright infringement cannot be evaluated.

Comment. Prior to retrial, the parties settled. O'Keeffe took "Seaweed," Snyder took another painting, and to pay the expenses of the litigation, a third was sold at auction at Sotheby's.

---

c. Possible Exemption

Congress enacted legislation in 1990 requiring museums to inventory and return, upon request, sacred objects and other cultural artifacts to Native Americans. In order to retain the object, a museum must prove that its possession was obtained with the voluntary consent of one who had authority of disposition over it.

E. Acquisition by Gift

A gift is defined as a voluntary conveyance to another. No consideration is involved. As in the case of deeds, the gift must be intended (sometimes referred to as donative intent) and there must be delivery. An additional requirement is that the grantee (also called the "donee") must accept the gift. Delivery means that there must be a change of possession from the grantor ("donor") to the grantee. Manual delivery is not required if it is impractical. Instead the grantor can effect constructive delivery (*e.g.*, handing over the means of acquiring possession, such as the car keys). Some courts will permit the gift to be made by a written instrument if manual delivery is impractical (either due to the size of the object or due to the circumstances the parties are in). This form of delivery is called "symbolic" delivery. In addition to delivery, the intent to transfer must be a present intent. "I will give you my car next week," for example, does not evidence present intent. Finally, as with deeds, an escrow agent can be used in conveyance.

1. Gifts Inter Vivos

These are gifts made during the grantor's life when his death is not imminent. Once made, an inter vivos gift is irrevocable.

2. Gifts Causa Mortis

These are gifts made in contemplation of imminent death (this includes surgery that the grantor may not survive). This permits deathbed conveyances outside of a will. If the would-be donor survives, the gift is automatically revoked.

3. Revocable Gifts

If the grantor reserves the right to revoke the gift, the general rule is that there is *no* gift at all.

4. No Symbolic Delivery

Newman v. Bost
29 S.E. 848 (N.C. 1898).

Facts. The intestate, a widower without issue, was stricken ill and, due to paralysis, was confined to his bed. In the presence of a witness (Enos Houston), the intestate gave to Julia Newman (P), a woman of 28 who had been the intestate's live-in housekeeper since she was 18, everything he owned. The intestate, who had previously announced his intention to marry P, gave her several keys and announced that he was giving her everything in the house, then pointed out specific pieces of furniture, including a bureau, and repeated that everything in the house was hers. A few days later he died. P sued Bost (D), the intestate's administrator, for $3,000 (me amount of an insurance policy on the intestate, which was kept in a locked drawer in the bureau to which only P had the key); $300, the value of an insurance policy on a piano upon which D had collected; $200.94, the value of the household property sold by D; and $45, the amount D collected on the sale of property from P's bedroom. P claimed the $3,000 and $200.94 as gifts causa mortis and the $45 and $300 as gifts inter vivos. The trial court found for P, and D appeals.

Issue. Is constructive delivery of a gift sufficient if actual delivery is not possible?

Held. Yes. Judgment reversed.

♦ It is unclear whether the intestate meant to give to P merely the bureau the intestate pointed to, or the bureau along with the insurance policy and everything else in the bureau. If the latter had been his intent, he could have had Houston, who was present, get the policy out of the bureau and then have delivered it to P. Since actual delivery was possible, constructive delivery of the insurance policy was insufficient and thus the insurance proceeds belong to the estate and not to P.

♦ As to the furniture to which P had the keys given her (the bureau, etc.), constructive delivery of these items was sufficient since, due to their size and weight, manual delivery was impossible. Delivery of the keys was sufficient.

♦ As to the other articles of household furnishings, except the furniture in P's bedroom, title did not pass to P since they were not constructively or actually delivered to her.

♦ As to the furniture in P's bedroom, there was sufficient evidence to support the jury's finding that that furniture was given to P as a gift inter vivos.

♦ As to the piano, it was bought by the intestate, placed in the parlor, and called "Miss Julia's piano." But when the piano burned, the intestate used the insurance money as his own, and although he said he would, he never did buy P another piano; thus P cannot recover the piano insurance money since there never was delivery.

---

5. Retention of Chattel by Donor

Gruen v. Gruen
496 N.E.2d 869 (N.Y. 1986).

Facts. When Gruen (P) was a college student, his father wrote him a letter telling him he was giving him a Klimt painting for his birthday. P's father stated he would retain possession for his lifetime, however. For tax reasons, P's father later sent another letter describing the gift without referring to the life estate. P's father also asked that P destroy the first letter, which P did. When P's father died 17 years later, the painting was still in the possession of Gruen (D), P's stepmother. P had never had physical possession of the painting. D refused P's request for possession of the painting and P sued. The trial court found that the elements of an inter vivos gift were not satisfied and that a donor cannot retain a possessory life estate after purportedly giving personal property to another. The appellate court reversed, and on remand the trial court awarded P $2,500,000, which was the value of the painting. D appeals.

Issue. May a donor make a valid inter vivos gift of a chattel if the donor retains a life estate in the chattel and never surrenders possession to the donee before the donor's death?

Held. Yes. Judgment affirmed.

♦ To be valid, an inter vivos gift must have three elements: (i) an intent by the donor to make a present transfer; (ii) actual or constructive delivery of the gift to the donee; and (iii) acceptance by the donee. Thus an inter vivos gift differs from a testamentary disposition, which is an intent to make a transfer only upon the donor's death. The critical test is whether the donor intended the gift to transfer a present interest or intended the gift to have no effect until after the donor died. Once an inter vivos gift is made, it is irrevocable and title vests immediately in the donee.

♦ In this case, the evidence clearly shows that P's father intended to give the painting to P while retaining a life estate. D claims that reservation of the life estate defeated the gift. However, there is a difference between ownership and possession, which is recognized in real property law and also applies to personal property.

♦ The element of delivery may be satisfied by constructive delivery, depending on the circumstances. While physical delivery is usually the best form of delivery, it is not always practical. In this case, for example, it would have been impractical and useless for P to have gone to his father's residence to receive the painting and then redeliver it to his father. The delivery of the letters satisfies the delivery requirement in this case.

♦ The acceptance element may be satisfied by the presumption that a recipient accepts a gift of value. In addition, P here showed that he had told others about the gift and he kept the second letter for over 17 years to verify the gift.

Part II

The System of Estates

A. Possessory Estates

1. Historical Background

The law pertaining to freehold estates has its roots in the feudal ages. An understanding of these feudal roots is necessary to make sense of modern real property law.

a. The Feudal System

Starting with William the Conqueror, England developed a feudal ladder. William claimed the whole of England as his own property. In return for certain services (providing yearly a given quantity of food, a certain sum of money, and/or a number of knights and soldiers), William gave vast tracts of land to his tenants-in-chief. These tenants-in-chief, in order to fulfill their obligations to the king, subdivided, so to speak, their vast landholdings to subtenants who provided a given quantity of services. The subtenants would subdivide their land and obligations in turn. In time, a feudal ladder was built with, on the bottom rung, the man in possession who actually grew the wheat, plucked the goose, etc. Since the services were fixed and the value of the land increased, landlords were anxious for their tenants to either die without heirs (in which case the land returned to the landlord) or to breach their obligations (in which case the landlord retook the land).

b. Statute Quia Emportes

Some 200 years after William conquered, the lords who were high on this feudal ladder had the Statute Quia Emportes enacted. This statute prohibited further subdividing of the land and services. In return for this concession, the lords had to give the tenants the right to alienate their land without the lord's consent. The principle that the land should be freely alienable was thus established. This principle of free alienability is the keystone of English and American freehold law.

c. Death of Feudalism

The Statute Quia Emportes marked the beginning of the decline of feudalism. In a few centuries the land was once again owned and controlled by the king.

d. Estates in Land

1) History

From the feudal ages evolved a system of estates in land. The system gradually simplified until **all** estates had to be one of six types (three freehold and three leasehold). The leasehold estates (tenancies at will, periodic tenancies, and tenancies for a fixed term) are discussed *infra*.

2) The Three Freehold Tenancies

a) Fee Simple

A fee simple estate has the potential to endure forever. The various types of fee simple estates are discussed hereafter. The granting language was often "to B and his heirs."

b) Fee Tail

A fee tail estate has the potential of lasting forever, but will cease whenever the tenant does not have a lineal descendant to succeed him. This was important in feudal times as it was a common mechanism to keep land in the family of the wealthy nobles. This type of estate is recognized in only a handful of American jurisdictions. The granting language was "to B and the heirs of his body."

c) Life Estate

This is an estate that will end at the death of some person. The granting language could be "to B, so long as he lives" or "to B for his life." At the death of the measuring life, the estate ends.

3) Seisin

The concept of "seisin" was extremely important in feudal times and is often spoken of in modern real estate cases. Only the holder of a freehold estate could have seisin. One was "seised" of the land if he had a freehold estate and was in possession or a tenant was in possession from him. Using the example of a landlord-tenant situation, it is the landlord who has seisin. In ancient times, a grantor delivered seisin to a grantee. This was accomplished by actually going onto the land and the grantor's giving the grantee, in front of witnesses, a clod of dirt or twig from the freehold estate. In a time when few persons could read or write, this formal ceremony was important to protect from fraud, duress, etc. As England evolved and more and more business began to be conducted in London, this ceremony came to be abandoned.

e. How Estates Are Created

Estates are created by language in a deed or other instrument describing the estate. For example, "I, John Doe, convey to John Brown and his heirs, the following real property . . ." would convey to Brown a fee simple estate.

f. Present and Future Estates

This is where the system of estates begins to get complicated. All estates can be classified as one of two types, present (the word "possessory" is sometimes used) or future.

1) Present Estates

These are estates that give the grantee the immediate right of possession.

2) Future Estates

These are estates that do not give the grantee immediate possession. The grantee will (or "may" as will be seen hereafter) receive possession at a later date.

3) Examples

Suppose G dies, leaving Blackacre "to A and his heirs," Whiteacre "to B for life, then to Z and his heirs," and Greenacre "to my nephew C, if he marries before he turns 25, else to T." A and B both have present estates. Z has a future estate that will vest in him or his successors. C and T both have future estates that may vest.

g. Miscellaneous Matters

Just as there are estates in real property, there may be estates in personal property. Finally, the only estates permitted are those that have been described. No new types of estates may be created.

2. Fee Simple

This is one of the simplest estates to understand. It is an absolute grant by the grantor to the grantee with no limitations as to its duration. The occurrence of no event can cut it short (hence, it is absolute). It has the potential of enduring forever (hence, it is simple). Typical language is "to A and his heirs." Anciently the phrase "and his heirs" was a requisite to creating a fee simple estate. The archaic practice is no longer required, but attorneys often use it when drafting instruments to be absolutely certain that there is no question that a fee simple estate is intended. Modern statutes often provide that it is rebuttably presumed that a grantor conveyed the largest estate that he could. As a practical matter, this usually means a fee simple.

a. Example

G conveys Blackacre "to A and his heirs." A receives a fee simple absolute from G. If A is alive, his heirs receive nothing, the words "and his heirs" being merely words that describe the type of estate conveyed to A. If A is dead, then Blackacre is parceled out as called for in A's will. If A has no will, then the state's intestate succession laws are applied to parcel out Blackacre.

b. Defeasible Estates

A fee simple may be defeasible, as explained *infra*. The fee simple absolute is not defeasible.

3. Fee Tail Estate

a. Introduction

If G conveys Blackacre "to A and the heirs of his body," then A has received a fee tail estate. The significance of this is that if A does not have lineal descendants, then the estate reverts back to the grantor. Since the grantor is usually dead, the land effectively passes to grantor's successor (typically his eldest son, if living, or else to his eldest son's eldest son, etc.). This operates to keep land in the family. In essence then, a fee tail is a fee simple subject to the condition that the grantee always have descendants. This amounts to the grantee having only a life estate, since if he did not have issue, the estate goes back to the grantor. If the grantee has children, then it has to be passed on to them. This type of estate is recognized in only a few states.

b. Disentailing

In time, the fee tail fell into judicial disapproval. As a result, a lineal descendant could "cut off the tail" of the fee tail either by means of a specific lawsuit or by means of deeding a fee simple estate to a "straw man," who in turn reconveyed the estate to the lineal descendant.

c. Modern Results of Conveying a Fee Tail

Most states hold such a conveyance to be a fee simple absolute. A few others hold it to be a fee simple subject to the condition subsequent that the grantee have children. In these states, once the grantee has children, it becomes a fee simple absolute. In other words, the condition subsequent does not pass down from generation to generation as in the case of a true fee tail. The states that recognize fee tails also permit disentailing.

4. Life Estates

a. Introduction

A life estate is one that lasts for the life of some person. There are two types, pur autre vie and for the life of the grantee. The corresponding future interest is called a reversion if the future interest is in the grantor, or remainder if it is in someone else.

1) Life of Grantee as Measuring Life

This is the usual life estate. Typically, G will convey to A "for her life." When A dies, the life estate is terminated and, unless otherwise specified, the estate reverts to G. Of course, G could specify that the estate is to go to anyone else he chooses when A dies.

2) Pur Autre Vie

This French phrase means "for another's life." In this type of life estate, the measuring life is someone other than the grantee. Typical language is "to A for the life of X, then to her son B." Until X dies, the estate belongs to A. If A predeceases X, the estate devolves as A specified in her will, etc.

b. Defeasible Life Estates

Just as in the case of fee simple estates, life estates can be made defeasible or subject to a condition subsequent.

c. Transferability

The holder of a life estate, a life tenant, may lease the estate, convey it, encumber it, etc. However, the transferee gets nothing more than the life tenant has. Thus, if A has a life estate that she leases to X, once the life estate ends, X no longer has an interest. X's interest terminates simultaneously with A's.

d. Preference for Largest Estate in Construing Wills

White v. Brown
559 S.W.2d 938 (Tenn. 1977).

Facts. Lide devised her home to White (P), "to live in and not to be sold." P contended that she received title to the home in fee simple. Brown and the testator's other heirs at law (Ds) claimed that the will conveyed only a life estate to P, leaving the remainder to pass to Ds by intestate succession. The Chancellor held for Ds and the court of appeals affirmed. P appeals.

Issue. Should the language of the will be construed to create in P a fee simple interest in the home?

Held. Yes. Judgment reversed and case remanded.

♦ When the intent of the testator is so ambiguous or obscure that it cannot be ascertained from the language of the instrument or the surrounding circumstances, rules of construction must be applied in interpreting the instrument.

♦ This court will apply statutory rules of construction in effect in Tennessee. The statute provides that unless the "words and context" of the instrument clearly demonstrate an intention to convey a lesser estate or interest, the will should be construed as passing the testator's entire interest. This Tennessee statute is in contrast to the common law presumption that a life estate is intended unless the intent to pass a fee simple is clearly expressed in an instrument.

♦ In the instant case, we find that the will failed to supply sufficient evidence of an intent to limit P's interest to a life estate. Accordingly, the home passed to P in fee simple.

♦ We note that doubts should be resolved against limitation and in favor of the absolute estate. So interpreted, the caveat "not to be sold" expresses an attempt to impose a restraint on alienation of the fee, rather than an attempt to create a life estate. The attempted alienation, being inconsistent with the principle of free alienability of a fee estate, is void as contrary to public policy.

Dissent. The admonition that P was to have the house to live in and "not to be sold" clearly and unambiguously creates a life estate, precluding the need to resort to statutory rules of construction.

Comment. The majority resort to rules of construction is supported by the judicial preference for that construction that disposes of the whole estate, rather than one that results in partial intestacy.

----

e. Limitations on Life Tenants

Life tenants cannot do anything to the estate to detract from its value. They cannot commit waste; if they improve it, the party who receives it after the grantee's life estate is terminated is not liable to the life tenant for the value of the improvements. In other words, the life tenant makes improvements at her own financial risk. Furthermore, life tenants must maintain the estate in good order. Due to the limitations on life estates and their inflexibility, trusts are often a better way of providing someone with an estate for her lifetime. Finally, if the estate is damaged, the majority of jurisdictions hold that the life tenant can recover only for the damage to her life estate, not for the damage to the estate as a whole.

f. Equitable Intervention

Equity may intervene and order sale of the life estate, if the sale is necessary for the best interest of all the parties. If the holders of the remainder are legally incapable of consenting to the sale (underage, insane, etc.), the court may consent for them. This is a flexible remedy, which equity exercises sparingly.

1) Approval of Sale of Property

Baker v. Weedon
262 So.2d 641 (Miss. 1972).

Facts. Weedon (P) sought an order permitting her to sell certain real property against the interests of Weedon's grandchildren (Ds). Weedon bequeathed by will certain property to his third wife, P. The will gave P a life estate with the remainder interest in P's children, if any. If P had no surviving issue, Ds were named as beneficiaries. The will expressly failed to provide for Weedon's children. P remarried after Weedon's death in 1932 and continued to live on the land bequeathed to her. In 1964, the Department of Highways sought a right-of-way through the land P was living on. At that time, Ds were made aware of their remainder interests in the property. P and Ds made an agreement giving P part of the award from the sale to the government. P then sought a court order permitting her to sell the remainder of the land because she needed the money for living expenses. Ds opposed the sale. Although the land was of negligible agricultural value, it was of rapidly increasing commercial value. The chancellor in the lower court approved the sale, finding the property of negligible agricultural value. Ds appeal.

Issue. Can a court approve the sale of property when there are future interests in that property?

Held. Yes. However, case reversed and remanded for a determination upon a motion by P to sell only enough of the land to adequately provide for P's reasonable needs.

♦ A court in equity has the power to order the sale of property in which there are future interests to preserve the estate from waste or deterioration.

♦ Here we do not follow the test of waste or deterioration, but the test of whether a sale is necessary for the best interests of all the parties. The best interests of all the parties would not be served by a judicial sale of *all* the property. The case is remanded for consideration of P's motion to sell only as much of the property as is sufficient for her needs.

Comment. As noted in the discussion of life estates, totally unproductive property can be put to more economically justifiable uses.

---

5. Defeasible Estates

Although any type of estate may be made defeasible, the fee simple defeasible is the most common example of a defeasible estate. There are two distinct types of fee simple defeasible estates; each one has a related future interest.

a. Fee Simple Determinable

This is a fee simple estate that will automatically end if some specified event occurs. This is a fee simple because it may last forever. It is "determinable" because at the occurrence of the specified event, it will automatically end. Typical language is "to A so long as . . . ," "to A while . . . ," or "to A until. . . . " The grantor's future interest is a "possibility of reverter."

1) Example

G conveys Blackacre "to School Board so long as Blackacre is used for an elementary school," or "to A until my son Paul returns from Rome," or "to City while Blackacre is used as a public park." In each of these cases, G has conveyed a fee simple determinable. In each case, if the specified event occurs (Blackacre is no longer used for elementary school, Paul returns from Rome, or City ceases to use the land for a park), then the estate automatically reverts to G. If G is dead, then it passes to G's successors.

b. Fee Simple Subject to a Condition Subsequent

This is a fee simple estate (thus it may last forever) that will be cut short at the occurrence of some specified event. It does not automatically end, however. The grantor may end it, if he wishes, after the occurrence of the specified event. Typical language is "to A, but if A is ever adjudicated insane, then G has the right to reenter." The grantor's future interest is a "right to reenter."

1) Example

G conveys Blackacre "to A and her heirs, but if A does not live to be 18, then G has the right to reenter." If A does not live to be 18, then G may, if he chooses, retake Blackacre. If G does not retake Blackacre, then it goes to A's heirs in fee simple (or to whomever A specifies in her will). Once A reaches 18, the condition is satisfied and A has a "fee simple absolute" estate in Blackacre. G must affirmatively act to retake Blackacre in the event A does not live to be 18.

c. Difference Between Fee Simple Subject to a Condition Subsequent and Fee Simple Determinable

The key difference is the word "automatically." Any fee simple determinable automatically ends at the occurrence of the specified event. Any fee simple subject to a condition subsequent may be ended by the grantor, if he so chooses, after the occurrence of the specified event. Of course, if the grantor is dead, then his successors are entitled to exercise the "right of entry." Note also the difference between the respective future interests. The grantor of a fee simple determinable has a "possibility of reverter" since it is possible that the land will revert back to him. In the case of a fee simple subject to a condition subsequent, the grantor has "a right to reenter" because at the occurrence of the specified event he has the right to reenter, but he does not have to do so. In case of ambiguity, the court will always declare the estate to be a fee simple subject to a condition subsequent. The reason for this is that courts disfavor the automatic divesting of estates.

d. Fee Simple Subject to an Executory Limitation

This is the same thing as a fee simple determinable except that it, by definition, divests in favor of a third person rather than the grantor. Typical language is "to A so long as he is sane, else to B." The respective future interests (the "springing executory interest" and the "shifting executory interest") are discussed later in this outline.

1) Example

G conveys Blackacre "to A unless B returns alive from the war, then to C." If B returns alive from the war, then A's estate automatically terminates and C gets it.

e. Distinctions Between a Fee Simple Subject to a Condition Subsequent and a Fee Simple Determinable

Mahrenholz v. County Board of School Trustees
417 N.E.2d 138 (Ill. App. Ct. 1981).

Facts. On March 18, 1941, W.E. and Jennie Hutton deeded one and one-half acres out of 40 acres of property that they owned to the Trustees of School District No. 1 and their successors in interest (Ds). The deed provided that the land was "to be used for school purpose only; otherwise to revert to Grantors herein." In July 1941, the Huttons conveyed to Earl and Madeline Jacqmain the remaining 38 1/2 acres surrounding the school property, specifically excluding the tract conveyed to Ds. W.E. and Jennie Hutton died, leaving Harry E. Hutton as their only legal heir. On October 9, 1959, the Jacqmains conveyed to the Mahrenholzes (Ps) the 38 1/2 acres, including a reversionary interest in the school grounds. Ds held classes on the property until May 30, 1973, after which time it was used for storage purposes only. On May 7, 1977, Harry Hutton conveyed to Ps all his interest in the school property. On September 6, 1977, Harry disclaimed his interest in the property in favor of Ds. Both conveyances were recorded. The trial court held for Ds. Ps appeal, contending that the deed of March 18, 1941, did not convey a fee simple subject to a condition subsequent, followed by a right of reentry for condition broken, but instead created a fee simple determinable followed by an automatic possibility of reverter.

Issue. Did the trial court correctly interpret the legal effect of the language of the deed so as to preclude Ps from acquiring any interest in the school property?

Held. No. Judgment reversed and case remanded.

♦ The trial court did correctly rule that Ps could not have acquired any interest in the property from the Jacqmains by the October 9, 1959, deed. Whether the future interest is characterized as a possibility of reverter or as a right of reentry for condition broken, Illinois statute forbids the transfer of either interest by will or inter vivos conveyance. The future interest remaining in the grantors could only be inherited by Harry Hutton.

♦ If the grantors retained a possibility of reverter, Harry became the owner of the school property by operation of law when the property ceased to be used for school purposes. If the grantors had retained a right of reentry, Harry becomes owner only after he acts to retake the property (which he did not do). Although the deed did not contain the classic language used to create a fee simple determinable ("for so long as," "while," or "until"), we find that the grantors intended to create such an estate followed by a possibility of reverter.

♦ The word "only" following the grant "for school purpose" constitutes a limitation within the granting clause. This suggests that a limited grant was intended, rather than a full grant subject to a condition.

♦ When read in conjunction with the phrase "otherwise to revert to Grantors," the granting clause seems to trigger a mandatory return rather than a permissive return. There is no language, such as the words "may reenter," indicating that the grantors must act affirmatively to retake possession of the land.

Comment. The appellate court declined to decide whether the 1977 conveyance from Harry Hutton was legally sufficient to convey his interest in the property to Ps. It also refrained from determining the legal effect of Harry's disclaimer in favor of Ds, as well as the question of whether in fact Ds had ceased to use the property for school purposes.

---

f. Restraints on Alienation

Mountain Brow Lodge No. 82, Independent Order of Odd Fellows v. Toscano
64 Cal.Rptr. 816 (Cal. Ct. App. 1968).

Facts. Action to quiet title to real property. James and Marie Toscano deeded a lot to Lodge (P). The deed contained a clause that provided that if (i) the land failed to be used by P or (ii) P sold or transferred the lot, then the lot reverted back to James and Marie, their successors, heirs, and assigns. James and Marie subsequently died. P sued the Toscano heirs (D) to quiet title in itself. P lost and appealed. P contends the restriction was an absolute restraint on alienation and thus void. D contends the covenant created a fee simple subject to a condition subsequent.

Issue. May a grantor restrict the use of the land?

Held. Yes. Judgment affirmed, as modified.

♦ Conditions restraining the alienation of land are void. Clearly, forbidding P to sell the land is an invalid restraint on alienation. However, the clause limiting the property to P's use is not an invalid restraint on alienation.

♦ A grantor may restrict the *use* of land. Here, James was a member of P. It is obvious that the clause limits the land to P's use in order to ensure the land was used for P's purposes as a fraternal lodge.

- Thus, we conclude the clause created a fee subject to a condition subsequent with the title to the reverter in the grantors.

- Covenants such as this one, restricting land use and creating a defeasible estate, have long been recognized in this state.

- The trial court judgment is modified to conform to this holding.

Dissent. The entire clause is invalid as a restraint upon alienation. The clause the majority allows to stand has the same effect as the clause forbidding the sale of the land; it limits who can use the land without reverting to the grantors. This is impermissible.

Comment. The dissent distinguished between restrictions that limit who can use the land and restrictions that limit to what use the land can be put.

---

g. Determinable Fee and Right of Partial Entry

Ink v. City of Canton
212 N.E.2d 574 (Ohio 1965).

Facts. In his memory, descendants of Henry Ink gave 33 1/3 acres to the city of Canton (D) for use as a park "and for no other use and purpose whatsoever." When this condition was not met, the land was to revert to the grantors. Also, the park had to be named after Henry Ink. The land was used for a park until 1961, when the state appropriated the bulk of the land for use as a roadway. The state deposited $130,000 in a fund. The sum represented the value of the taken land and the amount the remaining land declined in value. Ink (P), descendant of the grantors, sued D for the deposited money. D won and P appeals.

Issue. Should the owner of the reverter be paid when, through no fault of the grantee, the land is no longer used for its conditionally granted purposes?

Held. Yes. Judgment reversed.

- Traditionally, in cases such as this, the grantee gets everything and the owner of the reverter gets nothing. This is unfair if the grantee has paid nothing for the land. It gives the grantee a windfall. He gets the value for the land as if he had put it to a more rewarding use than the restriction allows. On the other hand, the owner of the reverter would get a windfall if he was given the land or its value.

- For these reasons, we hold that where the land is given to the grantee, the owner of the reverter is entitled to the following amount: The greater value of the land, less the value of the land with the restriction, which equals the amount due the owner of the reverter. The grantee gets that amount representing the value of the land with the restriction.

- Some courts hold that when eminent domain is involved, the grantee is excused from the restrictive covenant, since the grantee has done nothing to violate the covenant. We reject this, since it still gives the grantee value for something he has not lost. We do not see any reason to distinguish eminent domain cases from the other cases.

- D, by accepting the conveyance, undertook the fiduciary obligation to use the land as a park named after Henry Ink.

- Thus, the money is to be divided as follows: (i) D gets the value of the taken land insofar as this represents the value of the land as a park; (ii) P gets the excess value of the taken land; (iii) D gets the money for the decreased value of the remaining land, but only to the extent such money is, or reasonably can be, used for Ink Park purposes; (iv) D gets to keep the remaining land for as long as it uses it for Ink Park purposes; and (v) D gets the entire sum of money paid by the state for taking the structures D built in the park.

Comment. This case also shows that the holder of a right of entry may exercise a partial right of entry.

B. Future Interests

1. Introduction

This is one of the most complex areas of real property law. Attention must be paid to details. The exact language used is important, as is the sequence of events.

a. Definition

A future interest actually exists at the present time, but will or may become possessory only at some time in the future. For instance, if G deeds Blackacre to A, reserving a life estate for himself (G), A has a future interest in the property. At the end of G's life, A's interest in Blackacre will become possessory.

b. Limited Forms of Future Interest

There are a limited number of future interests. All future interests retained by the *transferor* fit into one of three categories: (i) reversion, (ii) possibility of reverter, and (iii) right of entry. A future interest created in a *transferee* may be: (i) a vested remainder, (ii) a contingent remainder, or (iii) an executory interest. Remainders may be either vested or contingent.

c. Future Interest Is Fixed When Created

The moment a future interest is created it is fixed. If it is subsequently transferred, that does not change its original character.

d. Alienability of Future Interest

While it was not always the case at common law, all future interests are alienable with the exception of rights of entry. Many states apply the common law and do not allow a right of entry to be alienated. Some states do allow alienation.

e. Statutory Termination of Future Interest

The Rule Against Perpetuities, which is discussed hereafter, prevents executory interests from being handed down perpetually. However, the Rule does not apply to possibilities of reverter and rights of entry. Some states, by statute, have limited the duration of such interests, typically to 30 years.

2. Future Interests in the Transferor

There are three possible types of future interests that a transferor may have, depending on the type of estate created: (i) a reversion, based on a life estate; (ii) a possibility of reverter, based on a fee simple determinable; and (iii) a right of entry, based on a fee simple with condition subsequent.

a. Reversion

This is a future interest left in the grantor (or his heirs if the conveyance is by will) after he conveys a lesser estate than he holds. For example: Suppose G, who owns Blackacre in fee simple, conveys it "to A for life." A has a life estate and G has a reversion, since a life estate is less than a fee simple. The key word to understanding reversions is "lesser."

b. Possibility of Reverter

This is a future interest that arises when G conveys a determinable fee of the same quantum. It almost always follows a fee simple determinable. For example: If G conveys Blackacre "to A, so long as A remains unmarried," A has a fee simple determinable. G has a possibility of reverter, since Blackacre will automatically revest in G if A marries.

c. Right of Entry

This is the future interest that follows an estate subject to a condition subsequent. For example: If G conveys Blackacre "to A subject to the condition that she marry before she is 45, or G may reenter," G has a right of entry. Recall that a grantor only has the right of entry. The estate in A does not automatically terminate if A does not marry before she is 45.

3. Future Interests in Transferees

All future interests in transferees are vested remainders, contingent remainders, or executory interests.

a. Remainders

This is a future interest in a grantee that can become possessory at the expiration of the prior estate. It cannot divest or cut short the prior estate. For example: G conveys Blackacre "to A for life, then to B and his heirs." B has a remainder that will become possessory at A's death. B's interest does not divest A of her life estate.

1) Vested Remainders

All remainders are either vested or contingent. Vested remainders are both created in an ascertained person (*e.g.,* "Paul," "my children" (and G already has children), etc.) and are not subject to a condition precedent.

2) Contingent Remainders

Contingent remainders are remainders that are either not created in an ascertained person, or are subject to a condition precedent.

3) Three Subcategories of Vested Contingent Remainders

a) Indefeasibly Vested

This is a remainder that meets two tests. First, the holder of the remainder is certain to acquire a possessory estate. Second, once he receives the estate, he is entitled to retain it permanently. For example: G conveys Blackacre "to A for life, then to B and his heirs." B has an indefeasibly vested remainder. B is certain to acquire the estate when A dies, and once acquired, B is entitled to keep it permanently.

b) Vested Remainder Subject to Open

This is the same as an indefeasibly vested remainder with one exception. The "holder" of the remainder is a class of people which may expand; *e.g.,* G conveys Blackacre "to B for life, remainder to B's children." Suppose B has three children. The class of people entitled to the remainder is sufficiently clear ("B's children"). However, B may yet have other children, and if so, they would be entitled to their pro rata share of Blackacre.

(1) Closing the Class

If other people can conceivably join the class, it is open. When no other person can join the class, it is said to close. The "rule of convenience" dictates that the class close the moment the vested remainder subject to open becomes possessory. In the example above, this would be at B's death.

c) Vested Remainder Subject to Complete Defeasance

If the vested remainder is subject to being divested by the occurrence of a condition subsequent or there is an inherent limitation of the remainder, it is a vested remainder subject to complete defeasance. For example: G conveys Blackacre "to A for life, then to B, but if B does not survive A, then to B's eldest surviving son." B has a remainder. However, if B does not survive A, then B will be divested of the remainder. This may not matter to B but it would to his children other than his eldest surviving son.

4) Examples of Contingent Remainders

a) "To A for life, then to A's children" (A has no children). Until A has a child, the remainder is contingent since there is no ascertainable person. Once A has a child it becomes a vested remainder subject to open.

b) "To A for life, then to B's heirs" (B is Alive). No one is an heir until B dies; thus there is no ascertainable person and the remainder is contingent.

c) "To A for life, then to B if B returns from the war alive prior to A's death." This is a contingent remainder since there is a condition precedent to it vesting in B, to wit: he must return from the war alive. Conditions precedent must be stated in the conveying instrument. Further, the condition must be fulfilled prior to the interest vesting. It is perhaps easy to think of this as the "you will get it if . . ." remainder.

5) Separating Conditions Subsequent from Conditions Precedent

It becomes quite sticky trying to separate conditions subsequent from conditions precedent. It all depends on the language used. The intent of the grantor is irrelevant to the analysis. If the conditional language is incorporated in the description of the gift to the grantee of the remainder, it is a condition precedent. On the other hand, if the conditional language follows words giving a vested remainder to the grantee, the remainder is vested subject to a condition subsequent ("to A for life then to B's children who are then alive"). If the language is ambiguous, the law favors vesting the remainder.

6) Alienability

At common law, no contingent interest was alienable. Most jurisdictions allow alienation of inter vivos contingent interests. Most courts also allow alienation of them by will as long as survivorship is not a condition precedent.

b. Executory Interests

This is a future interest in a grantee that either divests (cuts short) the prior estate or springs out of G at a later date.

1) Shifting Executory Interest

G conveys Blackacre "to A, but if B returns from the war alive, then to B." B has an executory interest that will divest A when B returns from the war alive. The estate will shift from A to B and hence is called a shifting executory interest.

2) Springing Executory Interest

G conveys Blackacre "to A, if A returns from the war alive." When A returns alive, A's future interest will spring from G (the grantor) to A. G's fee simple will then be divested. This is called a springing executory interest.

4. Trusts

A trust arises when a person called a trustee holds legal title to property (the "res") for the benefit of another person, the beneficiary. The person creating the trust is called the trustor or settlor. A common example of a trust is a parent (settlor) setting aside a sum of money (the res) for the benefit of his children (the beneficiaries), the trust being managed by a bank (the trustee). An express trust is one expressly created by the settlor either inter vivos or by will. There are also two forms of implied trusts, resulting and constructive (technically, a constructive trust is not a trust at all, but an equitable remedy).

a. Resulting Trusts

These trusts arise in two situations. In the first instance, a resulting trust will arise if an express trust fails. The second instance arises when someone gives an agent (using the term broadly) money to make a purchase. If the agent takes title, in his own name, to the property purchased with his master's money, he is said to hold the property in a resulting trust for the benefit of his master. The key with resulting trusts is that the person holding legal title did not furnish the consideration for the trust res.

b. Constructive Trusts

This trust arises to prevent unjust enrichment. In such a case the person unjustly enriched is said to be trustee for the person who has been cheated; *e.g.*, A fraudulently induces G to convey Blackacre to A. Blackacre is said to be held in a constructive trust for G as beneficiary.

c. Requirements for an Express Trust

The trustor must manifest the intent that the res be held in trust by a trustee for the benefit of someone. Unlike gifts, there is no delivery requirement. Further, a settlor can make himself a trustee for someone else. In any case, the trustee has a high fiduciary duty to not use the res for his own benefit; he must also prudently invest or manage the res. A trustee may, however, charge for his services. If there is no res, or trustee, or beneficiary, there is no trust. However, a settlor can provide for a trust to arise in the event certain res does come into existence. A life insurance proceeds trust created by the settlor prior to his death is a common example.

d. Judicial Modification of Trusts

It is clear that a settlor cannot anticipate every possible future contingency when creating a trust. If there is a change of circumstances, the trustee or beneficiary can petition the court to modify the trust. Modification will not be allowed if the settlor anticipated the change in circumstances, or if compliance with the trust terms does not substantially impair the accomplishment of the trust's goal.

e. Trust Income Not Subject to Seizure by Beneficiary's Creditors

Broadway National Bank v. Adams
133 Mass. 170 (1882).

Facts. Charles Adams (D) was a trust beneficiary under the provisions of his brother's will. The trust income was to be paid to D semiannually. The terms of the trust provided that the trust income was to be free from the interference or control of D's creditors and was not to be anticipated by assignment. Broadway National Bank (P) brought a bill in equity to apply the trust income as payment of D's debt to P.

Issue. May the founder of a trust by will secure the trust income to the beneficiary by providing that it cannot be alienated or subject to seizure by the beneficiary's creditors in advance of its payment to him?

Held. Yes. Bill dismissed.

♦ The intention of the testator is clear in this case, and if the court were to order the trustee to pay income to P, it would be in direct violation of the testator's intention and the will provisions. This court will not compel the trustee to do what the will forbids him to do, unless the provisions and intention of the testator are unlawful.

♦ Under common law, a man cannot attach to a grant or property transfer, which is otherwise absolute, the condition that it cannot be alienated. By such a condition, the grantor tries to deprive the property in the hands of the grantee of one of its legal incidents and attributes—its alienability. This is against public policy.

♦ However, where there is a transfer of property in trust, the trust property passes wholly to the trustee, who takes legal title to the property, along with the power of alienation. The trust beneficiary takes the whole legal title to the accrued income at the moment it is paid over to him.

♦ Courts have differed as to whether the common law rule should apply to equitable life estates created by will or deed. Some courts have held that the founder of a trust may not provide that the income of the trust cannot be taken for the beneficiary's debts. Other courts have upheld such provisions.

♦ The precise question at issue here has not been adjudicated in Massachusetts, but previous decisions of this court have recognized the principle that if a founder of a trust, like the one at issue here, intends to give an equitable life tenant a qualified and limited, not an absolute, estate in the income, such life tenant cannot alienate it by anticipation, and his creditors cannot reach it at law or in equity. This principle appears to apply to this case.

♦ Here, the founder owned his property absolutely. He had the complete right to dispose of it, in a manner not repugnant to law, either by an absolute gift or by a gift with restrictions or limitations. His intention was not to give his brother an absolute right to the trust income, with the power of alienating it in advance, but only to give him the right to receive the income of the fund semiannually. At the time of payment to him, not before, the income was to become his absolute property. The founder's intentions should be carried out unless they are against public policy. The power of alienating in anticipation is not a necessary attribute of D's interest here, and the restraint of alienation would not be repugnant.

♦ P argues that creditors are misled by the appearance of a beneficiary's wealth, which induces them to give the beneficiary credit. This argument fails because all wills and most deeds are public records. Creditors may reach a debtor's property not exempted by law, but they may not enlarge a founder's gift of a trust and take more than he has given. A debtor's property is subject to the payment of his debts, but a donor's property is not subject to the debts of his beneficiary.

5. Destruction of Contingent Remainders

The common law rule, still recognized in a minority of states, was that if the contingent interest did not vest at the termination of the prior freehold estate, the remainder was destroyed and never took effect; *e.g.*, G conveys Blackacre "to A for life, then to A's children who marry before 25." If when A dies none of her children have married before 25, then the remainder is destroyed and the estate returns to G, who is said to have the reversionary interest.

a. Rule in Shelley's Case

Also at common law (recognized in a few states) the Rule in Shelley's Case was applied. Under this rule if one instrument (i) creates a freehold estate in A and (ii) also creates a remainder in A's heirs, and (iii) both of the estates are either equitable or legal, then the remainder becomes a fee simple remainder in A. The doctrine of merger (discussed next) then steps in to merge the fee simple remainder and the life estate into a fee simple estate for A. This rule applied to fee tail estates as well; *e.g.*, if G conveys Blackacre "to A for life, then to her heirs," since one instrument has created a freehold estate (in this case a life estate) in A and a remainder in her heirs, under the Rule in Shelley's Case, A has a fee simple remainder. This remainder merges with the life estate and A winds up with fee simple title to Blackacre.

b. Doctrine of Merger

Under this doctrine, if A has both a life estate and a remainder, unless there is some vested estate that intervenes between the life estate and the remainder (or one estate is subject to a condition precedent to which the other is not subject), then the life estate and remainder merge and A has fee simple title to Blackacre. If an intervening estate was only a contingent remainder, it would be destroyed when the two interests merged.

c. Doctrine of Worthier Title

Under this doctrine, if (i) an inter vivos conveyance (ii) creates a future interest in the heirs of the grantor, then the future interest is void and the grantor has a reversion. *Example*: G while alive conveys Blackacre "to A for life, remainder to my heirs." Since an inter vivos conveyance is involved, which creates a future interest in G's heirs, G has a reversion. At common law this doctrine was a rule of law (and thus had to be applied in every case); most jurisdictions today recognize it as a rule of construction that can be rebutted. Note that the doctrine applies to any future interest in G's heirs. Today this rule applies to real and personal property.

6. The Rule Against Perpetuities

a. Introduction

This rule is the downfall of many unwary practitioners. Gray has stated the Rule as: No interest is good unless it must vest, if at all, not later than 21 years after some life in being at the time of the creation of the interest. The Rule applies to contingent remainders and executory interests. It does **not** apply to future interests in the grantor, nor to vested remainders.

b. Purpose of the Rule

The purpose of the Rule is to prevent the vesting of contingent future interests in the distant future. It is a rule of proof, not of construction. If there is any possibility, however remote, that the contingent future interest involved will vest outside of the "life in being plus 21 years," the future interest is void.

c. Corporations

Corporations have the potential of lasting for hundreds of years. Thus, for purposes of the Rule, a 21-year period is used.

d. Gestation

For purposes of the Rule, a life is in being from the time of conception, if the person is later born alive.

e. Vesting

The materials earlier in this outline on vesting vs. contingent become critical in applying the Rule. There is one exception to the previous discussion on vesting.

1) Special Rule

Although for most purposes a grant to a class vests as soon as there is a member of the class, for purposes of the Rule, a grant to a class does not vest until the class closes and all conditions precedent are satisfied. The Rule applies if there is any possibility of vesting outside of the prescribed time period. The presumption is that so long as a person is alive, she may have children.

2) Unborn Widows

Widows may yet be born. *Example*: G conveys Blackacre "to A for life, then to A's widow for life, then to their children." Even if A is now married, his wife could die and he could marry someone who was not yet born at the time of the conveyance. Thus, while the grant to A's widow is valid because it will vest immediately upon the death of A (a life in being), the grant to their children is void since their gift may not vest within 21 years after A's death. Thus, G has a reversion.

f. Blue Penciling

When applying the Rule, the invalid interests are stricken and legal effect is given to what is left. *Example*: G conveys Blackacre "to Klamath Falls so long as used for a library, but if Blackacre ceases to be used for a library, then to A and her heirs." If the Rule did not apply, G would have conveyed to Klamath Falls a fee simple subject to a condition subsequent. (Language of both fee simple determinable and fee simple subject to a condition subsequent is present. Since there is an ambiguity and the law disfavors the automatic termination of estates, the estate would be a fee simple subject to a condition subsequent.) A would have a shifting executory interest. However, since Blackacre could clearly cease to be used for library purposes later than 21 years after a life in being at the time the future interest was created, the Rule does apply. Applying the Rule, we "blue pencil" the impermissible portion of the conveyance, leaving "to Klamath Falls so long as used for a library." This is a fee simple determinable with a possibility of reverter in G.

g. Reforming the Rule Against Perpetuities

As you have seen, application of the Rule can lead to undesirable results. There has been a trend in recent times to reform the Rule.

1) The Wait and See Doctrine

A majority of states apply the wait and see doctrine in different forms. For example, some jurisdictions wait to see if vesting occurs within the common law period (21 years); others wait and see the length of measuring lives of persons statutorily listed. The Uniform Statutory Rule Against Perpetuities provides a 90-year wait and see period.

2) Cy Pres

Some courts will apply this doctrine and permit the conveying instrument to be modified to comply with the presumed intent of the grantor. Thus, if a contingent future interest would be void under the Rule ("then to A's children who reach 30"), the court will modify to comply with the apparent intent of the grantor. In the example, this would be changing the age from 30 to 21.

3) Reformation

Some states have enacted reformation statutes to cure violations of the Rule, *e.g.*, setting a realistic age for cessation of child-bearing.

h. Applying the Rule to Option to Purchase

The Symphony Space, Inc. v. Pergola Properties, Inc.
669 N.E.2d 799 (N.Y. 1996).

Facts. Broadwest Realty owned a two-story commercial building on Broadway between 94th and 95th in Manhattan and was unable to secure a tenant for 58% of the square footage (a theater). Broadwest also owned an adjacent residential complex and an adjacent commercial building and was operating at a net loss. On December 1, 1978, Broadwest and Symphony (P), a nonprofit organization devoted to the arts, executed a contract for sale of the building to P for a below-market price of $10,010. P leased back the commercial space to Broadwest, excluding the theater, for $1 per year. Broadwest maintained liability for the $243,000 mortgage and other maintenance obligations. As a condition of the sale, P, for $10 consideration, granted Broadwest an option to repurchase the entire building. Since P was a not-for-profit corporation, it could seek a tax exemption for the whole property. The sale and leaseback reduced Broadwest's real estate taxes by $30,000 per year while retaining the $140,000 annual rental income. On December 31, 1978, the parties executed a deed from Broadwest to P; a lease from P to Broadwest at $1 per year for the term January 1, 1978 to May 31, 2003, unless terminated earlier; a 25-year, $10,000 mortgage and note from P as mortgagor with full payment due on December 31, 2003; and an option agreement. The option agreement provided that Broadwest could exercise its right to purchase during any of the following "Exercise Periods: (a) at any time after July 1, 1979, so long as the Notice of Election specifies that the Closing is to occur during any of the calendar years 1987, 1993, 1998 and 2003. . . . " P obtained a tax exemption for the theater. In 1981 Broadwest sold and assigned its interest under the lease, option agreement, mortgage, and note, as well as its interest in the two adjacent buildings for $4.8 million. The purchaser contemporaneously transferred its rights to Pergola Properties and others (Ds) as tenants in common. Pergola initiated a cooperative conversion of the residential property, which received landmark designation in 1982, and the property's value substantially increased. In 1988, an appraisal of the entire blockfront, including unused air and other development rights, valued the property at $27 million, assuming the option was enforceable. The value of the leasehold interests and the adjacent commercial building without the option was $5.5 million. In 1985, Pergola, on behalf of Ds, notified P it was exercising its option with a closing date of January 5, 1987. P filed this declaratory judgment The parties cross-moved for summary judgment. The trial court granted P's motion. The appeals court affirmed. Ds appeal.

Issue. Are options to purchase commercial property exempt from the prohibition against remote vesting embodied in New York's Rule Against Perpetuities?

Held. No. Judgment affirmed. Ds' option is unenforceable.

- New York's Rule Against Perpetuities has been statutory since 1830, and predicated on the public policy of the state; it is a non-waivable legal prohibition. Under its common law, options to purchase land are subject to the Rule. The common law evaluates the reasonableness of a restraint based on duration, purpose, and designated method for fixing the purchase price.

- Options to purchase grant the holder the right to compel the owner to sell whether the owner is willing or not, unlike the preemptive right or right of first refusal in commercial and government transactions, which only minimally impede alienability. Here, the option to purchase provides the exact type of control over future disposition of the property that the common law rule against remote vesting seeks to prevent.

- Commonly, an option to purchase land that stems from a lease provision and is not exercisable after the lease expires and cannot be separated from the lease is valid even though the interest may vest after the perpetuities period. These options "appurtenant" to leases encourage the holder to maintain and develop the property by guaranteeing him the ultimate benefit of the improvements. Here the holder does not lease all of the property subject to the option and the option is not appurtenant. There is no incentive for P to improve the theater because it knows the property will eventually be claimed by D. The option significantly deters development of the property. Refusing to enforce it would further the purpose and rationale underlying the statutory prohibition against remote vesting.

- Ds' claim that the option must be exercised within the statutory period is contradicted by the plain language of the instrument. The parties are corporations and no measured lives are stated in the instruments; thus, the period is 21 years. With the required notice, the option could be exercised in 2003, as late as 24 years after its creation in December 1978.

- The "saving statute" cannot be invoked; rules of construction apply if a "contrary intention" does not appear in the instrument. The language here expresses the intent that the option be "exercisable 'at any time' during a 24-year period." This language does not permit a construction that the parties only intended 21 years.

- This court has refused to apply the "wait and see" approach. To look at what actually occurs during the perpetuities period offends the Rule, which mandates that "an interest is void from the outset if it may vest too remotely. . . . "

- Rescission of the parties' contract of sale if the option fails is not an appropriate remedy. While contracts entered into under mutual mistake of fact are subject to rescission, whether mistake of law may be a basis of rescission is a matter of discretion. To rescind here would give the option effect, which would be directly contrary to the Rule and undermine what the Rule was intended to prevent.

C. Co-Ownership and Marital Interests

1. Common Law Concurrent Tenancies

At common law, the three basic forms of concurrent tenancies were tenancies in common, joint tenancies, and tenancies by the entireties.

a. Tenancies in Common

This form of concurrent ownership is the simplest of the three basic tenancies. It is created by an express conveyance or when the property is inherited. Each tenant (co-owner of an interest) has a stated share of the property. Moreover, each tenant has an undivided interest in the whole property. That is, each tenant has an equal right to possess the whole property. Thus, unless his co-tenants object, one tenant can enter and use the whole property. When one tenant dies, his interest goes to his heirs (there is no "right of survivorship"). Tenants in common can have unequal shares of the property and need not have the same estate. The significance of this will become apparent when examining joint tenancies.

1) Presumption

Unless otherwise stated, it is presumed that a conveyance creates a tenancy in common.

2) Partitioning

Tenants in common can petition the court to divide the property among them. The court will do so if it is in the interests of the tenants as a whole.

b. Joint Tenancies

In this form of tenancy, each tenant has an undivided interest in the whole property, just as in the case of tenancies in common. The distinctive characteristic of this tenancy is the right of survivorship. When one tenant dies, the surviving joint tenants receive the decedent's interest in the property. The decedent's interest can never pass to his heirs (unless, of course, one of them happens to be a joint tenant).

1) Special Requirements in Creating a Joint Tenancy

At both common law and modern law, there are four requirements in creating a joint tenancy. These requirements are rooted in the old common law and are called the "four unities." If there is a failure of one of the four unities, the tenants are tenants in common, not joint tenants.

a) Unity of Title

Every one of the joint tenants must acquire title by the same conveyance, be it a will or a deed. This requirement must be carefully scrutinized for its pitfalls. Often a husband will desire to convey property to himself and his wife as joint tenants. If he does this by "granting Blackacre to myself and my wife, as joint tenants," all he has created is a tenancy in common. The reason for this is that at common law no one could convey property to himself. Thus, the husband's conveyance to himself and his wife amounted to a conveyance to his wife of one-half of the property, with him retaining the other half. Hence, there was no unity of title. Modern statutes sometimes give this type of conveyance effect as a joint tenancy.

b) Unity of Time

Each joint tenant's interest must vest at the same time. If G conveys Blackacre "to A for life, then to her heirs and the heirs of B as joint tenants," all that is created is a tenancy in common. The reason for tins is that A's heirs are determined at the time of A's death and B's heirs at the time of B's death. There is thus a failure of the concurrent estate to vest in A's heirs and B's heirs at the same time.

c) Unity of Interest

Each joint tenant's interest must be equal and must be the same type of estate. Thus, a conveyance of one-third of Blackacre to A for life and the other two-thirds to B in fee simple fails because (i) the interests are not equal (one-third vs. two-third) and (ii) because the estates are not equal (one is a fee simple, the other a life estate).

d) Unity of Possession

When each joint tenant acquires his interest, he must have the right to possess the whole. Of course, after the tenancy is created, the tenants can agree that only one of them is to have actual possession of the property.

2) Split Conveyance

A conveyance can be split. That is, it may create a joint tenancy in combination with some other tenancy. Thus G can convey Blackacre "one-half to A and B as joint tenants, the other half to B and C as tenants in common." This does not offend the unity of interest requirement.

3) Grantor's Intent

At common law it was presumed that a grant to two or more persons was a joint tenancy. This presumption has been abolished. Currently the various jurisdictions require a clear intent on the part of the grantor to create a joint tenancy.

4) Bank Accounts

It is common for holders of concurrent interests in bank accounts to be joint tenants. A special set of rules applies to joint interests in bank accounts. This topic is beyond the scope of this outline.

2. Severance of Joint Tenancies

A joint tenant may sever the right of survivorship by severing any of the four unities. The common law viewed this strictly. Modern law generally requires that the joint tenant intend to sever one of the unities. Many states have enacted statutes providing that divorce converts a joint tenancy between spouses into a tenancy in common.

a. Elimination of Common Law Fictions

Riddle v. Harmon
162 Cal.Rptr. 530 (Cal. Ct. App. 1980).

Facts. Mr. Riddle (P) and his wife acquired a parcel of real estate as joint tenants. Mrs. Riddle decided to terminate the joint tenancy so she could dispose of her share by will. Her attorney had her execute a deed granting herself an undivided one-half interest in the real estate. The deed specifically stated that the purpose of the deed was to terminate the joint tenancy. The trial court quieted title to the real estate in P. Harmon (D), the executrix of Mrs. Riddle's will, appeals.

Issue. May a joint tenant terminate a joint tenancy by granting her one-half undivided interest to herself?

Held. Yes. Judgment reversed.

♦ A joint tenancy may be converted to a tenancy in common by destruction of one of the four unities: interest, time, title, and possession. Each joint tenant clearly has the right to destroy the joint tenancy without the consent or knowledge of the other joint tenant by conveying her separate estate by gift or otherwise. Even if the recipient reconveys the property to the joint tenant, the unities remain destroyed and there is no joint tenancy.

- ♦ At common law, the only way for a person to create a joint tenancy with another person was to use a "strawman," who would receive the property, then reconvey it to the original owner plus the other joint tenants. California changed this rule by statute so that a joint tenancy conveyance may be made from a sole owner to herself and others.

- ♦ Prior cases have held that a joint tenancy cannot be terminated without using a strawman; *i.e.*, the joint tenant would have to convey the property to the strawman who would then reconvey to the former joint tenant. This is an outdated requirement that is easily met by using a trust or an associate of the attorney involved as the strawman. Because there is no reason other than tradition for following the feudal law requirements, the strawman procedure is no longer necessary.

- ♦ The elimination of the strawman requirement does not give new powers to a joint tenant, because such tenants had the power to destroy the tenancy by conveying to another person. Thus, one joint tenant may unilaterally sever the joint tenancy without using an intermediary.

Comment. The court noted that there are several alternative ways to create an indestructible right of survivorship. These include creating a joint life estate with a contingent remainder in fee to the survivor; a tenancy in common in fee simple with an executory interest in the survivor; and a fee simple to take effect in possession in the future.

---

b. Effect of a Mortgage on a Joint Tenancy

Harms v. Sprague
473 N.E.2d 930 (Ill. 1984).

Facts. Harms (P) and his brother took title to some real estate as joint tenants with right of survivorship. P's brother obtained a mortgage on the joint tenancy. When his brother died, P sued Sprague (D), the executor and sole devisee, as well as the mortgagees, to quiet title and to obtain a declaratory judgment. D counterclaimed seeking recognition of D's interest as a tenant in common. The trial court found that the mortgage severed the joint tenancy and survived the death as a lien against D's one-half interest. The appellate court reversed, and D appeals.

Issue. If one joint tenant mortgages his interest in the joint property, is the joint tenancy severed?

Held. No. Judgment affirmed.

- ♦ Cases involving severance of a joint tenancy typically rely on the four unities of interest, title, time, and possession. The courts have held that a judgment lien on one joint tenant's interest does not sever the joint tenancy unless a deed is conveyed and the redemption period has passed.

- ♦ If a mortgage is merely a lien, and not a conveyance of title, the execution of a mortgage by a joint tenant would not destroy the unity of title. Early cases followed the title theory of mortgages and would have resulted in the severance of the joint tenancy in this case. However, this court has since characterized a mortgage as a lien. Consequently, a joint tenancy is not severed when one joint tenant executes a mortgage on his interest because the unity of title has not been severed.

- ♦ Because the joint tenancy survived the execution of the mortgage, P became the sole owner of the property upon his brother's death. The mortgage does not survive. P takes the property through the conveyance that created the joint tenancy, not as his brother's successor. The mortgage was a lien on P's brother's interest, which was extinguished by his death.

---

3. Partition

Delfino v. Vealencis
436 A.2d 27 (Conn. 1980).

Facts. The Delfinos (Ps) and Vealencis (D) owned a 20.5-acre parcel of land as tenants in common. D occupied the land. Ps sought to develop the property into building lots. Ps brought an action to partition the property by sale; D moved for in-kind partition. The trial court held that partition in kind would result in material injury to the rights of the parties and ordered that the property be sold at auction and the proceeds distributed to the parties. D appeals.

Issue. Did the court properly order the sale, pursuant to statute, of the property owned by Ps and D as tenants in common?

Held. No. Judgment set aside and case remanded.

♦ It has long been the policy of this and other courts to favor partition in kind but to allow partition by sale in emergencies or when division cannot be well made otherwise.

♦ The burden is on the party requesting partition by sale to demonstrate that such sale would better promote the owners' interests.

♦ The court must consider the interests of all parties and not only the economic gain of one party. The court failed to consider that D had actual and exclusive possession of a portion of the property for a substantial period of time; D made her home on the property and derives her livelihood from the operation of a business on this portion of the property.

---

4. Sharing the Benefits and Burdens of Co-Ownership

Spiller v. Mackereth
334 So.2d 859 (Ala. 1976).

Facts. Spiller (D) and Mackereth (P) owned a building as tenants in common. When the lessee vacated, D entered the building, began using it as a warehouse and supplied new locks. P wrote a letter demanding that D vacate half of the building or pay half of the rental value. D refused. The court found for P. D appeals.

Issue. Is a co-tenant in possession liable to his co-tenants for the value of his use of the property in the absence of an agreement to pay rent or an "ouster"?

Held. No. Judgment reversed.

♦ Since there was no agreement to pay rent, ouster of a co-tenant must be established before D is required to pay rent to P. Ouster describes two distinct fact situations: (i) the beginning of the running of the statute of limitations for adverse possession, *i.e.*, a claim of absolute ownership and denial of the co-tenancy requirement; and (ii) the occupying co-tenant refuses a demand of the other co-tenants to be allowed into use and enjoyment of the land, regardless of a claim of absolute ownership. The second situation applies here.

♦ P's letter was not a demand for equal use and enjoyment of the premises.

♦ Whether a demand to vacate or pay rent is sufficient to establish an occupying co-tenant's liability has not been addressed here, but the majority view is that the occupying co-tenant is not liable for rent notwithstanding a demand to vacate or pay. The occupying co-tenant must have denied his co-tenants the right to enter. There is no evidence that D did so.

---

5. Leasing the Property

Special rules apply if one tenant leases the property to third parties without the consent of his co-tenants. At common law this effectuated a severance of the concurrent interest. The more modern view is contrary. The next case sets forth the modern trend and the principles surrounding it.

a. Lessee in Possession

Swartzbaugh v. Sampson
54 P.2d 73 (Cal. Ct. App. 1936).

Facts. Swartzbaugh (P) and her husband owned as joint tenants 60 acres of land. Her husband entered into an option to lease this property to Sampson (D). P sued her husband and D to have the lease canceled. Sampson leased the property in order to construct a boxing pavillion on it. P disapproved of this and would not sign any lease. Her husband and D then entered into the lease without P's knowledge. Subsequently the two men entered into a second lease involving the property. P lost in the lower court and appeals.

Issue. Can one joint tenant who has not joined in the leases executed between her cotenant and another maintain an action to cancel the leases where the lessee is in possession of all the leased property to the exclusion of the plaintiff?

Held. No. Judgment affirmed.

♦ An estate in joint tenancy can be severed by destroying one or more of the necessary unities, either by operation of law, by death, or by voluntary or certain involuntary acts of one joint tenant without the consent of the other. One of the essential unities is possession.

♦ Ordinarily a joint tenant out of possession cannot recover possession of the property to the exclusion of the other. Further, one joint tenant cannot sue the co-tenant for rent as a result of occupancy of the property (*i.e.*, she cannot sue a co-tenant in possession for rent if the co-tenant lives on the property) or for profits derived from his own labor. She can compel the tenant in possession to account for rent paid by third parties.

♦ During the lives of the co-tenants, the rules regulating the transfer of their interests are substantially the same whether they are tenants in common or joint tenants. Neither a joint tenant nor a tenant in common can do any act to the prejudice of his co-tenants in their estate. Thus, one tenant cannot without consent sell his co-tenant's interest.

♦ Generally, one joint tenant cannot, without the consent of his co-tenant, bind or prejudicially affect the rights of the other.

♦ An exception to this rule allows one joint tenant to lease all of the joint property without the consent of the co-tenant and put the lessee in possession. The theory behind this is that the one joint tenant is entitled to possession of the entire property and the lease merely gives to the lessee a right that he, the lessor, had been enjoying; thus, this is not prejudicial to the co-tenant. However, the lessor/joint tenant cannot convey that which he does not have (for example: he could not unilaterally give the lessee an option to purchase). The nonlessor co-tenant can recover from the lessor-tenant a pro rata share of the rents if the lessee refuses to allow her the use of her share of the estate.

♦ Thus, we conclude that a lease such as the one here is not a nullity but is valid. Hence, P cannot cancel the leases. P's concern that D will obtain title to the land by adverse possession is without merit.

Comment. Under the rule in this case P could have tried to use one-half of the land. If the lessee refused to let her do so, she could have recovered from her husband one-half of the rent. For purposes of this example, the effects of California law as a community property state were ignored.

b. Expenses

Each tenant must pay his share of the taxes, mortgage, etc. If one tenant is in actual possession of the property, he can make these payments and then turn around and sue his co-tenants for contribution. However, the co-tenant in possession cannot collect from the other tenants for improvements he makes to the property. Of course, rent from third parties must be divided among the co-tenants.

c. Ouster by Exclusive Possession

Sole possession by one tenant is not in itself adverse to the rights of a co-tenant. Even long, exclusive, and uninterrupted possession by one tenant, without any possession or claim for profits by the nonpossessory tenant, is not sufficient evidence of an actual ouster absent an explicit repudiation of the co-tenancy.

6. Marital Interests—The Common Law System

a. Marital Estates

At common law a system of marital estates evolved that had as their goal the protection of the surviving spouse. These estates were dower for the wife and jure uxoris and curtesy for the husband.

1) Dower

The wife had a one-third life estate in all land with which her husband was seised during the course of the marriage if that land would be inheritable by children born to the marriage. (There did not have to be children born to the marriage.) Thus, if the husband had a life estate, after his death the wife would have no dower claim (since the life estate terminated at the husband's death and hence could not be inherited by children of the marriage). Once the dower right attached (the moment the husband was seised of the land), any subsequent holder of the property (purchasers, creditors, etc.) took it subject to the wife's right to dower. Of course, the wife's dower interest was inchoate (not yet possessory) until her husband died.

2) Jure Uxoris

For the period of the marriage, all of the wife's personal property (except clothes and ornaments) was the property of her husband. This included her earnings and the right to possess, manage, and take all the profit from her real property.

3) Curtesy

This is the equivalent of dower for the husband. It was subject to the same conditions and limitations as dower. The chief difference between dower and curtesy was that the husband did not have a right to curtesy unless children were born to the marriage.

4) Rationale for Common Law Marital Estates

At common law a surviving spouse could not inherit the decedent spouse's property. The only rights of the surviving spouse were dower or curtesy.

5) Remarriage

Rights to dower and curtesy did not terminate if the surviving spouse remarried.

6) Curtesy and Dower Abolished

By statute, curtesy, dower, and jure uxoris have been abolished in most United States jurisdictions. They have been replaced by modern statutes such as the Uniform Probate Code, which provides for an "elective share" of the decedent's estate to go to the surviving spouse.

b. Tenancy by the Entirety

This form of tenancy can exist only between husband and wife. It is quite similar to a joint tenancy in that the four unities must be satisfied and there is the right of survivorship. However, severance by one of the tenants is impossible. In the states that still recognize this form of tenancy (many states no longer recognize it), it is rebuttably presumed that a conveyance to a husband and wife creates a tenancy by the entirety.

1) Common Law

At common law the husband had the exclusive right to manage the property and collect all the rents and other profits. If he survived his wife, he received the whole of the concurrent estate. The husband could transfer his right of survivorship to third parties, including creditors. The wife, on the other hand, had only the right of survivorship. This right remained with the wife even if the husband conveyed away his entire interest in the property. Her creditors could not reach her right of survivorship.

2) Modern Law

The Married Women's Property Acts, enacted in every state during the last century, changed this. It put the wife on equal footing with her husband in managing and disposing of real and personal property. Various jurisdictions apply their Acts differently as to tenancies by the entirety.

3) Spouse's Interest Not Subject to Levy and Execution by Individual Creditors

Sawada v. Endo
561 P.2d 1291 (Haw. 1977).

Facts. Mr. and Mrs. Sawada (Ps) were struck by a car driven by Kokichi Endo (D). On the date of the accident, D owned as a tenant by the entirety a parcel of real property. Shortly after the accident, D and his wife conveyed, without consideration, the real property to their sons. The deed was recorded shortly before the auto accident trial. Ps won the auto accident trial and, after being unable to satisfy their money judgment from D's personal property, sought to have the above conveyance set aside so they could satisfy the money judgment. (Kokichi's wife died a few days after the auto accident trial.) Ps lost and appeal.

Issue. Is the interest of one spouse in real property, held in tenancy by the entirety, subject to levy and execution by his individual creditors?

Held. No. The trial court is affirmed.

♦ Nineteen states and the District of Columbia continue to recognize tenancy by the entirety as a valid and subsisting institution in the field of property law. These jurisdictions can be divided into four groups.

♦ Group I: Three states hold that the estate is essentially the common law tenancy by the entirety, unaffected by the Married Women's Property Acts. As at common law, the estate is subject to the husband's exclusive dominion and control. The husband may convey the entire estate subject only to the possibility that the wife may become entitled to the whole estate upon surviving him. In two of these states the use and income from the estate is not subject to levy during the marriage for the separate debts of either spouse. One state allows only the husband's creditors to levy against the estate.

- ◆ Group II: Five states allow the interest of the debtor spouse to be sold or levied upon for his separate debts, subject to the other spouse's contingent right of survivorship. One of these states by statute allows levying against a debtor spouse's interest unless the property is a "homestead."

- ◆ Group III: Eleven jurisdictions hold that an attempted conveyance by either spouse is wholly void, and the estate may not be subjected to the separate debts of one spouse only.

- ◆ Group IV: Two states hold that the contingent right of survivorship appertaining to either spouse is separately alienable by him and attachable by his creditors during the marriage. The use and profits, however, may neither be alienated nor attached during coverture.

- ◆ Hawaii has long recognized that joint, common, and entirety tenancies are separate and distinct estates. In a tenancy by the entirety, both spouses are seised of the whole estate. Spouses do not take by moieties.

- ◆ The Married Women's Property Acts abrogated the husband's common law dominance over the marital estate and placed the wife on equal footing with her husband regarding the exercise of ownership over the whole estate. They also had the effect of insulating the wife's interest in the estate from the separate debts of her husband.

- ◆ Neither husband nor wife has a separate divisible interest in the property held by the entirety that can be conveyed or that can be reached by creditors. The estate is indivisible except by joint action of the spouses. Each spouse owns the entire estate.

- ◆ This holding is not unfair to creditors. They can require the signatures of both spouses, insist that debtors do not hold property as tenants by the entirety, etc.

- ◆ Were we to consider public policy we would reach the same result. By not permitting property held by tenants by the entirety to be subject to the individual spouse's creditors, the marital estate is secure for family purposes. This permits planning for children's educations, family emergencies, etc.

Dissent. I dissent on the ground that the majority misconstrues the Married Women's Act. A better interpretation is that since at common law the husband could alienate his right of survivorship, the Act enabled the wife to do likewise. Thus, the judgment creditors of either spouse may levy and execute upon their separate rights of survivorship. There is no logical reason to place a restriction upon the freedom of the spouses to deal independently with their respective interests.

---

4) Civil Forfeiture by Innocent Spouse

In *United States v. 1500 Lincoln Avenue*, 949 F.2d 73 (3d Cir. 1991), the United States sought civil forfeiture of property owned as a tenancy by the entireties and containing a pharmacy out of which Mr. Bernstein illegally distributed prescription drugs. Mrs. Bernstein averred that she had not known of the criminal activity; she did not occupy the premises. The federal government conceded that she had a valid innocent owner defense to the extent of the interest in the property that she was entitled to retain. The government argued that Mr. Bernstein's illegal use of the property resulted in severance of the entireties estate and that Mrs. Bernstein was entitled to a one-half interest. After the district court dismissed, based on Mrs. Bernstein's defense and her right to an interest in all of the property, the government's motion to alter or amend the judgment was denied. The appeals court reversed, remanding for a determination of whether Mr. Bernstein's interest was subject to forfeiture, and if it was found to be, Mrs. Bernstein's rights would be preserved by Mrs. Bernstein retaining exclusive use and possession during her lifetime, being protected against any conveyance without her consent or any attempt to levy upon the interest formerly held by her husband, and retaining the right to obtain title in fee simple absolute if she is predeceased by Mr. Bernstein.

c. Dissolution

Dissolution presents many difficult problems, which are normally studied separately in a family law course. However, the division of marital property involves certain basic property law principles with which any attorney should be familiar. The basic purpose of property settlements is to allocate to each spouse what equitably belongs to that spouse. The concepts of equity have changed over the years.

1) Common Law Approach

At common law, each spouse would retain the property to which he held title. A tenancy by the entirety would become a tenancy in common, and existing joint tenancies or tenancies in common would remain valid. Normally, the husband owned most of the property, but he would have to provide support, or alimony, to the wife.

2) Modern Approach

With the acceptance of no-fault divorce, the states replaced the common law approach to property division with a rule of equitable distribution, permitting the court to exercise discretion in dividing the property. Some states permit division of all property owned by the spouses; others restrict it to marital property, which can include all property acquired by whatever means during the marriage, or merely the property earned by either spouse during the marriage. Alimony is commonly called "maintenance" and is paid only for a period long enough to allow the dependent spouse to obtain employment.

a) Determining What Property Is Subject to Division

In re Marriage of Graham
574 P.2d 75 (Colo. 1978).

Facts. Mrs. Graham (P) put her husband (D) through one year of undergraduate school and three years of an M.B.A. program by working full-time as an airline stewardess. He worked part-time while going to school. P contributed 70% of the family financial support. Following his graduation D got a job as an executive assistant with a large corporation. After six years of marriage they filed for divorce. No marital assets were accumulated during the marriage. P did not claim financial support from D. The divorce court found that as a matter of law, the M.B.A. degree was jointly owned by P and D. The future earnings value of the M.B.A. were valued at $82,836. P appealed. The intermediate court held for D. P appeals.

Issue. Is a graduate degree marital property subject to division on divorce?

Held. No. Judgment affirmed.

◆ The applicable statute requires, without regard to misconduct, marital property to be divided in such proportions as it deems just after considering all relevant factors.

◆ It is clear that the statute intended for "property" to be broadly defined. Nonetheless, there are necessary limits upon what is considered "property."

◆ One helpful definition is "everything that has an exchangeable value of which goes to make up wealth or estate." For example, in one case we held that military retirement pay was not property for the reason that it did not have any of the elements of cash surrender value, loan value, redemption value, lump sum value, or value realizable after death.

- Even under the broad view of property, a graduate degree simply does not have an exchange value or any objective transferable value on an open market. It is personal to the holder. It is the result of many years of education, diligence, and hard work.

- We are unable to find any decisions, even in community property states, which hold that one spouse's education is a marital asset to be divided on dissolution; *e.g.*, a case has held that a physician's accrued goodwill in his medical practice is not property.

- This holding does not mean that a spouse who contributes to the other's education is without remedy. Contribution of financial support to a spouse getting a degree is a factor that may be taken into consideration in awarding the contributing spouse support. Here, P does not seek support from D.

Dissent. As a matter of economic reality, the most valuable asset acquired by either party during their six-year marriage was the graduate degree. By excluding the degree from the definition of "property," courts are impotent to provide a remedy for an obvious injustice. Future earning capacity is an asset considered in wrongful death actions; it should be the same in divorce actions. In awarding support (alimony), courts have broad discretion in considering relevant factors, such as contribution to one spouse's education. This case points out factors to be considered in determining whether or not something is "property."

---

b) Career and/or Celebrity Status

Elkus v. Elkus
572 N.Y.S.2d 901 (N.Y. App. Div. 1991).

Facts. Frederica von Stade Elkus (P) had just embarked on her career in opera at the time of her marriage, and during her marriage her career succeeded dramatically. In 1973, she earned $621,878. P is known internationally, has received numerous awards, and has performed for the President of the United States. P's husband (D) traveled with P, attending and critiquing her performances, and photographed her. D was also P's voice coach and teacher for 10 years of the 17-year marriage. D claims he sacrificed his own career to devote himself to P, and since P's celebrity status increased during the marriage due in part to his contribution, he is entitled to equitable distribution of this marital property. P and D have stipulated to mutual judgments of divorce and to joint custody of their two minor children. Trial on the remaining economic issues has been stayed pending P's appeal. The supreme court found that the enhanced value of P's celebrity status was not marital property. D appeals.

Issue. Is the enhanced value of P's career and/or celebrity status marital property subject to equitable distribution?

Held. Yes. Order reversed and case remanded.

- To the extent D's contributions and efforts led to an increase in the value of P's career, this appreciation was a product of the marital property subject to equitable distribution.

- Marital property is property acquired during the marriage regardless of the form in which title is held.

- Marital property need not be an asset with exchange value, salable, assignable, transferable, or licensed. However, a medical license has been held to enhance earning capacity, so as to enable a spouse who contributed to its acquisition to share its value.

- A marriage is an economic partnership to which both parties contribute. The enhanced skills of an artist such as P, albeit growing from an innate talent, which have enabled her to become an exceptional earner, may be valued as marital property. D's contributions and active involvement were direct and concrete. It is the nature and intent of the contribution by the spouse seeking equitable distribution, rather than the nature of the career, that should determine the status of the enterprise as marital property.

- - - - - - -

c) Professional Goodwill

Most jurisdictions treat professional goodwill, *e.g.*, reputation likely to generate future business, as a divisible marital asset.

7. Community Property

Arizona, California, Idaho, Louisiana, Nevada, New Mexico, Texas, Washington, and Wisconsin are community property states. Basically, community property means that all the property acquired during the period of the marriage belongs equally to the spouses, each having equal right to manage the property. In 1998, Alaska became an "elective" community property state; couples may elect to hold their property as community.

a. Two Classes of Property

In community property states property is divided into two classes, community and separate. All property acquired by a spouse before the marriage, or after marriage if the property was acquired by gift, descent, or devise, is that spouse's separate property. All other property acquired during the marriage is community property. This includes wages. Each spouse has a 50% interest in all community property.

b. Commingling

While the exact rules vary from state to state, generally commingling causes separate property to become community property unless a contrary intent on the part of the couple can be proven. Upon divorce each spouse gets her own separate property and one-half of the community property. The division of community property need not be exactly 50–50. In addition, from the time of separation each spouse's earnings are her separate property.

c. Migrating Couples

If a couple moves away from a community property state to a common law state, problems arise in characterizing property as community or separate. Generally, the law of the state where the couple is domiciled at the time they acquire the property governs. The chief exception to this rule involves real property. In that case the law of the state where the land is situated governs. If a couple moves to a community property state from a common law state, then all property acquired after the move is governed by community property law. The character of the property acquired prior to the move does not change.

8. Rights of Domestic Partners

In the ten states and the District of Columbia that still recognize common law marriage, the parties must manifest their intent to be and hold themselves out to the public as husband and wife. In common law jurisdictions the couple have the same rights as one married with traditional license and ceremony. Most jurisdictions abolished this practice for various reasons, the most common of which was the proof of marriage required for government benefits, pensions, and property claims. Contract theory stepped into the void in the 1960s when couples began to live together, with the most well-known case being *Marvin v. Marvin*, 557 P.2d. 106 (Cal.1976), where the state supreme court held that a contract could be implied from the parties' conduct. All states did not agree with *Marvin's* holding and in 2002, a different approach was adopted by the American Law Institute's Principles of the Law of Family Dissolution (Principles). The principle that legal rights and obligations arise from the conduct of the parties with respect to each other even though they have created no formal documentation or agreement stating such an understanding served as it basis. It is the same principle that underlays common law marriage. The Principles require that domestic partners share a primary residence and a life together as a couple for a significant amount of time. Sharing a life as a couple is determined by reference to a detailed list of circumstances. If both parties are living when the partnership ends, their property is divided according to the principles set forth for the division of marital property. If one partner dies, the survivor's rights depend on the state's law of intestate succession.

a. Marriage Not Limited to a Man and a Woman

Varnum v. Brien
763 N.W.2d 862 (Iowa 2009).

Facts. Six same-sex couples (Ps) lived in committed relationships but were prevented from marrying by the state statute that defined marriage as a union between a man and a woman. Ps requested marriage licenses from the county recorder (D), who, pursuant to law, refused to issue the licenses. Ps filed suit, claiming that the statute violated their fundamental right to marry and the rights to privacy and familial association and that they were being discriminated against on the basis of their sexual orientation. The case came before the court as a motion for summary judgment The record was developed through witness affidavits and depositions. Some of the Ps explained the disadvantages and fears they faced because they were unable to obtain a civil marriage in Iowa. These included: their legal inability to make many life and death decisions affecting their partners (*e.g.*, health care decisions and burial arrangements); their inability to share in their partners' state-provided health insurance, public employee pension benefits, and many private employer-provided benefits; the denial of some tax benefits; and the inability to obtain for themselves and for their children the personal and public affirmation that accompanies marriage. The district court found the statute unconstitutional under the due process and equal protection clauses of the Iowa Constitution and granted Ps summary judgment. It ordered D to begin processing marriage licenses for same-sex couples, but stayed the order during the pendency of this appeal.

Issue. Does the state statute limiting civil marriage to a union between a man and a woman violate the Iowa Constitution?

Held. Yes. Judgment affirmed.

♦ The doctrine of equal protection is the primary constitutional principle in this case. Like the Equal Protection Clause in the Fourteenth Amendment to the United States Constitution, Iowa's constitutional promise of equal protection "is essentially a direction that all persons similarly situated should be treated alike."

♦ Iowa courts pay deference to legislative decisions when determining whether the Iowa Constitution's equality mandate has been violated by legislative action. Most often, the rational basis test is applied; the plaintiff has the burden of showing *the* statute unconstitutional and must negate every reasonable basis upon which the classification may be sustained. But where reasons exist to suspect prejudice against discrete and insular minorities, a heightened level of scrutiny under equal protection analysis is applied. Classifications based on race, alienage, or national origin, and those affecting fundamental rights, are subject to strict scrutiny. These classifications are presumptively invalid and must be narrowly tailored to serve a compelling governmental interest.

♦ There is a middle tier of analysis between rational basis and strict scrutiny. This intermediate tier is applied to statutes classifying on the basis of gender or illegitimacy, and the party seeking to uphold the statute must demonstrate that the challenged classification is substantially related to the achievement of an important governmental objective. Groups entitled to this tier of review, known as "intermediate scrutiny" or "heightened scrutiny," are often called "quasi-suspect" groups. To survive intermediate scrutiny, the law must further an important governmental interest and be substantially related to that interest, and the justification for the classification must be genuine and not based on broad generalizations.

♦ D's threshold argument is that Ps are not similarly situated to heterosexuals because Ps cannot "procreate naturally." Equal protection does not require all laws to apply uniformly to all people, but it demands that those who are similarly situated with respect to the legitimate purposes of the law be treated alike. Plaintiffs must show as a preliminary matter that they are similarly situated, not identical, to people treated more favorably by the law in order for a court to consider whether their different treatment is permitted under the equal protection clause. A court cannot just look at the trait used by the legislature to define a classification under a statute and decide that a person without that trait is not similarly situated to persons with the trait.

♦ The equal protection guarantee requires that laws treat all those who are similarly situated with respect to the purposes of the law alike. Accordingly, the purposes of the law must be referenced in order to evaluate whether the law equally protects all people similarly situated with respect to those purposes. In this case, the trait asserted by D is insufficient to support its threshold argument.

♦ Our marriage laws, which provide an institutional basis for defining the fundamental relational rights and responsibilities of persons in our society, also serve to recognize the status of the parties' committed relationship. Thus, in accordance with the purposes of Iowa's marriage laws, we find that Ps are similarly situated compared to heterosexual persons. Official recognition of their status provides an institutional basis for defining their fundamental relational rights and responsibilities, just as it does for heterosexual couples.

♦ The marriage statute does not explicitly refer to "sexual orientation" and does not expressly prohibit gay and lesbian persons from marrying. However, it requires that if gay and lesbian persons marry, they must marry someone of the opposite sex. It is clear that the law is targeted at gay and lesbian people as a class since the benefit denied by the statute—the status of civil marriage for same-sex couples—is closely correlated with being homosexual. Thus, the ban on same-sex civil marriages differentiates implicitly on the basis of sexual orientation.

♦ In determining whether certain legislative classifications warrant more demanding constitutional analysis, the United States Supreme Court has looked to: (i) the history of invidious discrimination against the class burdened by the legislation; (ii) whether the characteristics that distinguish the class indicate a typical class member's ability to contribute to society; (iii) whether the distinguishing characteristic is "immutable" or beyond the class members' control; and (iv) the political power of the subject class.

♦ As to the first factor, gay and lesbian people have suffered a history of purposeful and invidious discrimination because of their sexual orientation. And until recently, homosexual conduct was criminalized in many parts of this country. This suggests that any legislative burdens placed on lesbian and gay people as a class are more likely than others to reflect deep-seated prejudice instead of legislative rationality in pursuit of a legitimate objective. Thus, elevated scrutiny should be applied to uncover such prejudice.

♦ Regarding the second factor, a classification unrelated to a person's ability to contribute to society is likely based on prejudice and typically reflects a view that those in the burdened class are not as worthy as others. None of the same-sex marriage decisions from other states have found sexual orientation to be indicative of a person's ability to contribute to society. And our legislature has recently declared as our state's public policy that sexual orientation is not relevant to a person's ability to contribute to numerous societal institutions other than civil marriage.

♦ Immutability is another factor in determining the correct level of scrutiny because the inability of a person to change a characteristic that is used to justify different treatment makes the discrimination violative of the concept that legal burdens should bear some relationship to individual responsibility. The permanency of the barrier imposed on the group depends on the ability of the individual to change the characteristic responsible for the discrimination. Temporary barriers are less burdensome, are more likely to advance a legitimate governmental interest, and thus, normally do not warrant heightened scrutiny.

♦ The nature-versus-nurture debate over the origin of sexual orientation need not be definitively resolved before plaintiffs' equal protection claims can be decided. The constitutional relevance of the immutability factor does not apply only to traits that are absolutely impossible to change. D acknowledges that sexual orientation is highly resistant to change.

♦ As to the fourth factor, D argues that gays and lesbians have secured many legal protections against discrimination and mat, therefore, they are not a politically powerless class. This implies that they must be characterized by a complete lack of political power before courts should subject sexual-orientation-based legislative burdens to heightened scrutiny. But Supreme Court cases show that absolute political powerlessness is not necessary. Women enjoyed a measure of political power when the Court first heightened its scrutiny of gender classification. Moreover, although the political power of gays and lesbians has been responsible for greater acceptance and decreased discrimination, it has done little to remove barriers to civil marriage. The political-power factor does not weigh against heightened judicial scrutiny of sexual-orientation-based legislation.

♦ The factors established by the Supreme Court all point to an elevated level of scrutiny. Therefore, we hold that legislative classifications based on sexual orientation must be examined under a heightened level of scrutiny under the Iowa Constitution.

♦ Intermediate scrutiny requires that a statutory classification be substantially related to an important governmental objective. The differential treatment or denial of opportunity for which relief is sought is used to identify the statutory classification. Here, Ps complain of their exclusion from the institution of civil marriage. The issues are whether the state has exceedingly persuasive reasons for denying civil marriage to same-sex couples and whether the exclusion of Ps from civil marriage is substantially related to an important governmental objective.

♦ D's proffered objectives include support for "traditional" marriage, optimal procreation and rearing of children, and financial considerations. We must determine whether the objectives purportedly advanced by the classification are important. If they are, the critical question is whether these governmental objectives are advanced by the legislative classification.

♦ Maintaining "traditional" marriage is just another way of saying that the governmental objective is to limit civil marriage to opposite-sex couples. The tradition is merely the classification expressed in the statute that is being challenged. When tradition is used as both the objective and the classification to further that objective, we are faced with a circular inquiry of whether the classification accomplishes the objective, which objective is to maintain the classification; the equal protection analysis is changed into the question of whether restricting marriage to opposite-sex couples accomplishes the governmental objective of maintaining opposite-sex marriage. This is empty analysis that allows a classification to be maintained for its own sake and permits discrimination to become acceptable because of tradition. Equal protection requires that the classification advances a state interest that is separate from the classification itself.

♦ D contends that social scientists say that child-rearing by a father and mother in a marriage is the best environment for raising children. This objective implicates the broader governmental interest in promoting the best interests of children, an important governmental objective. Ps, however, presented much evidence and research, confirmed by our independent research, that supports the proposition that same-sex couples can raise children as well as opposite-sex couples.

♦ Even if there were a rational basis to believe that a legitimate government interest is advanced by the legislative classification based on sexual orientation, it would not be sufficient to survive the equal protection analysis that applies in this case. Intermediate scrutiny requires a closer relationship between the classification and the purpose of the classification than rationality. The relationship between the goal and the classification must be substantial. A consideration of the under-inclusiveness or over- inclusiveness of the statute will help to determine this.

♦ An under-inclusive statute means that all people included in the statutory classification have the trait that is relevant to the purpose of the statute, but other people with the trait are not included in the classification. An over-inclusive statute means that the classification made in the statute includes more persons than those who are similarly situated with respect to the purpose of the law. As the degree of over- or under-inclusiveness increases, the difficulty of showing that the classification substantially furthers the legislative goal increases.

♦ D argues that a goal of the statute is that children will be raised in the optimal milieu. With this goal in mind, the statute is under-inclusive because it does not exclude from marriage other less than optimal parents, *e.g.*, child abusers and violent felons. Such under-inclusion suggests that the classification is based on prejudice and overbroad generalizations about gays and lesbians, rather than having a substantial relationship to an important objective.

♦ D could argue that the ban is only one step toward ensuring the best environment for raising children; by reducing the number of same-sex parent households, it is slowly moving the state towards the optimal milieu for children. However, this argument is flawed because the ban is over-inclusive—not all same-sex couples want to raise children. At the same time, the ban is under-exclusive—same-sex couples raise children in this state now without being married, and they will continue to do so. A law that is so simultaneously over-inclusive and under-inclusive is not substantially related to the government's objective. Also, the marriage statute denies the children of same-sex couples an environment supported by the benefits of marriage.

♦ Even if the ban on same-sex marriage could be justified as a means to ensure the asserted optimal environment for raising children, this does not mean that fewer children will be raised by same-sex couples or that more children will be raised in heterosexual marriages. Such outcomes would be accomplished only when people in same-sex relationships choose not to raise children without being married or when children are adopted by heterosexual couples who would have been adopted by same-sex couples if not for the same-sex civil marriage ban. There is no substantial support for this proposition.

♦ D asserts that maintaining traditional marriage will result in more procreation. But the only way that excluding same-sex couples from marriage could promote procreation is if it caused them to become heterosexual in order to procreate within a traditional marriage. Even if this were possible, the statute is under-inclusive because it does not include many other groups who do not procreate—the elderly, the physically disabled, and those who choose not to.

♦ D suggests that promoting stability in opposite sex relationships, an important governmental interest, is another rationale supporting the marriage statute. However, although the institution of marriage likely encourages stability in opposite-sex relationships, we can find and D offers no reasons showing that the statute achieves this end.

♦ D also puts forth the objective of conservation of state resources. If fewer people are allowed to marry, less state money will be expended on numerous governmental benefits, such as tax benefits, enjoyed by married couples. Excluding any group from civil marriage would achieve this result—African-Americans, illegitimates, aliens, but such classifications offend society's sense of equality.

♦ Also, many heterosexual married couples do not file joint tax returns or obtain any other tax benefit from marital status. If allowed to marry, many same-sex couples might not file joint tax returns or use more state resources than they use as unmarried couples. The two classes, opposite-sex couples and same-sex couples, may use the same amount of state resources. Hence, the two classes are similarly situated for the purpose of conserving state resources, but they are treated differently by the law.

♦ For these reasons, the sexual-orientation-based classification under the marriage statute does not substantially further any of the purported governmental objectives, as required by intermediate scrutiny.

♦ D has not addressed another reason for exclusion of same-sex couples from civil marriage, religious opposition. Our constitution does not allow any branch of government to resolve these types of religious debates and authorizes courts to ensure that the government avoids them. The free exercise of religion includes the freedom of a religious organization to define marriage as a union between a man and a woman. But the government must not endorse any religious view, either directly or indirectly. Civil marriage must be judged under our constitutional standards of equal protection rather than under religious doctrines. Our constitutional principles require that the state recognize both opposite-sex and same-sex civil marriage.

♦ The exclusion of gays and lesbians from the institution of marriage does not substantially further any important governmental objective. The legislature has excluded a historically disfavored class of individuals from an important civil institution without sufficient justification. Our constitutional duty to ensure equal protection of the law requires us to hold Iowa's marriage statute in violation of the state constitution.

♦ Therefore, the language in the Iowa marriage statute limiting civil marriage to a man and a woman must be stricken, and the remaining statutory language must be interpreted and applied so that gay and lesbian people are allowed full access to the institution of civil marriage.

———————

Part III

Leaseholds: The Law of Landlord and Tenant

A. Leasehold Estates

1. Introduction

Landlord-tenant law has changed significantly over the years as the courts and legislatures have recognized the inapplicability of traditional notions to modern circumstances. This area of law originated during the feudal ages when tenants were farmers who were primarily interested in the land. Buildings were maintained by the tenant, and the landlord typically had few duties other than to not evict the tenant. This agrarian model has proven inappropriate for the residential tenant, and the law has adapted to the needs of the modern tenant.

2. The Types of Tenancies

a. Term of Years

This type of tenancy is (i) for a fixed period of time (does not have to be measured in years) and (ii) the calendar dates for the beginning and ending of the lease period are ascertainable. For example, "one year from the date of signing of this lease," or "three years, five days after my 30th birthday." In both of these examples, once the lease is signed, the beginning and ending dates are ascertainable, so no notice is required.

b. Periodic Tenancy

This tenancy is for a fixed period of time until either the landlord or the tenant gives notice of termination. Examples of this are, "from month to month," "from year to year." Absent contractual provisions to the contrary, the terms and conditions carry over from period to period.

c. Tenancy at Will

It is easy to confuse the tenancy at will and the periodic tenancy. A tenancy at will lasts only so long as the landlord and tenant desire. Both are equally capable of terminating the lease at any time. The lease may provide for a given period of notice, such as 30 days, before the lease may be terminated.

d. Construing Lease Terms

Garner v. Gerrish
473 N.E.2d 223 (N.Y. 1984).

Facts. Donovan leased a house to Gerrish (D) for rent of $100 per month. The lease was to continue until D terminated the agreement at a date of his own choice. D moved in and had lived there for over four years when Donovan died. Garner (P), Donovan's executor, served D with a notice to quit the premises. D refused, and P initiated an eviction proceeding on the claim that the lease created a tenancy at will. D claimed the lease was a tenancy for life, but the court granted P summary judgment, holding that since the lease term was indefinite, it was a month-to-month term. The appellate court affirmed and D appeals.

Issue. If a tenant has the right to terminate a lease at a date of his own choice, does the tenant have a determinable life tenancy?

Held. Yes. Judgment reversed.

♦ At common law, a lease at the will of the lessee was also deemed to be at the will of the lessor. This rule arose from the requirement of livery of seisin to convey a life estate; if livery of seisin did not take place, a tenancy at will resulted.

♦ Livery of seisin has been abandoned, so there is no reason to convert a lease granting a tenant the exclusive right to terminate at will into a tenancy at will terminable by either party. The rule adopted by the Restatement recognizes that a lease such as D's creates a determinable estate in the tenant, terminable at the tenant's will or on the tenant's death.

♦ D's lease gives D the right to terminate the lease at a date he chooses. This is a common way to create a life tenancy terminable at the tenant's will. The lease is not indeterminate even though D could terminate it earlier than the time of his death.

---

e. Tenancy at Sufferance: Holdovers

A tenant who was rightfully in possession but wrongfully remains in possession after the tenancy expires becomes a tenant at sufferance. The tenant is not a trespasser and is not really a tenant because the possession is without the landlord's permission. The tenancy at sufferance lasts until the landlord either evicts the tenant or elects to hold the tenant to another term. The states apply varying rules as to the terms of the tenancy that apply if the landlord elects to hold the tenant to another term.

1) Rent Increases

If the landlord notifies that a higher rent will be charged for holding over, the tenant is liable for the increased rent unless he notifies the landlord that he will not pay it. This is one situation where silence on the tenant's part will be construed as consent to the rent increase.

3. The Lease

As mentioned above, landlord-tenant law originated in an agrarian culture. At first, a lease was primarily contractual, but in the 16th century the courts began recognizing the tenant's interest as a possessory interest in the land. A lease was a conveyance of an estate in land as well as a contract between the landlord and tenant. In recent years, the courts and legislatures have emphasized the contractual nature of leases in order to better protect tenants.

a. Conveyance

To the extent that a lease is a conveyance, the tenant typically acquires the right of exclusive possession, and the landlord can reenter only if the tenant breaches a covenant. The tenant assumes the responsibility of caring for the property.

b. Contract

The contractual nature of a lease involves the respective promises, or covenants, between landlord and tenant. The parties may allocate risks, expenses, and duties as they see fit. The promises are mutually dependent, so that if one party does not perform, the other is excused from performance.

4. Selection of Tenants

Traditionally, a landlord could lease or not lease to whomever she pleased for whatever reason she chose. Discrimination based on sex, race, and the like were possible in every case. Changes began by laws passed shortly after the Civil War.

a. Civil Rights Act of 1866

This Act prohibited racial, and only racial, discrimination in the leasing and selling of real and personal property. An aggrieved party could sue the landlord or seller for an injunction or damages.

b. Fair Housing Act of 1968

This congressional Act prohibits discrimination in selling or renting based on race, color, religion, or national origin. The Act was amended to prohibit discrimination based on sex in 1974.

1) Exceptions

The Act provides for certain exceptions. In the case of single-family dwellings a seller or lessor can discriminate if she owns fewer than four such dwellings, does not use a broker, and does not advertise in a manner that indicates her intent to discriminate. "Mrs. Murphy's" exception permits a resident owner of a building with four or fewer rooms or apartments (depending on whether it is the room or apartment for lease) to discriminate. Note that "Mrs. Murphy" must live in one of the four units, and she cannot advertise that she discriminates.

2) Remedies

Only the United States Attorney General (if he wishes), HUD (in certain cases), or the aggrieved party may sue the discriminating landlord or seller.

3) Prima Facie Case and Burden of Proof

Once the aggrieved party makes out a prima facie case, the burden of proof shifts to the landlord or seller.

5. Delivery of Possession

The landlord must give the tenant at the beginning of the lease term the right of possession. If the landlord does not then have the right of possession or if she fails to transfer it to the tenant, the landlord is in default.

a. Majority Rule

The majority rule (also known as the "English rule") imposes on the landlord the duty of giving the tenant both the legal right of possession and actual possession. If a prior tenant is holding over, it is the duty of the landlord to get him out.

b. Minority View ("American Rule")

In a minority of jurisdictions the landlord need deliver only the legal right of possession. Holdover tenants become the new tenant's problem and he has to sue to get them out at his own expense.

c. No Implied Covenant

Hannan v. Dusch
153 S.E. 824 (Va. 1930).

Facts. Dusch (D) leased some real property to Hannan (P) for a term of 15 years. When the term was to begin, the tenant who had possession prior to the agreement refused to relinquish the estate to P. D refused to take any legal action to remove the holdover tenant. P brought suit against D to recover damages resulting from D's inability to take possession of the leased land. The lower court held in favor of D. P appeals.

Issue. Does the landlord have the implied duty to deliver physical possession to the tenant at the beginning of the lease term?

Held. No. Judgment affirmed for D.

♦ There is no implied covenant that leased premises shall be open for possession by the tenant at the beginning of his term. The only right that the new tenant has is the right to possession. When the lease makes no provision for physical possession at the beginning of the term, and there is a tenant who is in possession and refuses to relinquish the leasehold, the new tenant has a remedy against the wrongdoer but not against the landlord.

♦ The rationale appears to be that the landlord should not be held liable for the wrongdoings of a third party.

Comment. The tenant's obligation to pay rent is dependent upon the landlord's fulfilling her obligation:

(i) To provide the legal right to possession;

(ii) Not to interfere either directly or indirectly with the tenant's physical possession; and

(iii) In most jurisdictions, to place the tenant in actual possession.

---

6. Subleases and Assignments

a. Assignments

Leases may be assigned by either the lessee or lessor absent some contractual provision to the contrary. The assignee (new tenant) is in privity of estate with the landlord, and unless otherwise provided, their obligations are the same as in the original lease.

b. Subleases

Subleases are different from assignments in that the tenant who subleases is a landlord to his sublessee. There is no privity of estate between the original landlord and the sublessee;

neither one can sue the other. Certain rules apply in determining whether a transfer is a sublease or assignment.

1) The Effect of a Reversion

At common law, if the subleasing tenant conveyed to the sublessee anything less than the whole leasehold estate (retained a reversion), it was a sublease and not an assignment. Conversely, if the new lessee received the whole (and not one bit less) of the leasehold estate, an assignment was involved.

2) The Effect of Retaining a Right of Entry

If a transferring tenant retains a right of entry in the event the transferee breaches a condition of the lease, the common law regards the transfer as an assignment, not a sublease. The modern view would hold the transfer to be a sublease.

3) Modern Trend

The modern trend is to examine the intention of the parties in determining whether a transfer is an assignment or a sublease. If the transferring tenant charges more rent than he has been paying, the courts view this as an indication of a sublease. If the transferee tenant pays a lump sum, the courts take this as an indication of an assignment.

c. Construing Terms of a Sublease

Ernst v. Conditt
390 S.W.2d 703 (Tenn. Ct. App. 1964).

Facts. Ernst (P) leased land to Frank Rogers for a term of 53 weeks. Rogers operated a go-cart business on the land. A few months later, Conditt (D) desired to purchase Rogers's business. P, Rogers, and D negotiated a two-year modification of the original lease. In the modification, P consented to Rogers's "subletting" the premises to D. However, Rogers remained personally liable to P. After D occupied the land and paid the rent for a few months he quit paying rent. D remained in possession until the end of the lease term. P sued D to recover back rent. D contended that he had sublet the land from Rogers, so there was no privity between P and D. Consequently, P could not sue D. The chancellor found for P. D appeals.

Issue. Are the words "sublease" and "subletting" in a transfer document controlling in determining whether a transfer is a sublease?

Held. No. Judgment affirmed for P.

♦   If a transfer is a sublease, there is no privity and the original landlord cannot recover directly from a sublessee. If a transfer is an assignment, there is privity and the landlord can recover from the assignee.

♦   At common law, if a transfer conveyed the whole leased estate, it was an assignment. If it conveyed less than the whole, even one day less, it was a sublease. (Under a sublease the sublessor had a reversionary interest, a right to reenter.)

♦   The modern rule looks to the intent of the parties rather than to formalistic ancient rules.

♦   Under either rule, the transfer to D was an assignment.

♦   This is true in spite of Rogers being personally liable. Under either sublease or assignment he still would have been personally liable to P absent a lease provision to the contrary. Rogers had no reversionary interest since he completely divested himself of the business and the leased property. Under the common law rule the transaction was an assignment.

♦ The use of the words "sublease" and "subletting" in the modified lease is not controlling. Under the common law rule, the effect of the transfer was controlling, rather than the words. Under the modern rule, it is the intent of the parties that is controlling, not the words.

Comment. Courts distinguish between a sublease and an assignment in the following way: When a lessee transfers all of her interest under the lease, *i.e.*, the right to possession for the entire term remaining, an assignment results; when a lessee transfers anything less, a sublease results (*e.g.*, where there are three years remaining on the lease and the lessee transfers two years, she has subleased and retains a reversion at the end of the two-year period).

---

d.   Commercial Lessor's Duty to Act in Good Faith

Kendall v. Ernest Pestana, Inc.
709 P.2d 837 (Cal. 1985).

Facts. Ernest Pestana, Inc. (D) leased hangar space at an airport that was subject to a preexisting sublease with Bixler. Bixler arranged to sell his business to Kendall and two other parties (Ps), but because Bixler's lease provided that the consent of the lessor was necessary for an assignment, Bixler sought D's consent. D refused to consent. Ps sued, claiming D's refusal to consent was an unlawful restraint on the freedom of alienation. The trial court sustained D's demurrer to the complaint and Ps appeal.

Issue. May a commercial lessor unreasonably and arbitrarily withhold consent to an assignment by the lessee?

Held. No. Judgment reversed.

♦ The common law rule of free alienability of a leasehold interest is still valid, but parties are permitted to restrict this alienability by contract. Such restraints are strictly construed against the lessor, however, especially when the lessor can terminate the lease if it is assigned without the lessor's consent. The lease in this case contained such a provision.

♦ The majority rule allows a lessor to arbitrarily refuse to consent to a proposed assignment, although in many cases the lessor is found by its conduct to have waived the right to refuse. An increasing minority has modified this rule by permitting a lessor to withhold consent only when it has a commercially reasonable objection to the assignment. This appears to be the better approach.

♦ Because a lease is a conveyance, it is subject to the public policy favoring reasonable alienation. Conditions unreasonably restraining alienation are deemed void. The Restatement (Second), section 15.2(2), adopts the minority approach while permitting a lessor to object to a proposed assignment on reasonable commercial grounds. The lessor is also protected because the original lessee remains liable as a surety.

♦ A lease is also a contract, and contracts include a duty to act in good faith and to deal fairly. Generally, a contract that gives one party discretionary power that affects the other party also imposes a duty to exercise that power in good faith. D here had discretionary power to disapprove an assignment. D must exercise that discretion in good faith.

♦ The reasonableness of the lessor's refusal to consent is a factual question. It would not be commercially reasonable to refuse consent solely because of the lessor's personal tastes, convenience or sensibility, or to charge a higher rent.

♦ While a lessor may have the freedom to choose its own tenant, this freedom is preserved by allowing the lessor to disapprove assignments for commercially reasonable reasons. Even though the lessee did not insist on reasonableness language in the lease, the lease does not forbid assignment, so the parties must have contemplated that if the lessee obtained a satisfactory subtenant, the lessor would consent.

♦ D claims it is entitled to charge higher rent to a sublessee because D is entitled to the benefit of increased property values. However, the lessee has already agreed to a particular rent. By ensuring a return to the lessor, the lessee assumes the risk of a decreased market value, and should also benefit from an increase in market value. D would get more than it bargained for if it were permitted to increase its rent.

---

7. The Tenant Who Defaults

The landlord has various common law, statutory, and, typically, contractual remedies to ensure the tenant's compliance with the lease. Most leases contain rent acceleration clauses, which provide that all the rent due under the contract is immediately due and payable if the tenant defaults. Of course, the landlord cannot accelerate the rent and take possession of the premises. Security deposits are also common in most leases. Common law remedies include "distress" (entry on the premises and seizure of the tenant's chattels to secure payment of the rent), although in some jurisdictions this has been either abolished or the entry must be peaceable. Statutory liens are also permitted in many jurisdictions. These statutes vary quite a bit, but basically, they allow the landlord a lien on the personal property of the tenant to secure payment of the rent.

a. Eviction

A tenant may be evicted if he breaches lease covenants or holds over beyond the lease term. There are two types of eviction, self-help and by judicial process. The self-help remedy has fallen into disfavor in recent years.

1) By Judicial Process

The most common judicial process for eviction is by a statutorily prescribed summary proceeding. In some places this is called "unlawful detainer," and in others, "forcible entry and detainer." Basically, this involves serving a tenant a notice to quit. If the tenant does not leave, the landlord files an unlawful detainer action, which is typically heard in five days or less. After the hearing, if the judge finds the tenant in breach of the lease, she will sign an order authorizing the sheriff to evict the tenant. Under these summary proceedings, a landlord cannot do anything more than obtain possession of the premises. She cannot get back rent. A landlord can also file a suit in ejectment, but this action does not get priority on the civil calendar and for that reason is seldom used. In Los Angeles County, for example, it could take five years for this to come to trial. No landlord wants a nonpaying tenant for that long.

2) Self-Help

At common law, a landlord could use self-help to evict a tenant. In America, a landlord has traditionally been allowed to use reasonable self-help to remove a tenant (changing the locks is a good example). The modern trend, however, has been to hold a landlord liable for damages if she uses self-help. This harshness is felt appropriate in light of the modern availability of summary judicial proceedings.

3) Damages for Wrongful Eviction

Berg v. Wiley
264 N.W.2d 145 (Minn. 1978).

Facts. Wiley (D) leased a restaurant to Berg (P) from 1970–1975. P, in violation of the lease, remodeled the restaurant without D's consent. P's restaurant was often cited for health code violations. This violated a lease provision regarding operating the business in a lawful manner. In 1973, D gave P two weeks' notice to make remodeling changes or, pursuant to the contract, D would retake possession. At about the same time, the Health Department gave P two weeks to remedy the health code violations. On the last day of the two-week period, P dismissed her employees, closed the restaurant, and put up a "closed for remodeling" sign. While P was gone, D changed the locks. P sued for damages and lost profits, claiming that she had closed the restaurant for a month to remodel it to D's specifications. P sued for wrongful eviction and won $31,000 for lost profits. D appeals.

Issue. May a landlord use self-help to regain possession of his property?

Held. No. Judgment affirmed.

- While the evidence is contradictory, it is sufficient to uphold the jury's determination that P was going to reopen the restaurant after remodeling.

- The second issue relating to a landlord's self-help is more difficult. At common law the landlord was legally entitled to retake possession if: (i) the landlord is legally entitled possession (such as where there is a reentry clause in the lease), and (ii) the landlord's means of reentry is peaceable.

- Public policy discourages landlords from taking the law into their own hands, especially when the self-help may result in breaches of the peace.

- Today, summary legal proceedings are available that can get the landlord possession in three to 10 days. This is a quick, easy, and safe way to retake a leased premises.

- Actual violence is not required for there to be forceful retaking. Changing the locks in P's absence is not a peaceable method of reentry but rather a forceful retaking.

- The modern trend to require landlords to use legal process, rather than self-help, is in direct contradiction to the common law.

- Thus, the only lawful means to dispossess a tenant who has not abandoned or voluntarily surrendered, but who claims possession adversely to a landlord's claim of breach of a written lease, is by resort to judicial process. There is no place and no need for self-help.

Comment The court here held that under either the common law or the modern rule, P had shown D's forceful eviction of P. The jury applied the common law in finding D's eviction of P wrongful. "Closed for remodeling" signs are a common ploy when a restaurant goes out of business and wants to delay its creditors.

---

4) Self-Help Authorized by Lease

Typically, courts uphold contractual provisions permitting the landlord to use self-help. A minority hold such provisions void as offending public policy.

8. Abandonment of Possession

a. Landlord's Options

If the tenant abandons the premises during the lease term, the landlord may leave the premises vacant and sue the tenant for the rent. (In most jurisdictions the landlord need not mitigate by seeking a new tenant. A minority of jurisdictions hold the opposite.) Or she may retake the premises and try to lease again. The courts are in conflict as to whether this effects a surrender of the premises (in such an event the tenant would only be liable for rent to the day of termination).

b. Duty to Mitigate Damages

Sommer v. Kridel
378 A.2d 767 (N.J. 1977).

Facts. This case is a consolidation of two cases. Sommer in one and Riverview Realty Co. in the other (Ps) sued Kridel in one and Perosio in the other (Ds) for rent due.

The facts of *Sommer v. Kridel* follow: D entered into a two-year lease agreement with P, with a rent concession for the first six weeks. Subsequent to the lease, but prior to occupancy, D wrote P a letter explaining that his expected wedding plans had been cancelled and that he could no longer afford to take the apartment. P made no reply to the letter. Thereafter, a third party went to look at the apartment and was ready and willing to move in, but she was told the apartment was rented. P did not reenter nor attempt to lease the apartment for at least three months. P then rented to a new tenant under the same terms as before, including a six-week rent concession. The new lease began September 1. Prior to reletting the premises, P sued D demanding the total amount due for the full two-year term. After reletting the premises, P amended the complaint asking for rent due between May and September. The trial court found for D, holding that P had a duty to mitigate damages by attempting to relet the premises. The appellate division reversed. D appeals.

In *Riverview Realty Co. v. Perosio* the facts are: D, the tenant, entered into a two-year lease with P. D took possession and occupied the premises for one year. At that time D vacated the premises. P sued for rent due on the one year remaining of the lease term. The trial court granted P's motion for summary judgment against D. The appellate division affirmed. D appeals.

Issue. Is a landlord seeking damages from a defaulting tenant under a duty to mitigate those damages by making a reasonable effort to relet the premises?

Held. Yes. Both decisions of the appellate division are reversed.

♦ The minority view, which is based on antitrust law, is that a landlord does have an obligation to make a reasonable effort to mitigate damages where a tenant has surrendered and abandoned the premises prior to expiration of the lease.

♦ The majority rule, which is based on property law, is that a landlord is under no duty to mitigate damages caused by a defaulting tenant. This court finds the majority view antiquated and will follow the minority view.

Comment. This case illustrates the continuing trend by the courts to apply principles of contract law rather than pure property law to residential leases. In this particular case, however, the court's opinion leaves some doubt as to whether the landlord has a duty to mitigate when she is seeking damages from the defaulting tenant or when she is recovering unpaid rent. Most of the language goes primarily to the landlord's duty to mitigate if she is seeking damages. However, Ps in these cases were seeking unpaid rent, not damages. Only a few states still follow the common law rule. However, some states require mitigation only for commercial leases and others only for residential leases.

B. Landlord's Duties

At common law, the landlord was under no duty to furnish habitable premises. Absent contractual provisions to the contrary, the premises were leased "as is." However, if there were defects or dangerous conditions known to the landlord and not easily discoverable, the landlord had a duty to disclose the defect. These rules have undergone significant development over the years.

1. Quiet Enjoyment and Constructive Eviction

a. Quiet Enjoyment

A tenant has the right to "quietly enjoy" the premises. This means that the landlord cannot interfere with the tenant's use of and enjoyment of the premises. This covenant is implied in every lease. Even at common law, where the general rule was caveat lessee, breach of this covenant absolved the tenant from his responsibility to pay rent. This covenant can be breached by either actual eviction or constructive eviction.

b. Actual Eviction

If the landlord evicts the tenant from the entire leasehold, the tenant may treat the lease as breached and terminate it. He no longer has to pay rent. If the tenant is evicted from only a portion of the leasehold, he may stay on the premises and refuse to pay rent until the landlord restores the entire premises to the tenant.

c. Constructive Eviction

If, through the landlord's fault, the tenant's quiet enjoyment of the premises is substantially interfered with, the tenant may treat the lease as terminated and vacate the premises. He is no longer liable for the rent. The theory behind this is that the landlord has so interfered with the tenant's right of possession that she might as well have evicted the tenant. The necessary elements are:

1) Substantial Interference

The tenant's use and enjoyment of the premises must be substantially interfered with. Of course, if the tenant knows of the interference when he signed the lease, the court may hold that he waived the interference.

2) Notice to the Landlord

The tenant must give notice to the landlord of the defect and give the landlord a reasonable time to cure the problem.

3) Tenant Must Vacate

The tenant cannot stay on and refuse to pay rent. He must vacate within a reasonable time.

4) Fault

The interference to the tenant's enjoyment and use of the premises must be the fault of the landlord. She must act, or fail to act, to the tenant's damage.

5) Village Commons

Village Commons, LLC v. Marion County Prosecutor's Office
882 N.E.2d 210 (Ind. Ct. App. 2008).

Facts. On June 2, 1999, then the Marion County Prosecutor executed a lease on behalf of the MCPO with Lombard to lease the basement of the Victoria Centre (the Lease). Lombard sold the Victoria Centre to Landlord and assigned the Lease to Landlord. The lease provided that the MCPO was to rent 9,356 square feet of lower level space in the Victoria Centre for a period of seven years and five months, commencing on August 1, 1999. The payment obligations increased over time, beginning with zero dollars owed per month for the first five months, increasing to $8,576.33 per month for months seventy-eight through eighty-nine of the lease term. The Lease provided that Landlord maintain all common equipment such as elevators, plumbing, heating, etc. and that it maintain the premises in good order and repair. The Lease provided that in the case of a breach by Landlord, MCPO could sue for injunctive relief or for damages, but could not terminate the Lease or withhold, setoff or abate rent. Starting in 2001, MCPO's property was damaged by a series of water intrusions from the outside and leaks from building equipment. From March 11, 2001, to September 10, 2001 there were leaks or water damage in the restroom, the evidence room, the "war" room, the electrical conduit, and other areas. Landlord hired Indoor Air Management (IAM) to conduct microbiological sampling and visual inspections. IAM repaired the sidewalk above the "war" room several times to no avail. Landlord got an estimate to replace the sidewalk above the "war" room, but took no action because of the costs. After more leaks in January, on Memorial Day 2002, the main water pipe in the building's air conditioning system broke, causing damage to 70 boxes in the evidence room. The MCPO devoted many person-hours to deal with the damaged evidence. In June, mold was detected in the evidence room. Landlord chose not to hire the mold remediation company because of its estimate of the costs, but had Landlord's maintenance man make the repairs. He did not perform several of the tasks the remediation company had recommended. In July, Landlord's maintenance man replaced more water-damaged ceiling tiles in the "war" room. IAM performed more testing and said more demolition was necessary and damaged boxes had to be discarded because of microbiological contamination. Other new leaks were discovered, new mold spores were found and fungal growth detected. IAM advised Landlord about potential allergic reactions to mold contamination. Landlord told MCPO there were no health risks. One MCPO employee suffered from coughing and sneezing. Another had headaches while in the building; when she was reassigned outside of the premises, the headaches stopped. In August, Landlord and the MCPO met with an IAM employee; the employee said there was an elevated mold count, but not the type of mold that requires a building to be quarantined. Problems continued until January 30, 2003, when the MCPO chose to vacate the leased premises. January was the last month that the MCPO paid rent to Landlord, leaving $380,477.37, unpaid according to the Lease terms. Landlord (P) sued the MCPO (D) in February, alleging breach of the Lease. D's answer asserted affirmative defenses and a wrongful eviction counterclaim premised on a wrongful eviction theory. In its counterclaim, MCPO first alleged it had been constructively evicted in January 2003; that date was later amended to August 2002. After a bench trial, the trial court held that D's claims were not barred by the Lease's exclusive-remedy provisions; that D was "actually" evicted in October 2002 and then "constructively" evicted in January 2003; and assuming the P could recover against D, P did not mitigate its damages reasonably. D was awarded $7,664 and costs on its wrongful eviction counterclaim. P appeals.

Issues.

(i) Does the exclusive-remedy provision of the Lease bar D from asserting that it was evicted by P's acts or omissions?

(ii) Were the trial court's findings that D was both actually evicted and constructively evicted clearly erroneous?

Held. (i) No. (ii) No. Judgment affirmed.

The exclusive-remedy provision, provides as follows:

"*Section 15.04. Default by Landlord and Remedies by Tenant.* It shall be a default under and breach of this Lease by Landlord if it shall fail to perform or observe any term, condition, covenant or obligation required to be performed or observed by it under this Lease for a period of thirty (30) days after notice thereof from Tenant; provided, however, that if the term, condition, covenant or obligation to be performed by Landlord is of such nature that the same cannot reasonably be performed within such thirty-day period, such default shall be deemed to have been cured if Landlord commences such performance within said thirty-day period and thereafter diligently undertakes to complete the same, and further failure to perform or observe any term, condition, covenant or obligation under this Lease is due to causes beyond the reasonable control of Landlord. *Upon the occurrence of any such default, Tenant may sue for injunctive relief or to recover damages for any loss resulting from the breach, but Tenant shall not be entitled to terminate this Lease or withhold, setoff or abate any rent due thereunder.* (emphasis added)."

The lease language unambiguously shows D did not have a right to terminate the Lease or withhold, setoff, or abate any rent due. However, this determination is not dispositive of the dispute before us. The unambiguous terms of the provision did not prohibit P from evicting D. The provision limited only D's ability to "terminate this Lease or withhold, setoff or abate any rent due thereunder." When eviction occurs, either actual or constructive, it is the lessor's act or omission that ends the obligation to pay rent, not the lessee.

We agree with the trial court that D was actually evicted beginning in October of 2002, and was then constructively evicted as of January 28, 2003, due to repeated and un-remedied water intrusions. In *Talbott v. English,* 156 Ind. 299, 59 N.E. 857 (1901), the court defined actual eviction as the tenant being deprived of the occupancy of some part of the demised premises, and constructive eviction as that which occurs when the lessor, without intending to oust the lessee, does an act that deprives the lessee of the beneficial enjoyment of some part of the premises, in which case the tenant may quit the premises and avoid the lease, or stay and seek his remedy in an action for the trespass. If the tenant wishes to relieve himself of liability for the rent, he must quit the premises. Whether or not that action is justified is for the jury.

The *Talbott* court went on to discuss the implied covenant of right of possession, occupancy, and beneficial use of every part of the leased premises. If a landlord deprives the tenant of the possession and enjoyment of any part of the premises, "the landlord shall not be entitled to any part of the rent during the time he thus deprives the tenant of this rights. The landlord may not apportion the rent by his own wrong."

After termination, the lease and all its attendant obligations for future rent are extinguished. After constructive eviction, if the tenant leaves within a reasonable period, he is no longer liable for rent under the lease. Therefore, since we find the trial court did not err in finding D had been wrongfully evicted, we hold that it was the P's own act or omission that resulted in extinguishing D's future rent payment obligations.

The trial court determined P had actually evicted D in October 2002 when P told D to stop using those areas of the leased premises "most vulnerable to water." It determined D was constructively evicted as of January 28, 2003, as a result of "repeated unremedied water intrusions." No eviction occurs when a transitory and fleeting interference by the lessor with the lessee's possession occurs; in that case, a mere trespass occurs for which the lessee is entitled to damages.

P's argument the D's problems were temporary and eventually fixed is not supported by the substantial evidence to the contrary. The water intrusions were recurring; indeed, it was P who suggested D should move evidence and materials out of areas vulnerable to water, revealing P's awareness that water leaks would recur.

---

d. Damages

After vacating, the tenant can recover damages for being wrongfully evicted. This would include damages for the additional cost of substitute premises, lost profits, increased expenses proximately caused by the eviction, etc.

e. Partial Constructive Eviction

Some courts have gone so far as to allow a tenant to recover for partial constructive eviction. This developed in light of judicial consideration for the situation of the modern city dweller.

2. Illegal Lease Agreements

a. Generally

Some local housing codes prohibit rental of premises in violation of the code. In such circumstances, the tenant cannot be forced to pay rent.

b. Limitations

For the tenant to be able to defend against the landlord's action for rent, the illegal condition must have existed at the time the lease was signed. Also, although the tenant need not pay rent, he is still liable for the reasonable rental value of the premises. Usually, if the illegal condition is substantial (renders the premises unfit for human occupation), this will not be very much money.

3. Implied Warranty of Habitability

a. Traditional Approach

At common law, the landlord had no duty to keep the premises in repair once the tenant moved in. Of course, the landlord and tenant could agree that the landlord will keep the premises in repair. This covenant, like contractual covenants in general, was independent. Thus, even if the landlord failed to keep the premises in repair, the tenant still had to pay rent, but could sue for breach of contract or specific performance.

b. Implied Warranty of Habitability

One of the areas of major reform in the law is in the area of implied covenants of habitability. Most courts will now imply, in every noncommercial lease, a covenant that the premises be delivered to the tenant in fit and habitable shape. The courts have further held that the landlord's fulfillment of this covenant is an antecedent condition to the paying of rent. While the exact application of this doctrine varies from state to state, typically the tenant can avoid the lease, or make the repairs and withhold the amount of the repairs from the rent. Several states have enacted statutes codifying this doctrine.

1) Commercial Leases

Some courts have extended this implied covenant to commercial leases.

2) Standards Applied

Courts and statutes differ on exactly what standard to use in assessing habitability. Some use the housing code standards, others follow a "fit for human habitation" standard. Some courts also require that the landlord be given notice of the unfit condition and time to make repairs.

3) Waiver

This implied covenant, according to the cases decided so far, cannot be waived by the tenant. Any waiver of it is held to violate public policy.

c. Tenant Need Not Abandon Premises

Hilder v. St. Peter
478 A.2d 202 (Vt. 1984).

Facts. Hilder (P) rented an apartment from St. Peter (D) for herself, her three children, and a newborn grandson. P agreed to pay $140 per month plus a $50 damage deposit. She paid the deposit and the first month's rent. P also cleaned up the apartment from the previous tenants in reliance on D's promise to refund the damage deposit, but D never refunded the money. P always paid her rent. P notified D of several problems, which D promised to fix but did not. These included a broken window, no key to the front door lock, a clogged toilet and inoperable bathroom electricity, falling plaster due to a roof leak, and raw sewage in the basement from a broken sewage pipe. P also paid for her own heat contrary to the rental arrangement. P finally sued for reimbursement of the rent paid and additional compensatory damages. The trial court awarded P the rent she paid of $3,445, plus the $50 deposit, and $1,500 as additional compensatory damages. D appeals, claiming P should not have been reimbursed for the rent because she occupied the apartment the whole time.

Issue. When a landlord breaches the implied warranty of habitability, must the tenant abandon the premises to obtain reimbursement of the rent paid?

Held. No. Judgment affirmed in part and case remanded on the damages issue.

♦ Traditionally, leases were deemed to be conveyances of real property, and possession by the tenant created a duty to pay rent. The landlord was not liable to make repairs unless the lease so specified. The modern approach, recognizing the inability of urban tenants to make effective repairs in complex apartment situations and the tenants' inferior bargaining position, treats leases as contracts. Thus, a tenant's duty to pay rent depends on the landlord's maintaining the premises in habitable condition. The tenant does not have to abandon the premises in order to bring suit.

♦ All rentals of residential dwelling units include an implied warranty of habitability that applies to latent and patent defects. The tenant does not assume the risk of defects in place when the lease is entered, and the implied warranty of habitability cannot be waived in writing or verbally.

♦ Whether the implied warranty is breached depends on the circumstances of the particular case, but if the defect impacts the tenant's safety or health, there is probably a breach. Before suing, the tenant must notify the landlord of the defect and allow a reasonable time for correction. The defects in this case, and P's response thereto, satisfy these requirements, and D breached the implied warranty.

♦ When there is a breach, the tenant may pursue rescission, reformation, and damages. The basic measure of damages is the difference between the value of the residence as warranted and its value as it actually exists. The tenant may also recover for discomfort and annoyance, as well as any costs of repair. The tenant may choose to withhold future rent. Finally, punitive damages may be awarded to punish landlords who are morally culpable.

♦ In this case, the trial court awarded damages for the proper reasons but did not adequately explain the basis for the additional compensatory damages.

---

4. Tort Liability

a. Conditions Existing at Time of Lease

The general common law rule was caveat lessee. The landlord was liable neither to the lessee nor his guests unless she failed to disclose a known, latent, dangerous condition or defect (one which the lessee probably could not discover). Once a latent defect was disclosed to the lessee, the landlord was no longer liable. If the latent, dangerous defect was discovered by the landlord after the tenant entered into possession, the landlord had a duty to disclose (but not repair).

1) Modern Rule

Most courts now hold landlords liable if they fail to disclose dangerous defects. This extends to defects that the landlord should have discovered, even if she had no actual knowledge.

2) Publicly Used Portions of the Premises

The landlord is liable for injuries occurring to the public on these portions of the premises if she knows, or should know, of the defect, has reason to think that the tenant will not fix the defect, and fails to use reasonable care to fix the condition. The landlord is not liable for the tenant's injuries under this rule. If the landlord does not know that that portion of the premises was going to be used by the public, she is not liable. A twist to this rule is that the landlord may be liable even if the tenant promises to make the repairs *if* the landlord has reason to know that the tenant will not make the repairs before admitting the public to that portion of the premises.

b. Conditions Arising After Execution of the Lease

The general rule is no liability. It now becomes the tenant's job to keep the premises safe.

1) Liability for Voluntary Repairs

Even if the landlord is under no duty to make repairs, if she does do so she must use reasonable care. She is liable if the repairs are made negligently. This is in accord with the general principles of tort liability.

2) Contractually Obligated Repairs

Modern cases treat this about the same as liability for voluntary repairs. The old view, still adhered to in some places, absolved the landlord of tort liability, leaving the tenant to sue for breach of contract.

c. Common Areas

If the landlord is in control of the common areas (hallways, walkways, elevators, swimming pool), she is liable for those injuries resulting from those defects of which she knew or which she reasonably could have discovered.

d. Legal Duty to Repair

In some locations, statutes or ordinances impose liability on landlords to make repairs. Sometimes liability is imposed by enforcing an implied covenant of habitability.

C. Tenant's Duties

1. Duty to Repair

At common law a tenant has the duty to keep the premises in as good a condition as when he leases it. He does not need to make substantial repairs.

2. Duty Not to Commit Waste

A tenant is liable for waste. Waste is one of two types, ameliorating or damaging.

a. Ameliorating Waste

If the tenant improves the premises (adds a room, paints the house, etc.), he commits ameliorating waste. At common law he was liable for this. The modern cases do not hold tenants liable for this as long as the value of the premises is not lessened.

b. Damaging Waste

If a tenant substantially damages the premises, he is liable. The injury must be one that extends beyond the end of the lease term. In certain conditions a landlord may get an injunction to stop the damage. A tenant is not liable for ordinary wear and tear.

c. Involuntary Waste

Also known as permissive waste, this occurs when the premises are allowed to fall into disrepair.

3. Duty to Pay Rent

Traditionally, the tenant had the obligation to pay the rent called for in the lease whether or not the landlord performed her part of the lease. If the value of the rent is not specified, it is presumed the tenant must pay a reasonable rental value. If the lease is illegal, the tenant must pay a reasonable rental value. He need not pay the price called for in the lease. At common law, the tenant was liable for rent even if the premises burned to the ground. Today, most jurisdictions excuse further performance from both parties in cases of accidental destruction. [*See Albert M. Greenfield & Co. v. Kolea*, 380 A.2d 758 (Pa. 1976)].

D. The Problem of Decent Affordable Housing

1. Rent Control

The shortage of affordable housing in many areas has led to an escalation in rent. Because of the serious impact on the public generally, many jurisdictions adopted rent control regulations. The courts have generally upheld these regulations, so long as the interests of landlords are fairly considered.

2. The Chicago Ordinance

Chicago Board of Realtors, Inc. v. City of Chicago

819 F.2d 732 (7th Cir. 1987).

Facts. In 1986 the Chicago Board of Realtors (Ps) challenged a newly enacted Residential Landlord and Tenant Ordinance that codified the implied warranty of habitability and established new landlord responsibilities and tenant rights. Ps argued that the ordinance violated the Contracts Clause, procedural and substantive due process, the void-for-vagueness doctrine, equal protection, the Takings Clause, and the Commerce Clause. The district court denied a motion for preliminary injunction. Ps appealed, contesting the court's ruling with regard to all but the Takings Clause and the Commerce Clause issues. The court of appeals affirmed. Ps appeal.

Issue. Is the ordinance sufficiently specific and, giving due deference to the legislative judgment, sufficiently reasonable in light of its stated purpose to promote public health, safety, and welfare?

Held. Yes. Judgment affirmed.

Note: The court's constitutional analysis written by Judge Cudahy is not presented; the policy analysis contained in a separately filed opinion follows.

- Judge Cudahy's opinion does not make the strongest case that can be made for the reasonableness of the ordinance. The stated purpose of the ordinance is to promote the public health, safety, and welfare and the quality of housing in Chicago. This is neither its real purpose nor its likely effect.

- Forbidding landlords to charge interest at market rates on large rent payments does not meet the purpose or improve the quality of the housing stock. Its effect will be to reduce landlords' resources and the resources they devote to improving housing.

- The provisions requiring that interest be paid on security deposits and that interest be kept in Illinois banks are equally remote from the stated purpose. Their only apparent rationale is to transfer wealth from landlords and out-of-state banks to tenants and local banks—making this an unedifying example of class legislation and economic protectionism rolled into one.

- The ordinance is not in the interest of poor people. It puts no cap on rents. The beneficiaries will be middle-class people who buy housing because the supply will be increased as landlords convert rental to owner housing, people willing to pay higher rent, and more affluent tenants who will be less likely to be late with rent or to abuse the right of a tenant to withhold rent. Landlords, out-of-state banks, and the poorest class of tenants will be the losers.

- The literature dealing with the effects of government regulation of the market for rental housing shows that the market for rental housing behaves as economic theory predicts; if price is depressed artificially, or if landlords' costs are increased artificially, supply falls and the poorer and newer tenants are hurt.

---

3. Government-Subsidized Housing

a. Legislation

The federal government became involved in housing in the 1930s. The United States Housing Act lets the local public housing authority ("PHA") sell tax-exempt government bonds to raise revenue. The revenue is used to construct local low-income housing. Currently this scheme is used by private parties who construct public housing.

b. Regulations

Of course, numerous regulations need to be complied with in building public housing. Building sites must be approved by the local government in accordance with federal guidelines. Regulations require that building sites be located outside areas of high minority concentration. PHAs, on the other hand, are more eager to locate the housing in racially segregated areas. The aid of federal courts has been invoked to force local compliance with the regulations.

c. Local Approval

A state's constitutional requirement that a low-rent housing project can be developed only after approval by a majority of the local residents has been upheld. The court held that the constitutional requirement was neutral on its face and not in fact aimed at racial minorities. Economic, but not racial, discrimination is permissible.

d. Admission to Public Housing

The PHA is free to decide its own admission requirements with the exception that preference is to be given to veterans and persons displaced by urban renewal. Some courts have held that a person is entitled to an informal hearing on his eligibility.

e. Rent Increases in Public Housing

It has been held that a tenant's right to low-rent housing is a property right that is subject to due process. With this as a rationale, courts have held that tenants are entitled to exercise certain rights prior to rent increases.

f. Eviction

Tenants may be evicted for destroying property or for being loud and unruly, etc. They may not be evicted for belonging to a tenants' organization or for exercising their constitutional rights.

Part IV
Transfers of Land

A. The Land Transaction

1. Real Estate Brokers

A real estate broker is an individual engaged in the buying and selling of property for another for something of value, most often a commission. Brokers are commonly licensed to perform tasks such as negotiating purchase agreements, aiding in arranging financing, and serving as intermediaries between buyers and sellers, among other services. Although brokers have a long history of aiding sellers in marketing their property, in recent years there has been an increase in the employment of buyers' brokers.

a. Breach of Fiduciary Duties

Licari v. Blackwelder
539 A.2d 609 (Conn. App. Ct. 1988).

Facts. Six brothers and sisters (Ps), unsophisticated regarding real estate matters, engaged Schwartz, a real estate broker, to sell property that Ps had inherited from their parents. Schwartz consulted with Blackwelder and Opert (Ds), brokers experienced in valuing and marketing property in the vicinity of Ps' home. Schwartz and Ds discussed several of Ds' prospective clients who might be interested in some of Schwartz's real estate listings. Ds and Schwartz agreed to a "co-broke arrangement" under which they would share the listings and divide the commissions evenly if one of Ds' prospective clients bought real estate listed by Schwartz. Opert then asked Schwartz to list Ps' property so it could be shown to a prospective buyer. Schwartz secured an exclusive 24-hour right to sell Ps' property at a price of $125,000, and Schwartz's sales agent immediately showed the property. Within the period of the exclusive listing, Ds made their own offer to purchase the property for $115,000. Ps accepted, believing they were selling at fair market value. Ds did not negotiate on Ps' behalf with a prospective buyer whom they had secured, nor did they wait for negotiations before they made their offer. Ds also failed to disclose to Ps their assessment of the value that the property might have to other buyers and led Ps to believe they would occupy the property themselves. Immediately after title was transferred to Ds, Opert contracted on behalf of Ds to sell the property for $160,000 to a neighbor of Ps whose interest in the property Ps were aware of, but whom Ps directed Ds not to contact. Title passed to this buyer six days after Ps sold to Ds. Ps filed suit, claiming that Ds breached their duty by withholding information of negotiations with other potential buyers for a higher price and that Ds intentionally misrepresented the identities of prospective buyers in order to mislead Ps into selling the property to Ds at a lower price. At trial, the court found for Ps. Ds appeal.

Issue. Must a real estate broker disclose to his client all facts within his knowledge that may affect his client's rights and interests and inform his client of his actions in relation to the subject matter of the employment?

Held. Yes. Judgment affirmed.

- ◆ A real estate broker is a fiduciary and is required to exercise good faith. A real estate broker acting as a subagent is under the same duty as a primary broker. Failing to communicate material information that a broker may acquire or acting contrary to his client's interest is a breach of the broker's duty.

- ◆ A failure to communicate that a more advantageous sale can be made renders the broker liable for whatever loss the client may suffer as a result and precludes payment of a commission for the broker's services.

---

2. The Contract of Sale

Typically, the sale of land involves two steps. First, a contract to sell/purchase the real property is signed. In it is specified the date for the second step, closing. At closing the seller gives the buyer a deed to the property and the buyer gives the seller the agreed-upon consideration. A discussion of this two-step method of conveying must begin with the basic premise that the transactions must conform to the Statute of Frauds, which requires, in essence, that the agreement to sell/purchase be in writing.

a. Statute of Frauds

The Statute of Frauds provides that no interest in real property can be conveyed, encumbered, etc., without a writing signed by the party to be charged. The "party to be charged" is the party against whom it is asserted there is a contract. The writing can consist of several documents that, when taken together as a whole, evidence an agreement affecting real property. Thus, formal contracts are not required.

b. Essential Terms

The writing must contain all the essential terms for the agreement. "Essential terms" are words of art meaning the following terms: description of the property sufficient to make clear what property the parties have in mind, price (some courts will imply a "reasonable price" or "market price"), the parties, and the other terms and conditions pertinent to the transaction (manner of payment, etc.).

c. Specific Performance

Since all real property is unique, courts will use their equity powers to compel a buyer or a seller to go through with a deal, rather than award damages. The aggrieved party must ask for specific performance.

d. Oral Revocation

Most states hold that the Statute of Frauds applies only to the making of a contract affecting an interest in land and will thus allow subsequent oral modification or revocation of the contract.

e. Time of Performance

Unless the contract specifies that time is of the essence, if the contract is not performed on the date called for in the agreement, each party has a "reasonable" time in which to complete its performance.

f. Specific Performance

Hickey v. Green
442 N.E.2d 37 (Mass. App. Ct. 1982).

Facts. The Hickeys (Ps) put a deposit on D's lot after orally agreeing to a sale for $15,000. D accepted the $500 check, marked on the back with "Deposit . . . Subject to variance from Town of Plymouth." No variance was required and Ps told D to fill in the name of the payee, which had been left blank because of uncertainty as to whether D or her brother and agent were to receive the check. D held the check, did not indorse it, and did not fill in the payee's name. Ps sold their house and accepted a deposit check. D told Ps she had decided to sell the lot to another for $16,000; Ps offered D $16,000. D refused. Ps sought specific performance. D claimed the Statute of Frauds barred relief. The court found for Ps based on stipulated facts and documents. D appeals.

Issue. May a contract for transfer of an interest in land be specifically enforced if there was no compliance with the Statute of Frauds if the party seeking enforcement reasonably relied on the contract and has so changed her position that injustice can be avoided only by specific performance?

Held. Yes. Case remanded.

- The rule is set forth in Restatement (Second) of Contracts, section 129 (1981).

- In the present case, D knew Ps were planning to sell their house and Ps did so rapidly without obtaining any adequate memorandum of the terms of what appears to have been a quick sale. Ps relied on D's oral promise and less than 10 days later accepted a deposit on their house.

- Ps bound themselves so that to avoid transfer of their home they might have had to engage in costly litigation.

- D does not deny that she made the oral contract and the promise on which Ps relied and that she promptly repudiated it. In equity, D's conduct cannot be condoned.

- Neither party has shown expectation of a written agreement.

- No public interest will be violated if D is held to her bargain by the principles of equitable estoppel subject to the following: (i) Ps have already conveyed or are still obligated to convey their property, and (ii) the case is remanded for the trial judge to require D to convey the property only upon payment to her in cash of the balance of the purchase price within a stated time. If Ps have no obligation to sell their house, the trial judge may require full restitution to Ps of all reasonable costs in respect to this transaction rather than specific performance.

---

3. Marketable Title

Absent an express provision to the contrary, it is implied in every contract for the sale of land that the seller will furnish the buyer "marketable title" to the property at closing. This is a title that is reasonably free from doubts; one that a prudent person would be willing to buy. Marketable title does not mean perfect title; it means one that is good enough for a title insurance company to be willing to insure in the regular course of business.

a. Good Record Title

Less frequently, contracts will call for the seller to furnish good record title. This means that the seller must furnish good title based on the documents in the chain of title. It precludes title by adverse possession.

b. Defects in Title

There are numerous possible defects in title. Some of the more common ones include a defect in one of the instruments in the chain of title, private encumbrances, unrecorded easements, covenants, and restrictions on the use of the property.

c. Curing Title Defects

Normally, the seller has until closing to cure any defects in title. Minor defects such as an unrecorded release of lien may be remedied by the seller setting aside from the purchase price sufficient funds to cover the lien until he procures the release. Generally, the seller is willing and able to discharge the mortgage at closing, then the mortgage does not render title unmarketable. Similarly, if an easement benefits the property, it does not make the title unmarketable. Zoning restrictions do not, except in unusual cases, make title unmarketable. Finally, easements and the like that are shown on official maps may make title unmarketable.

d. Violations of Building Codes and Zoning Restrictions

If there are violations of zoning restrictions for which the government can demand correction, title is usually held to be unmarketable. The policy behind this is that the law is loath to require someone to buy into the possibility of a lawsuit.

e. Violation of Public and Private Restrictions

Lohmeyer v. Bower
227 P.2d 102 (Kan. 1951).

Facts. Lohmeyer (P) contracted to buy a house. The contract provided that Bower (D), the seller, was to provide good merchantable title subject to all restrictions of record. In the event there were imperfections of title, D was to have a reasonable time to correct them. The abstract of title showed that the original subdivider imposed a restriction requiring that any home erected on the lot be two stories in height (the existing home was one story). Further, under a zoning ordinance no frame building could be erected within three feet of the lot line (the existing house was within 18 inches of the lot line). D offered to buy for P two feet of the adjoining lot so that the house was more than three feet from the new lot line. P refused this offer and brought suit to rescind the contract. D countersued for specific performance. The trial court found for D, awarding specific performance. P appeals.

Issue. Does the violation of private and public restrictions render title unmarketable?

Held. Yes. Judgment reversed.

♦ This case requires a determination of (i) whether the encumbrances to which the property was subject made the title unmarketable; and (ii) if so, did they fall within an exception provided for by the contract?

♦ P does not base his suit upon the fact that there existed both a private restrictive covenant on the property (the limitation as to building height) and a public zoning restriction (the three-foot requirement), but upon the violation of the two restrictions.

♦ Two general rules applicable here are (i) the existence of municipal restrictions, such as zoning, is not a ground for a buyer to rescind a contract, and (ii) private covenants or restrictions, such as the height requirement, may constitute encumbrances rendering title unmarketable.

♦ A "merchantable" (or "marketable") title is one that is free from reasonable doubt, and a title is doubtful and unmarketable if it exposes the party holding it to the possibility of litigation. Of course, defects in title must be substantial, not minor. Immaterial defects do not diminish the value of the property and are no grounds for a buyer to rescind the contract.

- It is clear that the two violations here exposed P to the hazard of litigation. Thus, D could not convey marketable title. While the contract provided that the conveyance was to be made subject to all restrictions, that provision referred to the existence of the restrictions. It did not permit the violation of the existing restrictions.

- On these grounds, the trial court erred in not granting P the relief sought.

---

4. Risk of Loss

Because the property is subject to being damaged or destroyed between the time the contract is entered into and the transaction is closed, allocation of the risk of loss is an important matter to be resolved.

a. Equitable Conversion

The two-step method of conveying, mentioned above, causes certain problems. In order to solve these problems, the doctrine of equitable conversion is often applied by the courts. Between the date of the contract to sell and closing, the doctrine steps in and treats the buyer as having title to the property. The doctrine treats the buyer as the equitable owner of the land with the seller as the legal owner. The seller's interest is deemed security for the debt owed him by the buyer. The buyer still does not have the right of possession until closing.

b. Alternative Approaches

The majority rule is that once the buyer acquires equitable title, the risk of loss passes to him. Thus, if the building burns down after the signing of the purchase agreement but prior to closing, and the buyer does not have the premises insured, it is his loss. He must still pay full price for the property. The minority rule is directly opposed. Risk of loss remains with the seller until closing. Under the minority view, if the damages are slight, the buyer must still go through with the sale but he is entitled to have the purchase price abated by the value of the damages.

5. The Duty to Disclose Defects

Stambovsky v. Ackley
572 N.Y.S.2d 672 (N.Y. App. Div. 1991).

Facts. P discovered that the house he had recently contracted to purchase was possessed by poltergeists seen by D and her family for nine years. The apparitions were reported in *Reader's Digest* and the local press, and D promoted the house's reputation, but P was not a local resident. P sought rescission of the contract for sale. The supreme court dismissed P's complaint, holding that P had no remedy at law in this jurisdiction. P appeals.

Issue. May the remedy of rescission be properly applied to the doctrine of caveat emptor where a condition that has been created by the seller materially impairs the value of the contract and is peculiarly within the knowledge of the seller or unlikely to be discovered by a prudent purchaser exercising due care with respect to the subject transaction?

Held. Yes. Judgment reversed; cause of action reinstated.

- The doctrine of caveat emptor imposes no duty on the vendor to disclose any information concerning the premises unless there is a confidential or fiduciary relationship between the parties or some conduct on the part of the seller that constitutes "active concealment."

- The doctrine requires the buyer to act prudently and operates to bar the purchaser who fails to exercise due care from seeking rescission.

- D is estopped to deny the existence of the apparitions and, as a matter of law, the house is haunted.

- The reputation of the house goes to the very essence of the bargain between the parties, greatly impairing both the value of the property and its potential for resale. The extent of this impairment may be presumed for the purpose of reviewing the disposition of this motion and represents merely an issue of fact for resolution at trial.

- The most meticulous inspection would not reveal the presence of poltergeists or unearth the property's ghoulish reputation. There is no sound policy reason to deny P relief for failing to discover a state of affairs that the most prudent purchaser would not be expected to even contemplate.

- D's contention that the merger or "as is" clause in the contract of sale bars P's recovery is unavailing. Even an express disclaimer will not be given effect when the facts are peculiarly within the knowledge of the party invoking it. Here, the merger clause expressly disclaims only representations made with respect to the physical condition of the premises and as broad as its language is, it does not extend to paranormal phenomena. Finally, if the language of the contract is to be construed as broadly as D urges to encompass the presence of poltergeists in the house, it cannot be said that she has delivered the premises "vacant" in accordance with her obligations.

Dissent. The existence of poltergeists is not binding on D or on this court.

---

6. Material Defect Known to Seller

Johnson v. Davis
480 So.2d 625 (Haw. 1985).

Facts. The Davises (Ps) agreed to purchase the Johnsons' (Ds') home for $310,000. Although Ds knew that the roof leaked, they affirmatively represented to Ps that there were no problems with the roof. Ps made a deposit of $31,000, and Ds vacated the home. Several days later, it rained heavily and Ps saw water gushing in from around the windows and from the ceiling. Ps brought an action for rescission of the contract and return of their deposit. Ds counterclaimed for liquidated damages. The trial court awarded Ps $26,000 of the deposit. Ps appealed, and Ds cross-appealed. The appellate court held that the affirmative representation that the roof was sound was a false representation, entitling Ps to rescind. Ds appeal.

Issue. May the seller of a home who fails to tell the buyer of a material defect known to the seller be liable for damages caused by the fraudulent concealment?

Held. Yes. Judgment affirmed.

- Under common law, there was no liability for nonfeasance. Ds' failure to tell Ps of the latent defect would not be actionable. However, it is not always easy to make a distinction between misfeasance and nonfeasance, active conduct and passive conduct. A failure to disclose a material fact when it is intended to induce a false belief is close to an affirmative representation. In such situations, both misfeasance and nonfeasance arise from the same motives and have the same effect.

- Modern notions of justice, equity, and fair dealing require that the doctrine of caveat emptor be restricted. Other jurisdictions have held a home seller liable for failing to disclose material defects of which he was aware. This is the better approach and should be applied in Florida.

♦ Accordingly, we hold that where the seller of a home knows of facts that materially affect the value of the home but are not readily observable and are unknown to the buyer, the seller has a duty to disclose them to the buyer. Ds' failure to tell Ps of the roof problems constitutes fraudulent concealment. Ps are entitled to the return of their deposit and also should be awarded costs and fees.

Comments.

♦ Although caveat emptor (let the buyer beware) is still applied in some states, the number grows smaller each year. Most states now have statutes that require sellers to give buyers a written statement disclosing facts about the property.

♦ Real estate brokers have been among those who have promoted seller disclosure laws. If a seller has a duty to disclose, the real estate broker also has a duty to disclose to a prospective buyer material defects that are known to the broker but are unobservable and unknown to the buyer.

---

7. Warranties from the Seller

The common law rigidly applied the doctrine of caveat emptor. Many modern courts have overruled the common law and held that there is an implied warranty that the building is fit for the use contemplated by both of the parties. This warranty is often implied in housing that was fairly recently constructed.

a. Implied Warranty of Workmanlike Quality

Lempke v. Dagenais
547 A.2d 290 (N.H. 1988).

Facts. The Lempkes' (Ps') predecessors in title contracted with D to build a garage. The original owners sold the property to Ps within six months after construction. Ps noticed structural problems with the garage shortly after the sale. Ps contend that separation of trusses from the roof of the garage was a latent defect that could not have been discovered until the separation and bowing became noticeable from the exterior. Ps contracted D, who agreed to make repairs but never completed them. Ps brought suit, and D filed a motion to dismiss, which was granted. Ps appeal.

Issue. May a subsequent purchaser of real property sue the builder/contractor on the theory of implied warranty of workmanlike quality for latent defects that cause economic loss, absent privity of contract?

Held. Yes. Judgment reversed and case remanded.

♦ Privity of contract is not necessary for latent defects that manifest themselves within a reasonable time after purchase and that cause economic harm. To require privity would be to defeat the purpose of the implied warranty of good workmanship and could leave innocent homeowners without a remedy.

♦ *Ellis v. Morris*, 513 A.2d 951 (N.H. 1986), upon which the trial court based its dismissal, remains controlling on Ps' claim for negligence, but denial of relief to subsequent purchasers on an implied warranty theory in *Ellis* was predicated on the court's adherence to the requirement of privity in a contract action and on the fear that to allow recovery without privity would impose unlimited liability on builders and contractors.

♦ Many other courts have found that implied warranty, whether based on contract or tort law, exists independently, imposed by the operation of law on the basis of public policy because of the parties' relationship, the nature of the transaction, and the surrounding circumstances. We agree.

- Recovery for purely economic harm in these circumstances has been allowed in other courts, which have found that to draw a line between mere economic loss and personal injury is without merit. We agree that there is no rational reason for such a distinction. The vendee has a right to expect to receive that for which he has bargained.

- Our extension of liability is limited to latent defects and to a limited period of time. The plaintiff has the burden to show that the defect was caused by the defendant's workmanship. The builder also has defenses such as the defects being the result of age and wear and tear, not attributable to him, or that previous owners have made substantial changes.

---

8. Remedies for Breach of the Sales Contract

a. Available Remedies

Both the buyer and the seller may seek certain remedies if a contract for sale of real estate is breached. The nondefaulting party may select from: (i) damages, (ii) retention of the deposit (sellers) or restitution of the deposit (buyers), or (iii) specific performance of the contract.

b. Measure and Type of Damages Determined

Jones v. Lee
971 P.2d 858 (N.M. Ct. App. 1998).

Facts. The Lees (Ds) negotiated with the Joneses (Ps) to purchase Ps' home for $610,000. After signing the purchase agreement in June and tendering $6,000 in earnest money, Ds informed Ps in August that they were unable to buy the property because of financial difficulties and presented a proposed termination agreement whereby Ds offered to void the contract in return for the forfeiture of the earnest money they had paid. Ps rejected Ds' offer, relisted the property, and sold it in November for $540,000. Ps filed suit seeking damages for breach of the purchase contract and were awarded damages of $70,000, plus special and punitive damages for a total of $157,118.94. Ds appeal.

Issue. May a court award compensatory, special, and punitive damages to a seller of real estate if a purchaser defaults on the contract to purchase the realty?

Held. Yes. Judgment affirmed in part and case remanded in part.

- Ps elected to sue for damages as their remedy for Ds' default on the contract to purchase real estate. Ps' burden is to provide evidence to support the claim so they may receive just compensation commensurate with their loss. This state follows the "loss of the bargain" rule in this matter, the measure of damages being the difference between the purchase price in the breached contract and the market value of the property at the time of the breach.

- The parties stipulated that the property was valued at $610,000 when Ds presented their proposed termination agreement, and Ds contend that Ps' property was valued at the contract price at the time of the breach. If this is the case, the sellers are limited to the recovery of only nominal damages or forfeiture of earnest money. Here, there was no determination of the date of the breach or the property's market value at the time of the breach. This case must be remanded for express findings of fact on these matters and to determine what effect to give the stipulation.

- Special damages may be awarded if they are shown to have resulted as the natural and probable consequence of the breach and if, at the time the contract was formed, the breaching party reasonably knew or should have anticipated that such damages would be incurred.

- Here, the court's awards for money expended for inspection of the solar heating system, for consultation on the system, and for a heating warranty were not in error. These were reasonably foreseeable requirements that a future purchaser might impose, and payment for the warranty was specifically provided for in the sales agreement.

- Mortgage interest payments awarded here, which were reduced by half because Ps lived in the property after Ds' default until the subsequent sale, were reasonably foreseeable.

- In attempting to persuade Ps to terminate the contract, Ds frightened Mrs. Jones and misrepresented their financial circumstances. At the time of the breach, Ds had $577,000 in a checking account and earned more than $16,000 per month. Ds' failure to consummate the contract was wanton, reckless, in utter disregard of their obligations, and sufficient to warrant the imposition of punitive damages.

---

c. Buyers Entitled to Restitution of Deposit Money in Excess of Damages

Kutzin v. Pirnie
591 A.2d 932 (N.J. 1991).

Facts. The Pirnies (Ds) agreed to purchase the Kutzins' (Ps') house for $365,000. Under a standard sales contract, Ds agreed to pay a partial deposit of $1,000 on signing the contract and the remaining deposit of $35,000 within seven days. There were no liquidated damages or forfeiture provisions in the contract. After Ds failed to go through with the purchase, Ps sued for breach of the sales agreement and were awarded $17,325 in damages. This consisted of: the $12,500 difference between the $365,000 that Ds had contracted to pay and the $352,500 for which the house later sold; $3,825 for utilities, taxes, and insurance expenses incurred between the originally anticipated closing date and the actual date of sale; and $1,000 for a new basement carpet purchased on the advice of Ps' realtor to enhance the value of their home. Ps did not recover interest they contended they would have earned on the original purchase price or damages for increased capital gains tax that Ps had paid, and they were ordered to return to Ds the $18,675 balance of Ds' deposit. The appellate court found that the contract was enforceable but that Ps' claims for interest and capital gains tax were too speculative. The court also found that Ps' loss was less than Ds' deposit but that Ps could nevertheless retain the deposit but were not entitled to recover any additional damages. Ps appeal. Ds cross-appeal.

Issue. If a real estate sales contract does not contain a forfeiture or liquidated damages clause, and the buyer breaches the sales contract, may the seller retain the buyer's entire deposit on the purchase price if the buyer shows that the deposit exceeds the amount of actual damages resulting from the breach?

Held. No. Judgment affirmed as modified.

- In the absence of a forfeiture clause in the sales contract, we have looked to the common law. It provides that a defaulting buyer may not recover her deposit, whether there is a forfeiture provision or not. While there is much authority for the appellate court's finding regarding damages, there has been growing recognition of the injustice that results from the common law rule. The Restatement (Second) of Contracts section 374(1) and courts in several jurisdictions have moved away from the common law rule to permit a defaulting buyer who can show that a deposit exceeds the amount of actual damages resulting from a breach to recover the excess.

- We overrule our state cases adhering to the common law rule and adopt the modern approach of the Restatement. To allow retention of the entire deposit would unjustly enrich the seller and would penalize the buyer, but a buyer who argues unjust enrichment has the burden of proving it.

- When a breaching buyer proves that his deposit exceeds the seller's actual damages resulting from the breach, the buyer may recover the difference. However, here we do not consider the validity or enforceability of a liquidated damages clause.

- Judgment of the appellate court is modified to reinstate the trial court's damage award. Ds are entitled to restitution of their deposit in excess of the loss caused by their breach. We accept the trial court's finding that Ps suffered $17,325 in damages because it is not challenged here. Ds are entitled to recover $18,675.

Comment. Unlike the court's holding in *Kutzin*, a majority of jurisdictions still hold that a buyer who defaults on a real estate contract without lawful excuse cannot recover his deposit, especially where the deposit does not exceed 10% of the contract price.

B. The Deed

1. Requirements

Usually the instrument used for transferring an interest in land is a deed, although sometimes more informal instruments may satisfy the Statute of Frauds. In the case of deeds the grantor, and only the grantor, must sign the instrument. It is a very good idea to have the grantor acknowledge his signature before a notary public so that the deed will comply with the recording acts. If it does not so comply, it cannot be recorded. Often the signature of the spouse will be required. It is always a good idea to have the spouse sign. This avoids problems caused by the spouse's right to community property, homestead, dower, curtesy, etc. As for the exact words required, any words evidencing an intent to make a transfer will suffice. (The common law required certain words of art. These technicalities have been rejected everywhere.) Further, the deed must name an ascertainable grantee ("John," "all my surviving children," etc.). Finally, the property to be conveyed must be described.

a. Consideration

A deed does not require consideration to support it. A grantor may give the property away.

b. Failures in the Description of the Property

Land can be described by metes and bounds, recorded plat, the name of the property, and the street address. (One must be careful in describing property by street address. Often mistakes are made when assigning house numbers. "1234 Lombard St." may legally be the address of the house next door.) Extrinsic evidence is normally admissible to clear up any ambiguity in the description of the property conveyed. The common law classified ambiguities as either latent or patent. A patent ambiguity (one on the face of the deed) could not be resolved by turning to extrinsic evidence. A latent ambiguity (one not on the face of the deed) could always be resolved by turning to extrinsic evidence.

c. Example

If a deed ambiguously describes property as "1234 Loma Linda Blvd." in one place and a paragraph or two later refers to the property as "2134 Loma Linda Blvd.," this constitutes a patent defect. If a deed refers to "my cabin in the mountains" and the grantor has two different mountain cabins, this is a latent ambiguity and extrinsic evidence would be admissible to show which cabin the grantor meant to convey.

d. Modern Trend

The modern trend is to admit extrinsic evidence to resolve both kinds of ambiguities.

2. Warranties of Title

a. Introduction

Almost all deeds contain what attorneys refer to as the "usual covenants." These covenants run from the seller of real property to the buyer. There are six "usual" covenants, although one of them is actually unusual in America.

b. Types of Deeds Warranting Title

1) Warranty Deed

This is the usual type of deed and it contains the "usual" covenants. It warrants title.

2) Special Warranty Deed

This type of deed contains the "usual" covenants but warrants title only from defects arising during the time the grantor has held the land. By contrast, a general warranty deed has no such limitation.

3) Quitclaim Deed

This form of deed does not warrant anything. It only transfers whatever interest the grantor has, or may have, in the property.

c. The Usual Covenants

1) Present Covenants

These are covenants that in essence state "I, the grantor, warrant that as of the date of this deed, I have not breached this particular covenant." Such covenants are breached, if at all, when the conveyance is made. Thus, the statute of limitations for these covenants begins to run as of the date of the conveyance.

a) Covenant of Seisin

The seller covenants he owns the property conveyed.

b) Covenant of Right to Convey

The seller warrants that he has the right to convey the property. For example, this covenant would be breached if the seller had the property in an irrevocable trust that gave only the trustee the right to convey.

c) Covenant Against Encumbrances

The seller promises that there are no easements, covenants, mortgages, or liens on the property. As a practical matter almost all property is subject to an encumbrance of some sort. What the seller will do is warrant against encumbrances "except as enumerated herein."

2) Future Covenants

These are continuing covenants that may be breached at the moment of conveyance or any time thereafter. The statute of limitations does not run until there is an actual breach.

a) Covenant of Quiet Enjoyment

The seller warrants that the buyer will not be disturbed in her possession of the property by the lawful claim of a third party.

b) Covenant of Warranty

This covenant meshes closely with the covenant of quiet enjoyment. The seller warrants that the title to the property is good and that, as grantor, he will defend at his own cost any suit from a party claiming paramount title.

c) Covenant of Further Assurances

This is the unusual covenant. It is rare in America and more common in England. By this covenant the seller promises to perform whatever acts are necessary to perfect the buyer's title to the property.

3) Merger

Because land sales in the United States involve two steps, sometimes there is a discrepancy between what is promised in the contract for sale and the deed. The general rule is that, absent provisions in the deed to the contrary, the contract of sale and the deed merge, leaving only those covenants that are contained in the deed. The modern trend is to hold that acceptance of the deed does not bar a suit on the contractual promises.

3. Breach of Covenants

Present covenants are breached, if ever, at the time of the conveyance. Future covenants may be breached anytime in the future. Generally, present covenants are "personal" and hence do not run with the land. Future covenants do run with the land. A minority of courts hold that the covenant against encumbrances runs with the land. From the definitions of the covenants above, it is fairly clear what constitutes a breach of one of these covenants. For example, if there is an encumbrance at the time of the conveyance, the covenant against encumbrances is breached.

a. Present Versus Future Covenants

Brown v. Lober
389 N.E.2d 1188 (Ill. 1979).

Facts. The Bosts bought 80 acres of land in 1947, the owner retaining a two-thirds interest in the mineral rights. In 1957, the Bosts conveyed the land to the Browns (Ps) under a general warranty deed containing no exceptions. Ps were going to convey the mineral rights to Consolidated Coal Co. for $6,000. Upon discovering that they had only one-third of the mineral rights, Ps sold that one-third interest for $2,000 and sued Lober (D), executor of the estate of the Bosts (both deceased), for $4,000 for breach of the covenant of quiet enjoyment. The 10-year statute of limitations had run, barring suit on the present covenants. The trial court found for D. The intermediate appellate court reversed. D appeals.

Issue. Does the warranty of quiet enjoyment constitute a warranty that the grantor is the owner of the entire estate as conveyed?

Held. No. Judgment reversed.

♦ The question is whether Ps have alleged facts sufficient to constitute a constructive eviction. Ps contend that when a covenantee fails in his efforts to sell an interest in land because he does not own what his warranty deed purported to convey, he has suffered a constructive eviction. We reject this argument.

- The covenant of quiet enjoyment only guarantees the covenantee (buyer) that his peaceable possession of the land will not be taken from him. It does not guarantee to the covenantee that there is no one with a paramount title. Thus, if the covenantee never attempts to occupy the land, his possession can never be other than peaceful.

- To possess a mineral estate, one must undertake the actual removal of the minerals from the ground. Possession of the surface does not carry possession of the minerals. Since no one has undertaken to remove the minerals, the mineral estate is "vacant." Accordingly, until such time as one holding paramount title interferes with Ps' right of possession (*e.g.*, begins mining coal), there can be no constructive eviction, and no breach of the covenant of quiet enjoyment.

- The protection of the covenant of quiet enjoyment should not be extended to an area governed by another covenant (that of seisin). Here, the fact that the Bosts had only a one-third interest in the mineral rights was of public record. Yet Ps failed to bring suit within the 10 years following delivery of the deed.

Comment. An action for breach of a covenant of seisin lies whenever there is a defect in title. In Illinois, the statute of limitations was 10 years for breach of that covenant.

---

b. Latent Land Use Violation

Frimberger v. Anzellotti
594 A.2d 1029 (Conn. App. Ct. 1991).

Facts. D's brother and predecessor in title conveyed to D by quitclaim deed property, upon which the brother had built a bulkhead, filled the property, and constructed a dwelling encroaching on the tidal wetlands boundary. D conveyed the property to P by warranty deed, free and clear of all encumbrances but subject to all building, building line and zoning restrictions, easements, and restrictions of record. P discovered a violation of a land use statute when he engaged an engineer to perform repairs. The Department of Environmental Protection ("DEP") informed D that he would have to submit an application to DEP demonstrating the necessity of maintaining the bulkhead and fill within the tidal wetlands in order to correct the violation. Instead, P filed suit, claiming breach of warranty against encumbrances and innocent misrepresentation. The trial court determined that the area had been filled in without obtaining the necessary permits, and found for P. D appeals.

Issue. Does a latent violation of a restrictive land use statute or ordinance, that exists at the time the fee is conveyed, constitute a breach of the warranty deed covenant against encumbrances?

Held. No. Judgment reversed.

- Latent violations of state or municipal land use regulations that do not appear on the land records, that are unknown to the seller of the property, as to which the agency charged with enforcement has taken no official action to compel compliance at the time the deed was executed, and that have not ripened into an interest that can be recorded on the land records do not constitute an encumbrance for the purpose of the deed warranty.

- Such a conceptual enlargement of the covenant against encumbrances would create uncertainty and confusion in the law of conveyancing and title insurance because neither a title search nor a physical examination of the premises would disclose the violation.

- P never filed an application; thus any damages P may have suffered were speculative.

- The proper way to deal with violations of governmental regulations is by contract provisions or language in the deed.

- Because we have held that the warranty of a covenant against encumbrances was not violated, no misrepresentation was made.

---

c. Remote Grantees

Rockafellor v. Gray
191 N.W. 107 (Iowa 1922).

Facts. Doffing conveyed 80 acres to Rockafellor (P). P assumed Doffing's mortgage to Gray (D). P subsequently defaulted and D foreclosed on the mortgage. Connelly purchased the land at a sheriff's sale and was given a sheriff's deed. He in turn sold the land to Dixon for $4,000 by means of a deed containing the usual covenants of warranty. Dixon sold the land to Hansen & Gregory (H & G) for $7,000 by means of a deed containing the usual covenants of warranty. Subsequently, P had the sheriff's deed to Connelly set aside and the foreclosure proceedings declared void. H & G sued Connelly, the remote grantor, for breach of warranty of seisin and recovered an award of $4,000. Connelly appealed on the ground that since he had no title to the land (due to the void foreclosure) and had never entered in possession, the warranty of seisin could not run with the land to a remote grantee.

Issue. Does covenant of seisin run to a remote grantee even if the original grantor never had actual possession of the land?

Held. Yes. Judgment affirmed.

♦ We have previously adopted the minority rule (English Rule) and held that a warranty of seisin runs with the land to remote grantees and is broken the instant a defective conveyance is delivered. (The majority rule is called the American Rule.)

♦ Because on the day Connelly conveyed the land to Dixon he had no title and no possession of the premises, the covenant of seisin was breached. The covenant ran with the land to H & G, Dixon's successors.

> H & G filed their cross-petition within the 10-year statute of limitations.

> The original covenantee, here Connelly, is bound even if he does not have title or actual possession at the time of the conveyance.

♦ This still leaves the issue of whether the covenant of seisin runs with the land since the original covenantee, Connelly, was never in possession of the premises. Some courts hold that possession (seisin) itself is what causes the covenant of seisin to run with the land. We reject this hypertechnical theory.

♦ As to the amount of the judgment ($4,000, with interest thereon from the date of the conveyance to Dixon):

> Proof of actual consideration would be admissible only in a suit between the grantor (Connelly) and the original grantee (Dixon).

> In all other cases the consideration recited in the deed is a conclusive admission by a defendant of the land's value. (Connelly contended that although the deed recited consideration of $4,000, the real consideration was nominal. Connelly had parol evidence to support this).

> The damages are limited to the amount paid by the original grantee to the original grantor ($4,000) plus interest. H & G cannot recover the amount it paid to Dixon ($7,000).

---

4. Delivery

One of the requirements of a deed is that it must be delivered by the grantor. If the grantor signs a deed and leaves it on his desk (fails to deliver it), the deed is ineffective.

a. Delivery Defined

"Delivery" has two requirements: (i) the grantor, by words or conduct, must manifest an intent to make the deed effective and (ii) the grantor must immediately give it to the grantee. Some modern cases have relaxed the manual delivery requirement where it is clear the grantor meant for the grantee to receive the property.

1) Evidence of Intent

Extrinsic evidence is admissible to prove delivery or nondelivery.

2) Delivery Cannot Be Cancelled

Once delivery of the deed has taken place, it cannot be cancelled because the grantor's interest in the property has already passed to the grantee. To get the property back, it must be deeded back to the grantor.

3) Estoppel

Even if there is no delivery, the grantor may be estopped from denying delivery if a subsequent good faith purchaser for value is involved.

b. Types of Delivery

There are two types of delivery: (i) those involving only the grantor and grantee and (ii) those involving a third-party intermediary.

1) Grantor-Grantee Delivery

When the grantor has possession of the deed, a rebuttable presumption arises that there was no delivery. Likewise, it is presumed that if the grantee has the deed, there was delivery. If a deed is recorded, it is presumed there has been a valid delivery. If the grantor has acknowledged his signature, one of the prerequisites to recording, then a presumption of delivery applies. Once delivery is shown, it is presumed to have taken place on the date of the grantor's signature.

2) Delivery Subject to a Condition

Assume the grantor delivers a deed to the grantee subject to a condition, such as "this deed to take effect only upon my death." If the condition is expressed in the deed, it is usually held that there has been a valid delivery of a future interest (the grantor retaining a life estate). Likewise, if the condition is that the grantee survive the grantor, the delivery is valid. The common law is to the contrary. The modern trend is to give effect to deeds that reserve in the grantor the power to revoke the deed prior to the date it passes legal title to the grantee. Oral conditions attached to a deed valid on its face are invalid. The courts simply ignore the conditions.

c. Unsuccessful Conditional Delivery

Sweeney v. Sweeney
11 A.2d 806 (Conn. 1940).

Facts. Maurice Sweeney deeded his farm to his brother John Sweeney (D). Then, as security in the event D predeceased Maurice, D immediately deeded it back to Maurice. The first deed was recorded;

the second was not. Maurice took both deeds to D, who kept them at his house. Maurice continued to possess the premises and leased part of the property to a third party. D never received any rent or made any repairs to the property. Maurice died. Sweeney, Administratrix (P), Maurice's estranged, but still lawful, surviving spouse, sought a declaration that the property was part of Maurice's probate estate. The trial court rendered judgment for D and P appeals.

Issue. May a delivery of a deed be deemed conditional when it is made to the grantee?

Held. No. Judgment reversed.

♦ Maurice, for only a short time, physically possessed the unrecorded deed that reconveyed the property to himself. Physical possession is not conclusive proof that it was legally delivered, however; to be effective, the delivery must have been made with the intent to pass title.

♦ The parties executed the attestation clauses on the deeds, which constitutes prima facie proof that the deed was delivered to Maurice. No facts rebut this presumption. In fact, the very purpose of the reconveyance was to protect Maurice if D predeceased him. This purpose would have been frustrated if no present intent to deliver had existed, because in that case the reconveyance would have been ineffective. Therefore, present delivery must have been intended by D.

♦ D claims that any delivery was only conditional on D's predeceasing Maurice. However, delivery to the grantee cannot be conditional. Delivery to a grantee vests absolute title in the grantee. Conditional deliveries can only be effected through the agency of a third person, who then delivers the deed to the grantee upon the occurrence of the condition.

---

d. No Intent to Part with the Power to Retake

Rosengrant v. Rosengrant
629 P.2d 800 (Okla. Ct. App. 1981).

Facts. Harold and Mildred Rosengrant, a childless elderly couple with six nieces and nephews, attempted to convey their farm to Jay Rosengrant (D). In the presence of their banker, Harold and Mildred signed the deed to their property and informed D to leave the deed at the bank until their deaths when D was to record the deed. Harold handed the deed to D to "make this legal." D accepted the deed, then handed it back to the banker, who put it into an envelope marked "J.W. Rosengrant or Harold H. Rosengrant." When Mildred was close to death, D and Harold checked with a lawyer regarding the legality of the transaction. They were told "it should be sufficient" but if they anticipated there would be problems with D's cousins, Harold should draw up a will. After Harold's death, D retrieved the deed and recorded it. A petition to cancel and set aside the deed was filed. The trial court found the deed was null and void for lack of legal delivery. D appeals.

Issue. Did the trial court err in its ruling?

Held. No. Judgment affirmed.

♦ The writing on the envelope indicates the deed was retrievable at any time prior to his death by Harold. Harold continued to farm the land, pay taxes, claim it as his homestead, and otherwise control the land.

♦ Harold attached a condition to delivery of the deed that it would become operative only after his and Mildred's death. He was attempting to use the deed as a will. The delivery to D was a symbolic delivery. It did not carry "all the force and consequence of absolute, outright ownership at the time of delivery."

Concurrence. A valid delivery requires actual or constructive delivery of a deed to the grantee or third party and the grantor's intention to divest himself of the interest conveyed. The Rosengrants' subsequent actions indicate they intended to reserve a de facto life estate or retain the power to revoke the conveyance.

Comment. The lawyer from whom D sought advice should have suggested Harold and Mildred establish a revocable trust whereby they would hold their land in trust for their joint lives and the life of the survivor and upon the death of the survivor have title pass to D. They would have accomplished what they set out to do and avoided probate. Also, under Oklahoma law, Harold and Mildred could have delivered the deed to a third party depository with instructions to deliver to D at their death, intending at the time of delivery to give up all ownership, control or power to retake. [*See* Anderson v. Mauk, 67 P.2d 429 (Okla. 1937)].

------

e. Delivery to Third Parties (Escrow)

Occasionally a grantor may want to make the transfer conditional on the occurrence of some event. This requires the use of a third party.

1) Escrow

If the grantor delivers the deed to a third party with instructions that he deliver it to the grantee on the occurrence of certain conditions, this is deemed an effective present delivery so long as the grantor does not retain the right to revoke the delivery. The third party is an "escrow agent" and the instructions given him are contained in an "escrow agreement." Typically the conditions are something like "deliver the deed to the grantee upon my death," or "deliver the deed to the grantee when he deposits the purchase price with you." Often commercial escrow companies are used. In order to avoid gaps in title, the grantee is deemed to have received title when the grantor delivered the deed into escrow.

2) Reservation of the Power to Revoke

The general rule is that by reserving the power to revoke, the grantor still has such control of the deed that there is no delivery. The modern trend is to recognize the delivery so long as there is no actual revocation. Some courts will consider the delivery valid only if the contingency is beyond the grantor's control.

f. Estoppel of Grantor

When dealing with deed delivery problems, the practitioner must not forget that estoppel may operate to prevent the grantor from denying that he delivered the deed to the grantee. Assume, for example, that the grantor gives a deed to Blackacre to the grantee to examine and the grantee breaches the trust and records the deed and sells Blackacre to C. If C is a BFP (bona fide purchaser for value), the grantor will be estopped from asserting nondelivery. The grantor's remedy is to sue the grantee. In cases involving wrongful delivery by the escrow agent, the majority rule is that the grantor is not estopped from asserting nondelivery. The minority view is the opposite.

g. Estoppel by Deed

If a grantor conveys an estate that he does not own, and later acquires the estate, the grantee gets that interest. This doctrine is founded on the proposition that by conveying what he does not own, the grantor has impliedly promised to immediately convey it to the grantee when he does acquire it.

C. Financing Real Estate Transactions

1. Introduction

In most real estate transactions, the buyer makes a relatively small down payment and finances the rest. The financing institution, usually a bank or savings and loan association, typically takes a note from the borrower as well as a mortgage. The borrower is personally liable on the note, but the mortgage gives the lender the right to sell the property to pay off the note if the borrower defaults. The lender is the mortgagee, and the borrower is the mortgagor.

2. Mortgages and Foreclosure

Under early common law, the lender would receive title in fee simple absolute if the borrower failed to pay promptly. Eventually, borrowers were given an equitable right to redeem the property. This right of redemption could be foreclosed by the lender through a judicial foreclosure proceeding, the result of which would be a decree that the property be publicly sold and the proceeds used to pay the debt, with any balance going to the mortgagor. Many state legislatures have enacted statutes permitting mortgagors to redeem property from the purchaser at the judicial foreclosure sale.

3. Mortgagee's Duty upon Foreclosure

Murphy v. Financial Development Corp.
495 A.2d 1245 (N.H. 1985).

Facts. The Murphys (Ps) bought a house and financed it with a mortgage loan. They later refinanced the home, using Financial Development Corp. (D) as the mortgagee. D assigned the note and mortgage to Colonial Deposit Corp. (D). About a year later, Mr. Murphy became unemployed and Ps began failing to pay their mortgage payments. Ds notified Ps of their intent to foreclose. Ps made up the mortgage arrearage, but did not pay certain costs and legal fees incurred due to the foreclosure. Ds postponed the sale to give Ps more time, but Ps did not make the necessary payments. Ds refused to postpone the sale further. The only parties present at the sale were Ps, Ds, and an attorney. Ds bid the amount owed on the mortgage, plus costs and fees, and acquired the property for $27,000. Later that day, one of the attorney's other clients offered to buy the property for $27,000. Ds refused, but made a counteroffer to sell for $40,000. Ds sold the property to this person two days later for $38,000. Ps sued to have the foreclosure sale set aside, or alternatively for money damages. The trial court found for Ps on the ground that Ds had not exercised good faith and due diligence in obtaining a fair price at the foreclosure sale. The court awarded Ps $27,000, representing the difference between what it found to be the fair market value on the date of foreclosure, $54,000, and the price paid by Ds, $27,000. The court also awarded legal fees. Ds appeal.

Issue. Does a mortgagee who is foreclosing on a property have a duty to secure a portion of the mortgagor's equity if it is reasonably possible to do so?

Held. Yes. Judgment reversed in part and case remanded.

♦ A mortgagee who forecloses on a property has a dual role as seller and potential buyer. In its seller role, the mortgagee has a duty to act in good faith and with due diligence, in a fiduciary capacity. The mortgagee must use reasonable efforts to obtain a fair and reasonable price.

♦ Inadequacy of price alone does not prove the mortgagee acted in bad faith in selling the property; the circumstances of the particular case are controlling. In this case, Ds did comply with the statutory requirements and did postpone the sale once to assist Ps. Ds did not sell the property with any awareness of the subsequent purchaser. Thus, Ds did not act in bad faith.

♦ The evidence does demonstrate that Ds failed to use due diligence in obtaining a fair price. The home had been appraised at $46,000 about two years before the sale. Ds thus had reason to know that they could make a quick turnaround sale. This knowledge was demonstrated by their rejection of the $27,000 offer made the day of the sale and Ds' counteroffer for $40,000. Ds should have done more to ensure a higher sales price.

♦ A mortgagee does not necessarily have to secure a portion of the mortgagor's equity in all cases, but Ds did have a duty to do so here. Ds' officer testified that Ds were only concerned with making Ds whole, not with obtaining the fair market value for the property. Ds' advertising was ineffective since no one showed up at the sale. Compliance with the strict requirements of the law was not enough in this case.

♦ Even though Ds failed to exercise due diligence, the award to Ps of the difference between the fair market value and the price actually obtained was improper. This measure of damages may be appropriate for a case of bad faith, but it produces greater damages than a measure based on a "fair" price which is the result of due diligence. Ps are only entitled to the difference between a fair price and the price actually obtained.

---

4. Unfair Subprime Mortgage Loans

Commonwealth v. Fremont Investment & Loan
897 N.E.2d 548 (Mass. 2008).

Facts. The Commonwealth of Massachusetts (P), through its attorney general, filed a consumer protection enforcement action against Fremont Investment & Loan and its parent company (D), claiming that D, by originating and servicing certain "subprime" mortgage loans (*i.e.*, loans made to borrowers who generally would not qualify for traditional loans offered at the generally prevailing rate of interest for conventional mortgages), between 2004 and 2007, acted unfairly and deceptively in violation of Massachusetts's consumer protection statute. All of the loans at issue were secured by mortgages on the borrowers' homes. About 50% to 60% of D's loans in Massachusetts were subprime. Because they present a greater risk to the lender, the interest rate for a subprime loan is typically higher than the rate charged for conventional or prime mortgages. D's subprime loan products offered different features that catered to low-income borrowers. Most were adjustable rate mortgage ("ARM") loans with fixed interest rates for the first two or three years, which then adjusted every six months to a much higher variable rate for the remaining 30 years of the loan. When qualifying borrowers for a loan, D usually required a debt-to-income ratio of less than or equal to 50%; *i.e.*, the borrower's monthly debts, including the applied-for mortgage, could not exceed 50% of their income. However, D took into account only the monthly payment required for the introductory period of the loan, not the payment that would be required when the interest rate increased. At the time that P intervened, a large number of D's loans were in default. P's investigation showed that all were ARM loans with a substantial increase in payments required after the first two or three years.

The court found no evidence that D encouraged or condoned misrepresentation of borrowers' incomes or that D concealed or misrepresented the terms of the loans. It did find, however, that P was likely to prevail on its claim that D's loans with the following characteristics were unfair: (i) the loans were ARMs with an introductory period of three years or less; (ii) the introductory rate was at least 3% below the fully indexed rate; (iii) the borrowers' debt-to-income ratio would have been greater than 50% if D had measured the borrower's debt by the monthly payments that would be due at the fully indexed rate rather than under the introductory rate; and (iv) the loan-to-value ratio was 100%, or the loan featured a prepayment penalty greater than the conventional prepayment penalty or a prepayment penalty that extended beyond the introductory rate period.

The court said that D should have known that the loans with the first three characteristics were doomed to foreclosure unless the borrower could refinance the loan at the end of the introductory rate period and get a new, low introductory rate. But the fourth factor would make refinancing impossible for subprime borrowers unless housing prices increased. Without an increase, the borrowers would not have enough equity or financial capacity to get a new loan. The judge stated that, with the fluctuations and uncertainties in the housing market, it was unfair to issue a home mortgage loan that D expected would fall into default when the introductory period ended unless the fair market value of the home had increased.

A preliminary injunction was granted in favor of P. Under the terms of the injunction, D had to notify P of its intent to foreclose on any mortgage loan. As to loans with the four characteristics of unfair loans that were secured by the borrower's principal residence ("presumptively unfair" loans), D had to work with P to resolve their differences through a restructure or workout of the loan. If the loan could not be worked out, D had to get court approval to foreclose. Borrowers were obliged to prove that their loans were unfair. D appeals from the preliminary injunction.

Issue. Did D act unfairly in violation of the consumer protection statute by originating the subprime mortgage loans?

Held. Yes. Grant of preliminary injunction affirmed.

- D argues that, under the standards applicable to the mortgage lending industry when the loans were originated, it did not violate any established concept of fairness. D contends that the judge applied new rules or standards for what is "unfair" retroactively or in an ex post facto manner.

- D emphasizes the judge's statement that, when D made the loans at issue, loans with the four characteristics the judge deemed unfair were not considered by the industry to be unfair. However, this does not mean that the loans were fair. Instead, D knew or should have known that the combination of the four characteristics in a subprime loan would operate together to guarantee that the borrowers would be unable to pay and would default unless real estate prices continued to rise indefinitely, an assumption already shown to be unreasonable in 2004. The court correctly determined that P would likely be able to prove that, by originating loans with terms that in combination would lead to default and foreclosure, D's actions were unfair at the time the loans were made.

- Like other lending institutions making subprime loans, D was warned by state and federal regulatory agencies mat, even if D made subprime loans that complied with banking-specific laws and regulations, their policies could still be considered unfair and deceptive practices under consumer protection law.

- Before 2004, the principle had been stated that loans made to borrowers on terms showing that they would be unable to repay and thus were likely to default were unsafe, unsound, and probably unfair. Hence, an interagency federal guidance published in 2001 stated that loans to borrowers who did not show the ability to repay the loans, as structured, from sources other than the collateral were considered unsafe and unsound. In 2003, a federal agency warned that a loan was unfair to consumers when it was made based on the foreclosure value of the collateral, rather than on a determination that the borrower had the capacity to make the scheduled payments under the terms of the loan. The lender anticipated seizing the borrower's equity in the collateral to satisfy the obligation and to recover high fees.

- The record suggests that D made no effort to determine whether borrowers could make their scheduled payments. As the judge determined, D made loans in the understanding that they would have to be refinanced before the introductory period ended. D claims that it believed housing prices would improve during the introductory loan term and that borrowers would be able to refinance before the higher payments began. But it was unfair to the borrower for D to structure its loans on such unsupportable optimism. D ignored warnings to consider the performance of its loans in declining markets and cannot now claim that it was taken by surprise by the economic downturn.

♦ Furthermore, D entered into a consent agreement with the FDIC in March 2007, the day D stopped making loans. D did not admit to wrongdoing, and we do not consider the agreement as evidence of liability. However, we do see it as evidence of existing policy and guidance provided to the mortgage lending industry. The fact that the FDIC ordered D to stop using the loan features that are in the judge's list of presumptively unfair characteristics shows that the FDIC considered that, under established mortgage lending standards, the marketing of loans with these features constituted unsafe and unsound banking practice with harmful consequences for borrowers. Such conduct qualifies as unfair under the consumer protection statute.

♦ D contends that the preliminary injunction order does not serve the public interest and will make lenders unwilling to risk doing business in an environment of uncertainty where the rules may change after the fact. We disagree that the injunction order has created an environment of uncertainty. The order balances the borrowers' and the lender's interests. Where the loan terms include all four features deemed presumptively unfair, D must explore alternatives to foreclosure and then seek the court's approval. If the court does not approve foreclosure, the injunction remains until P has an opportunity to try to prove that the loan violated the statute; the burden never shifts to D. We find that the order serves the public interest.

---

5. No Authority to Foreclose

U.S. Bank Natl. Assn. v. Ibanez

941 N.E.2d 40 (Mass. 2010).

Facts. There are two mortgages involved here. We discuss each separately.

The Ibanez mortgage. On December 1, 2005, Ibanez took out a $103,500 loan for the purchase of property at 20 Crosby Street in Springfield, secured by a mortgage to the lender, Rose Mortgage, Inc. (Rose Mortgage). The mortgage was recorded the following day and assigned in blank (no assignee designated) a few days later. Option One Mortgage Corporation (Option One) was later designated as the assignee, and that assignment was recorded on June 7, 2006. Before the recording, on January 23, 2006, Option One executed an assignment of the Ibanez mortgage in blank. Option One assigned the Ibanez mortgage to Lehman Brothers Bank, FSB, which assigned it to Lehman Brothers Holdings Inc., which assigned it to the Structured Asset Securities Corporation, which then assigned the mortgage, pooled with approximately 1,220 other mortgage loans, to U.S. Bank, as trustee for the Structured Asset Securities Corporation Mortgage Pass-Through Certificates, Series 2006-Z. With this last assignment, the Ibanez and other loans were pooled into a trust and converted into mortgage-backed securities that can be bought and sold by investors—a process known as securitization. U.S. Bank claims the assignment of the Ibanez mortgage to U.S. Bank occurred pursuant to a December 1, 2006, trust agreement, which is not in the record. Instead, the record contains the private placement memorandum (PPM), dated December 26, 2006, a 273-page, unsigned offer of mortgage-backed securities to potential investors. The PPM describes the entities involved, the mortgage pools, and summarizes the trust agreement; one representation in the agreement is "that mortgages 'will be' assigned into the trust." According to the PPM, each mortgage loan transfer from the Seller (Lehman) through to the Trustee (U.S. Bank) "will be intended to be a sale of that loan and will be reflected as such in both the Sale and Assignment Agreement and the Trust Agreement. The PPM states that each loan will be identified in a schedule appearing as an exhibit to the Trust Agreement. P provided the court no schedule listing the Ibanez mortgage. On April 17, 2007, in a foreclosure proceeding necessitated by the Servicemembers Civil Relief Act (Servicemembers Act), which restricts foreclosures against active duty members of the uniformed services, U.S. Bank (P) filed a complaint to foreclose on the Ibanez mortgage in the Land Court. P represented it was the "owner (or assignee) and holder" of the mortgage. The court allowed the foreclosure on June 26, 2007. P published the notice of foreclosure sale and identified itself as "the present holder" of the mortgage. On July 5, 2007, U.S. Bank, as trustee for the securitization trust, purchased the property for $94,350, a price much less than the outstanding debt and the estimated market value of the property. The foreclosure deed (from U.S. Bank, trustee, as the purported holder of the mortgage, to U.S. Bank, trustee, as the purchaser) and the statutory foreclosure affidavit were recorded on May 23, 2008. On September 2, 2008, more than one year after the sale, and more than five months after recording of the sale, American Home Mortgage Servicing, Inc., "as successor-in-interest" to Option One, which was until then the record holder of the Ibanez mortgage, executed a written assignment of that mortgage to U.S. Bank, as trustee for the securitization trust. This assignment was recorded on September 11, 2008.

The LaRace mortgage. On May 19, 2005, Mark and Tammy LaRace gave a mortgage for the property at 6 Brookburn Street in Springfield to Option One as security for a $103,200 loan; the mortgage was recorded that same day and Option One executed an assignment in blank of this mortgage. Wells Fargo (P2) asserts that Option One assigned the LaRace mortgage to Bank of America in a July 28, 2005, flow sale and servicing agreement. There is no copy in the record of the flow sale and servicing agreement; thus, there is no document showing an assignment of the LaRace mortgage by Option One to Bank of America. (P2 produced an unexecuted copy of the mortgage loan purchase agreement as an exhibit to the PSA. That agreement provides that Bank of America agrees to sell and convey to the purchaser (ABFC) all of its right, title and interest in each mortgage loan; again, a schedule is referred to that lists the assigned mortgage loans, but it is not in the record. There is no document showing the LaRace mortgage was among the loans assigned to the ABFC. P2 provided a schedule that it represented identified the loans assigned in the PSA; it contained no property addresses, names of mortgagors, or any number that corresponds to the loan number or servicing number on the LaRace mortgage. P2 argued a loan showing the LaRace property zip code and city is the loan at issue because the payment history and loan amount match the LaRace loan.) Bank of America then assigned to Asset Backed Funding Corporation (ABFC) in an October 1, 2005, mortgage loan purchase agreement. Finally, ABFC pooled the mortgage with others and assigned it to Wells Fargo, as trustee for the ABFC 2005-OPT 1 Trust, ABFC Asset-Backed Certificates, Series 2005-OPT 1, pursuant to a pooling and servicing agreement (PSA). On April 27, 2007, P2 filed a complaint under the Servicemembers Act in the Land Court to foreclose on the LaRace mortgage, representing P2 as the "owner (or assignee) and holder" of the mortgage. A judgment issued on P2's behalf on July 3, 2007. In June, 2007, P2 published the statutory notice of sale, identifying itself as the "present holder" of the mortgage. On July 5, 2007, at the foreclosure sale, P2, as trustee, purchased the LaRace property for $120,397.03, very much below its estimated market value. P2 did not execute a statutory foreclosure affidavit or foreclosure deed until May 7, 2008 when Option One, still the record holder of the LaRace mortgage, executed an assignment of the mortgage to P2 as trustee; the assignment was recorded on May 12, 2008. Although executed ten months after the foreclosure sale, the assignment declared an effective date of April 18, 2007, a date that preceded the publication of the notice of sale and the foreclosure sale.

In September and October of 2008, P and P2 (together Ps) brought separate actions in the Land Court to quiet title. Both complaints sought a judgment that the right, title and interest of their respective mortgagors in their property was extinguished by foreclosure; a declaration that there was no cloud on the title as a result of publication in the *Boston Globe*; and that title was vested in the Ps as trustees in fee simple. Ps each asserted it had become the holder of the respective mortgage through an assignment made after the foreclosure sale. Ibanez and the LaRaces (Ds) did not answer the complaints and Ps moved for default judgment. Judgment was entered against Ps. The judge found the foreclosure sales were invalid because the notices of the foreclosure sales named P (in the Ibanez foreclosure) and P2 (in the LaRace foreclosure) as the mortgage holders where they had not yet been assigned the mortgages. The judge found, based on each P's assertions in its complaint, that the Ps acquired the mortgages by assignment only after the foreclosure sales and thus had no interest in the mortgages being foreclosed at the time of the publication of the notices of sale or at the time of the foreclosure sales. Ps moved to vacate the judgments. At a hearing on the motions on April 17, 2009, the Ps conceded that each complaint alleged a postnotice, postforeclosure sale assignment of the mortgage at issue, but they now represented to the judge that documents might exist that could show a prenotice, preforeclosure sale assignment of the mortgages. The judge permitted Ps to produce these documents so long as they were produced in the form they existed at the time the foreclosure sales were noticed and conducted. Ps produced hundreds of pages, most of which related to the creation of the securitized mortgage pools in which the two mortgages were purportedly included. Ps motion to vacate judgment was denied. Ps appeal.

Issue. Did the court err in concluding that the securitization documents submitted by Ps failed to demonstrate that they were holders of the mortgages at the times of the publication of the notices of the foreclosure sales and of the sales themselves?

Held. No. Judgment affirmed.

♦ With the exception of the limited judicial procedure aimed at certifying that the mortgagor is not a beneficiary of the Servicemembers Act, a mortgage holder can foreclose on a property, as Ps did here, by exercise of the statutory power of sale, if such a power is granted by the mortgage itself.

♦ Unless the mortgagor files an action and obtains a court order enjoining the foreclosure, the sale goes forward even if there is a dispute as to whether the mortgagor was in default or whether the party claiming to be the mortgage holder is the true mortgage holder.

♦ Because of the power the statutory scheme gives to the mortgage holder, we follow the rule that "one who sells under a power [of sale] must follow strictly its terms. If he fails to do so there is no valid execution of the power, and the sale is wholly void." The terms of a power of sale of a mortgage must comply strictly with its terms.

♦ Who is entitled to exercise the power of sale is one of the foremost matters that demands strict compliance. If a party lacks jurisdiction or authority to carry out a foreclosure, the effort is void.

♦ The notice requirement, that provision that mandates that no sale is effectual under a power to sell unless advance notice has been provided to the mortgagor and other interested parties by publication in a newspaper published in the town where the property lies or one of general circulation in the town, is another provision that requires strict compliance.

♦ Since only the present mortgage holder may foreclose, and because the mortgagor is entitled to know who is foreclosing and selling the property, the failure to identify the holder of the mortgage in the notice of sale may render the notice defective and the foreclosure sale void.

♦ If Ps wish to obtain a judicial declaration of clear title, they must prove their authority to foreclose under the power of sale and show compliance with the requirements on which this authority rests. Here, Ps were not the original mortgagees to whom the power of sale was granted. Instead, Ps claimed authority as the eventual assignees. The statute clearly provides Ps had the authority to exercise the power of sale only if they were the assignees of the mortgages at the time of the notice of sale and the subsequent foreclosure sale. Ps' authority cannot be based on an assignment dated four months after the foreclosure proceedings began.

♦ Ps' claim that their securitization documents establish valid assignments that made them the holders of the Ibanez and LaRace mortgages before the notice of sale and the foreclosure sale is completely without merit.

♦ We turn, then, to the documentation submitted by the plaintiffs to determine whether it met the requirements of a valid assignment. The assignment of a mortgage is a conveyance of an interest in land that requires a writing signed by the grantor.

♦ Here, the mortgages are pooled in a trust and converted to mortgage-backed securities, but the mortgages securing the notes are still legal title to someone's house or land.

- P1 argues it was assigned the mortgage under the trust agreement described in the PPM, but it did not provide a copy of that agreement to the court. However, the PPM described the trust agreement as one Focusing first on the Ibanez mortgage, U.S. Bank argues that it was assigned "to be executed." It shows only evidence of intent to assign, not assignment.

- Even if there were an executed agreement, P1 did not produce the schedule allegedly showing the Ibanez mortgage was among those to be assigned by that agreement.

- Finally, even if we had an executed trust agreement and the schedule, P1 did not produce any evidence that the entity assigning the mortgage ever held the mortgage. The last assignment on record is from Rose Mortgage to Option One. There is nothing showing Option One ever assigned the mortgage to anyone before the foreclosure sale. Based on the documents before us, Option One was the mortgage holder at the time of the foreclosure sale. P1 had no authority to foreclose.

- P2 also claims it had authority to foreclose under the PSA. Unlike P1's PPM, P2's PSA uses language of a present assignment ("does hereby . . . assign . . .") rather than an intent to assign. However, the mortgage loan schedule P2 provided does not identify with specificity the LaRace mortgage as one of those assigned in the PSA. Furthermore, P2 provided the court with no document that showed ABFC held the LaRace mortgage that it was purportedly assigning in the PSA. Again, Option One was the record holder of the loan and there is nothing to show that Option One ever assigned it to anyone before the publication of the notice and the sale.

- A plaintiff who cannot show proof that the foreclosing entity was the mortgage holder at the time of the notice of sale and foreclosure cannot claim that it was unfairly denied a declaration of clear title.

- We are not saying an assignment must be in recordable form at the time of the sale; where a pool of mortgages is assigned to a securitized trust, the executed agreement that assigns the pool of mortgages, with a schedule of the pooled mortgage loans that clearly and specifically identifies the mortgage at issue as among those assigned, may suffice to establish the trustee as the mortgage holder. In all circumstances, however, there must be proof that the assignment was made by a party that itself held the mortgage.

- Assignments in blank do not constitute a lawful assignment of the mortgages. Without the name of the assignee, nothing is conveyed. In the absence of a valid written assignment of a mortgage or a court order of assignment, the mortgage holder remains unchanged. Neither may a postforeclosure assignment be treated as a preforeclosure assignment simply by declaring an "effective date" that precedes the notice of sale and foreclosure, as did Option One's assignment of the LaRace mortgage to P2. An assignment of a mortgage is a transfer of legal title; it becomes effective with respect to the power of sale only on the transfer; it cannot become effective before the transfer.

Concurrence. I concur fully and write only to emphasize the carelessness with which Ps documented the titles to their assets. What would be the effect of such conduct on a bona fide third-party purchaser who relied on the bank's foreclosure title and the confirmative assignment and affidavit of foreclosure recorded by the bank after that foreclosure but before the purchase by the third party, especially where the party whose property was foreclosed was in fact in violation of the mortgage covenants, had notice of the foreclosure, and took no action to contest it.

---

6. Deeds of Trust

Most states permit use of a deed of trust, under which the borrower conveys title to the property to a trustee. If the borrower defaults, the trustee can sell the property without going to court. This power of sale is subject to statutory and judicial restrictions with respect to notice and procedure, but it avoids the burdensome judicial foreclosure proceeding.

7. Installment Contracts

A seller may finance the sale of real estate instead of a third-party lender. The common instrument used for doing so is an installment land contract. The seller promises to convey title to the buyer once the purchase price is paid; in the meantime, the seller retains title. The buyer takes possession and assumes responsibility to pay taxes and insurance. The terms of the ordinary installment contract provide that if the buyer defaults, the seller can keep all payments already made, but the courts normally hold such forfeiture clauses invalid. Instead, the seller's interest is treated as a lien that may be satisfied only through a judicial sale.

8. Defaulting Vendee

Bean v. Walker
464 N.Y.S.2d 895 (N.Y. App. Div. 1983).

Facts. The Walkers (Ds) purchased a home from Ps for $15,000 to be paid over a 15year period. Ps retained legal title to be conveyed upon payment in full. Ds were entitled to possession and were obligated to pay taxes, assessments, water rates, and insurance. The contract provided that if Ds defaulted and failed to cure within 30 days, Ps could elect to call the balance due immediately or terminate the contract and repossess the premises. If Ps chose to terminate, the contract provided that Ps could retain all money paid as liquidated damages and the money paid would be considered payment of rent. Ds defaulted after nine years, during which time they had paid almost one-half of the purchase price plus interest. Ps commenced an action in ejectment and the court granted summary judgment.

Issue. Does a vendee under a land sale contract acquire an interest in the property of such a nature that it must be extinguished before the vendor may resume possession?

Held. Yes. Judgment reversed and case remanded.

♦ A vendee acquires equitable title and the vendor merely holds legal title in trust for the vendee, subject to the vendor's equitable lien for payment of the purchase price in accordance with the terms of the contract. The vendor may not enforce his rights by an action in ejectment but must foreclose the vendee's equitable title or bring an action at law for the purchase price.

♦ Forfeiture may be an appropriate result where a vendee abandons the property or absconds or where he has paid a minimal sum on the contract and upon default seeks to retain possession while the vendor is paying taxes, insurance, and other upkeep.

D. The Recording System

1. Introduction

Recording does not directly affect the rights of the grantor and the grantee vis-à-vis themselves. It does affect the right of people who subsequently receive the property from the grantee. The purpose of recording is to give notice to the public as to who has what interest in the property. Recording furnishes constructive (also called "record") notice to everyone.

2. Method of Recording

To record, a grantee files the deed with the county recorder. Furthermore, the deed must be "acknowledged" (*i.e.*, it has to be signed in front of a notary public). The deed is typically filed one of two ways:

a. Grantor-Grantee Index

The conveyance is filed chronologically. Record of the filing is kept in two books, one for grantors and one for grantees. The names in the books are listed alphabetically. Typically, a new book is begun each year. Tracing title through grantor-grantee index books, especially if a date or two is missing, becomes quite laborious. One must first determine the year of the conveyance and look up the grantee's name. One can then determine from the book who his grantor was. After finding the grantor's name, one looks for his name as a grantee. When one finds it, one determines who his grantor was and looks for him as a grantee. The process is repeated until reaching the initial conveyance of the land.

b. Tract Index

In localities using tract indexes, each plot of land is given a tract, block, and lot number (*e.g.*, 'Tract A, Block 57, Lot 23"). Recorded documents are filed in chronological order under each tract, block, and lot number. This simplifies title searching considerably. One looks up the tract, block, and lot number and there will be a list of all the documents pertaining to that particular lot.

3. The Indexes

Luthi v. Evans
576 P.2d 1064 (Kan. 1978).

Facts. In 1971, Owens specifically assigned her interest in seven Coffey County, Kansas, oil and gas leases to defendant International Tours (Dl). Included in the assignment was a clause stating that Owens also assigned "all interest of whatsoever nature in all . . . oil and gas leases in Coffey County, Kansas." This instrument of conveyance was recorded. In 1975 Owens assigned her interest in an oil and gas lease known as the Kufuhl lease (which was located in Coffey County) to defendant Barris (D2). Prior to this assignment D2 personally checked the records in the office of the register of deeds and after the assignment, D2 secured an abstract of title to the real estate in question. The controversy on this appeal is whether Dl or D2 owns the lease. D1 contends that it owns the oil and gas rights due to the language of the prior assignment, which, it argues, gave constructive notice to all subsequent purchasers, including D2. D2 contends the 1971 assignment was sufficient as between the parties to that instrument. D2 argues, however, that it was not sufficient to give constructive notice to subsequent innocent purchasers for value who did not have actual notice of the prior assignment, since the general language of the instrument failed to state with specificity the names of the lessor and lessee, the legal description, etc. The trial court found for D2. The intermediate appellate court reversed.

Issue. Is a general assignment, when recorded, sufficient to give constructive notice to an innocent purchaser for value?

Held. No. Judgment reversed.

♦ A clause in a conveyance describing the property to be conveyed as "all of the grantor's property in a certain county" is commonly referred to as a "Mother Hubbard" clause. Although they are seldom used in Kansas, they have been upheld for many years as binding between the parties to the instrument. At the outset it must be noted that:

Here, both D2 and Dl agree that the "Mother Hubbard" clause in Owens's assignment to Dl was valid as between the parties to that instrument.

Further, it is recognized that a single instrument may convey separate tracts by specific description and by general description capable of being made specific.

Finally, a subsequent purchaser who has actual notice or knowledge of an instrument takes subject to the rights of the assignee or grantor. This is not applicable here since D2 did not have actual notice.

♦ The central issue is whether a "Mother Hubbard" clause constitutes constructive notice to a subsequent innocent purchaser without actual notice.

♦ Kansas recording statutes evince a legislative intent that instruments of conveyance should describe the land conveyed with sufficient specificity to enable the register of deeds (i) to determine the correctness of the description from the numerical index and (ii) to make it possible to make any necessary changes in address records for mailing tax statements.

♦ It seems obvious that the purpose of the recording statutes is to impart knowledge to subsequent purchasers of the instrument that affects one's title to a specific tract of land. Thus, we hold that the specific land conveyed must be described sufficiently to be identified. Hence, since the Kufuhl lease was not described in the instrument, recording that instrument was not sufficient to be constructive notice to D2, who did not have actual notice of the Kufuhl lease.

♦ This does not mean that as between Owens and Dl the conveyance was ineffective, nor does it mean that a properly recorded but improperly indexed instrument is not constructive notice to subsequent purchasers.

---

4. Misspelled Name

Orr v. Byers
244 Cal.Rptr. 13 (Cal. Ct. App. 1988).

Facts. Orr (P) obtained a judgment against William Elliott. Elliott was identified erroneously as William Duane Elliot on the judgment, and on an abstract of judgment later filed, as William Duane Elliot and William Duane Eliot. Elliott obtained title to a parcel of property, which became subject to P's lien. When Elliott sold the parcel to D, a title search failed to disclose the abstract of judgment and the judgment was not satisfied from the sale proceeds. P sued D and others, seeking a declaration of the rights and duties of all parties, requesting a judicial foreclosure of his lien. The court found for D. P appeals.

Issue. Does an abstract of judgment containing a misspelled name impart constructive notice of its contents under the doctrine of *idem sonans*?

Held. No. Judgment affirmed.

♦ The doctrine of "idem sonans" provides that although a person's name has been inaccurately written, the identity of such person will be presumed from the similarity of sounds between the correct pronunciation and the pronunciation as written. Therefore, absolute accuracy in spelling names is not required in legal proceedings, and if the pronunciations are practically alike, the rule of idem sonans is applicable.

♦ The rule is inapplicable where the written name is material, as it is here.

♦ The rule is viable for purposes of identification but not to give constructive notice to good faith purchasers for value.

♦ To apply the doctrine here would place undue burden on the transfer of property.

5. Types of Recording Acts

At common law the first person to record had priority. All states have recording acts replacing the common law.

a. Race Statutes

Few states have race statutes. Under the race statutes the first to record had priority, even if the person recording knew of prior unrecorded conveyances.

b. Notice Statutes

Under these statutes, a subsequent purchaser for value ("BFP") prevails over a prior grantee who has not recorded unless the BFP has actual or constructive notice of the prior conveyance at the time of the conveyance to him.

c. Race-Notice Statutes

Under these statutes, in order to cut off a prior grantee, the BFP must both record first and have no actual or constructive notice of the prior conveyance.

d. Example

G deeds Blackacre to A. Subsequently G sells Blackacre to B. Under a race statute, whoever records first (A or B) wins, even if both know of both conveyances. Under a notice statute, B will prevail provided he did not know of the prior conveyance at the time he bought Blackacre, Remember, notice can be either constructive or actual. Under a race-notice statute, to prevail against A, B must (i) not have notice of the prior conveyance and (ii) must record before A.

e. Improperly Acknowledged Deed

Messersmith v. Smith
60 N.W.2d 276 (N.D. 1953).

Facts. On May 7, 1946, Caroline Messersmith executed a quitclaim deed to Frederick Messersmith (P), her nephew, on property of which both she and P were the owners of record. On April 23, 1951, Caroline deeded to Smith (D) an undivided one-half interest in the mineral rights of the same property. Smith discovered an error in the deed Caroline had signed in front of the notary, so he tore it up and took a corrected deed to Caroline. She signed it. Smith took the deed to the same notary, who acknowledged the deed without Caroline's being present (the notary called Caroline on the phone to see if she had voluntarily signed the deed). On May 9, 1951, Smith deeded his interest in the mineral rights to Seale (D). Both the deed to Smith and the deed to Seale were recorded May 26, 1951. In July 1951, P recorded his deed from Caroline. P claimed that since Smith's deed was improperly acknowledged, Smith's deed was a nullity and did not have priority over P's deed (North Dakota had a race-notice recording statute). At trial Seale won and P appeals.

Issue. Is an improperly acknowledged deed capable of being recorded?

Held. No. Judgment reversed.

♦ Seale claimed title to the land under a statute that voided all unrecorded real estate conveyances (such as P's) if there was a subsequent purchaser (such as Seale) who (i) bought the land in good faith, and (ii) for valuable consideration, and (iii) recorded first.

♦ However, Seale cannot prevail since the deed was improperly acknowledged (Caroline did not sign it in front of the notary) and as such was legally incapable of being recorded. Thus, Seale does not fall within the protection of the statute.

Rehearing. This holding has a narrow scope. It applies to situations involving a prior unrecorded valid deed and a subsequent deed that was improperly acknowledged and thus not worthy of being recorded. This situation differs from a prior properly acknowledged deed not entitled to be recorded because of a latent defect.

Comment. One of the important aspects of this case is that the court examined Seale's *entire* chain of title (which was defective because of Smith) and not just the conveyance from Smith to Seale. Many jurisdictions hold the direct opposite of this case.

---

6. Effect of Recording

By recording, all subsequent prospective purchasers are put on notice of the existence and contents of the recorded document. Thus, no subsequent purchaser can be a BFP since to be a BFP one must take the property without notice of prior conveyances. Recording does not make an invalid deed valid nor does it protect one from interests in the land arising by operation of law (tax liens, implied easements, etc.).

a. Effect of Not Recording

A subsequent BFP can cut off one's interest in the property, leaving one to sue his grantor.

b. What Is a BFP?

Only a BFP is protected under the notice and racenotice statutes. A BFP (i) must purchase the property (or be a creditor or mortgagee), (ii) must take the property without notice of prior conveyance (this means without either constructive or actual notice), and (iii) must give valuable consideration.

E. Chain of Title Problems

1. Introduction

To give notice to subsequent would-be purchasers, an instrument must be recorded in the "chain of title." "Chain of title" refers to the title established by the grantor's predecessors up to the time of the conveyance to the grantee. Special problems arise when instruments are improperly recorded. The next case will illustrate what is included in a chain of title.

a. Prior Unrecorded Deeds in Chain

Board of Education of Minneapolis v. Hughes
136 N.W. 1095 (Minn. 1912).

Facts. On May 16, 1906, Hughes (D) offered to buy a lot from Hoerger. The offer was accepted and the deed forwarded by mail the next day to D. The name of the grantee was blank. On April 27, 1909, Hoerger quitclaimed the lot to certain real estate agents, Duryea & Wilson, who subsequently sold the lot to the Board of Education of Minneapolis (P) on November 19, 1909, under warranty deed, which was recorded on January 27, 1910. D recorded his deed from Hoerger on December 16, 1910, shortly after he finally filled in his name as grantee. Duryea & Wilson recorded their deed from Hoerger on December 21, 1910. In the action to determine adverse claims to the lot, judgment was rendered for P. D appeals from an order denying a new trial.

Issue. Is a record of a deed from an apparent stranger to the title notice to a grantee of a prior unrecorded conveyance by the grantor?

Held. No. Judgment reversed and new trial granted.

♦ There is a conflict in authority, but the better rule is that because the deed was complete in all other respects, the insertion of D's name by him did not invalidate the otherwise valid deed. D had authority to fill in his name, which, if not express, could at least be implied from the circumstances. For that reason, the deed to D was operative once he inserted his name as grantee.

♦ Because D's deed was only effective when he filled in his name as grantee, D was a subsequent purchaser. The record of the deed from Duryea & Wilson to P was not notice to D of the prior unrecorded conveyance by Hoerger; it was merely the record of a deed from an apparent stranger to the title. As a subsequent purchaser, D was protected by recording his deed before the prior deed from Hoerger to Duryea & Wilson was recorded.

♦ The recording statute does not give priority to a prior recorded deed that shows no conveyance from a record owner. P's deed would only have priority if the deed to P's grantor had been recorded before D's deed.

---

b. Deeds Recorded Before Grantor Obtains Title

As may be recalled, if a grantor does not have title at the time he conveys but subsequently obtains title, the doctrine of estoppel by deed applies. Under this doctrine the grantor must then convey the property to the grantee. The jurisdictions are split as to whether a recorded deed taken from a grantor without title is in the chain of title.

c. Subdivision Restrictions

The courts are also split as to whether subdivision restrictions contained in the deeds to the other lots in the subdivision are outside the chain of title. To hold that they are within the chain of title imposes on a would-be buyer the burden of searching all the deeds flowing from a common grantor.

1) Restrictions in Neighbor's Deed

Guillette v. Daly Dry Wall, Inc.
325 N.E.2d 572 (Mass. 1975).

Facts. Guillette (P) purchased a lot in a subdivision from Gilmore. P's deed contained restrictions imposed for the benefit of the other lots on the recorded subdivision plan and stated that the same restrictions were imposed on each of the lots owned by Gilmore. The restrictions were intended to maintain the subdivision as single-family dwellings. Four years later, Daly Dry Wall, Inc. (D) purchased a lot by a deed that made no reference to the restrictions. D sought to construct a multifamily apartment building on its lots and P and other landowners obtained an injunction to prevent all but single-family dwellings. D appeals.

Issue. Is a grantee bound by restrictions in deeds to its neighbors from a common grantor when it took without knowledge of the restrictions and under a deed which did not mention them?

Held. Yes. Judgment affirmed.

♦ The Statute of Frauds prevents enforcement of restrictions when the common grantor has not bound his land by writing. In this case, Gilmore did bind his remaining land by writing, so D as a subsequent purchaser from Gilmore takes title subject to the restrictions in P's deed.

- D claims it was only required to determine whether there were restrictions in prior deeds in its chain of title. However, P obtained not only one lot but also an interest in the rest of the land still owned by Gilmore. P's deed was properly recorded. Even though it may be burdensome for a title examiner to search all deeds given by a grantor in the chain of title while he owned the premises in question, it is not an impossible task.

- As a purchaser of part of restricted land, D took subject to those restrictions that could have been discerned from the records. D's deed referred to a recorded subdivision plan even though the restrictions were not mentioned.

Comment. Other courts hold that a restrictive covenant on one parcel created by a deed on a separate parcel is not in the first parcel's chain of title.

---

d. Recorded Instrument That Refers to Unrecorded Instrument

Generally, if a recorded instrument refers to an unrecorded instrument, the buyer must make inquiry into the contents of the unrecorded instrument.

e. Recorded Instrument That Is Defective

Similarly, if the prior instrument is defective, inquiry must be made.

f. Knowledge

The courts are split on the question of constructive notice when a prior deed from an owner is recorded after a later deed from the same owner. In *Woods v. Garnett,* 16 So. 390 (Miss. 1894), Riley borrowed $3,500 from Pond in 1891 and secured the note with a deed of trust (Tranthorn as trustee). The acknowledgment of the deed of trust stated that Riley had "signed" the deed, but omitted the words "and delivered." These latter words were required by statute. A deed without them was defective. This defective deed of trust was recorded. In 1892 Riley owed Cocke & Co. $397.22 and secured the debt with a deed of trust on the same land. Cocke's agent (Lester) did a title search and discovered the 1891 deed of trust. Lester saw the defect in that deed and, being of the opinion that the deed was ineffective, accepted the 1891 deed of trust as security for the $397.22 debt. Pond assigned the note to Wood pursuant to provisions of the 1891 deed of trust. About this time the defect in the 1891 deed was discovered. Wood had the deed of trust properly acknowledged and rerecorded it. Subsequently, on November 19, 1892, the land was sold under each of the two deeds of trust, sales being at different places. At the sale under the 1891 deed of trust, Wood was the purchaser. At the sale under the 1892 deed of trust, Garnett was the purchaser. Garnett had no notice of the other sale. Thus, Wood had the deed first made but junior in record. Garnett had the deed second made but senior in record. Wood sued Garnett as noted above. The trial court found for Garnett. On appeal the judgment was reversed. The court found that a subsequent grantee is under the duty to make further inquiry if he has actual knowledge of a prior conveyance, even if that conveyance is defective; and if a person fails to make such inquiry, his grantee who has no actual knowledge of the prior instrument, but who buys after the defect in the prior instrument is cured (and the instrument is properly rerecorded), does not have an interest superior to that of the grantee of the prior instrument. Cocke & Co., the court said, was not a bona fide encumbrancer of the land without notice of the Pond mortgage.

Having actual knowledge of the prior defective deed, Cocke & Co. was under the duty of making further inquiry. Having faded to make such inquiry, Cocke & Co. was held to having the knowledge such inquiry would have revealed. *Morse v. Curtis,* 2 N.E. 929 (Mass. 1885) is the leading case holding that a purchaser is not required to examine the record after the date of a recorded conveyance to discover a prior conveyance recorded at a later time.

2. Persons Protected by the Recording System

Some statutes vary regarding which persons come within the protection of a recording statute. Although creditors and subsequent purchasers are often protected, donees and devisees are not. Thus, it has been necessary for courts to determine whether a person is a purchaser or a donee and what constitutes valuable consideration for purposes of the recording act.

a. Equitable Conversion Theory Waived

Daniels v. Anderson
642 N.E.2d 128 (Ill. 1994).

Facts. Daniels (P) contracted to buy two parcels of land from Jacula. The contract also provided P with right of first refusal on an adjacent parcel. The sale contract was not recorded. The deed, which was recorded, did not mention the right of first refusal. Eight years later, Jacula contracted with Zografos to buy the adjacent parcel. Zografos paid Jacula $10,000 and provided him with a note for the balance. After Zografos made two more payments, P's wife told Zografos about P's right of first refusal. Zografos made the final payment and recorded his deed. P sued Jacula and Zografos (Ds) for specific performance. Zografos claimed he was a subsequent bona fide purchaser without notice. The trial court found for P, holding Zografos had actual knowledge of the option when he took title, and ordered Zografos to convey the parcel to P. P was ordered to pay Zografos the full purchase price plus property taxes Zografos had paid. The appellate court affirmed. Zografos appeals.

Issue. Was Zografos a bona fide purchaser because he took equitable title when he entered into the contract of sale prior to receiving notice from P's wife?

Held. No. Judgment affirmed.

♦ Zografos raised the theory of equitable conversion for the first time on appeal. It has been held that an issue not considered by the trial court cannot be raised for the first time on review. The doctrine of equitable conversion has been waived.

♦ Regarding the point at which a buyer becomes a bona fide purchaser, it is well established that a buyer who prior to the payment of any consideration receives notice of an outstanding interest, pays the consideration at his peril with respect to the holder of the outstanding interest. A consummation of the purchase, after notice of the outstanding interest, is a fraud upon the holder of the interest.

---

b. Lis Pendens Recorded but Not Indexed

Lewis v. Superior Court
37 Cal.Rptr.2d 63 (Cal. Ct. App. 1994).

Facts. In February 1991, the Lewises (Ps) contracted to buy property from Shipley. On February 24, Fontana recorded a lis pendens on the property, but it was not indexed until February 29. Ps paid Shipley $350,000 on February 25, and, at the closing on February 28, gave Shipley a note for $1,950,000. The note was paid and additional money was spent renovating the property. In September 1993, Ps were served in the pending Fontana lawsuit and first learned of the lis pendens. Ps brought suit for summary judgment to have the lis pendens removed. The trial court denied the motion. Ps appeal.

Issue. Was the lis pendens properly recorded before it was indexed?

Held. No. Superior court to vacate its order and issue a new order granting Ps' motion for summary judgment.

♦ *Davis v. Ward,* 109 Cal. 186, 41 P. 1010 (1895), the case upon which Fontana relies to assert that Ps were not bona fide purchasers because they did not make full payment for the property until after the indexing, does not apply to this case.

♦ In *Davis,* Ward mortgaged property to Davis's predecessor. The mortgage identified the wrong land parcel. Ward later sold half of the property to Fleming, who paid cash, and half to Brown, who paid part cash and part notes. At trial to have the mortgage reformed and foreclosed, Fleming and Brown were shown to be bona fide purchasers because they could not have discovered the error by searching the record of the purchased property. Fleming and Brown won nonsuits. On appeal the supreme court reversed Brown's nonsuit, finding he was not a bona fide purchaser because he could not show the purchase price had been paid before notice.

♦ The payment of value rule in *Davis* cannot be reconciled with modern property law and should be strictly limited to its facts. Any purchaser without notice who makes a down payment and unequivocally obligates himself to pay the balance has every reason to believe that, if he makes the payments when due, his right to the property will be secure.

♦ *Davis* permits the correct result, but for the incorrect reasons. Davis should have prevailed, not because Brown was a good faith purchaser, but because Ward continued to hold an interest that, in equity, belonged to Davis.

———————

c. Purchase Not Completed

In *Alexander v. Andrews,* 645 S.E.2d 487 (W. Va. 1951), Thomas Alexander's father conveyed his interest in real estate to his daughter Sarah Andrews on May 8, 1946, the consideration for which was stated in the deed to be love and affection. Andrews did not record until July 8, 1946. On May 14, Alexander's father conveyed the same interest to Alexander and Alexander's deed was recorded on the same day. The consideration for Alexander's deed, as testified to, was Alexander's obligation to bury his father and to take care of him during his declining years. Alexander also paid his father $1,000. Alexander sought to have his title quieted in a suit in equity. The trial court found for Andrews. The applicable statute read: "Every . . . deed conveying . . . real estate . . . shall be void as to . . . subsequent purchasers for valuable consideration without notice, until and except from the time that it is duly admitted to record in the county wherein the property . . . may be." The money and other consideration paid by Alexander was sufficient to give Alexander the benefit of the statute had it been paid in full at the time Alexander first received notice of the former deed. To sustain a plea of purchaser without notice, the court stated, the party must be a complete purchaser before notice; that is, must have obtained a conveyance and paid the whole purchase money. Alexander's transaction was not a completed one.

3. Inquiry Notice

The third form of notice (in addition to actual and constructive) is inquiry notice. It imposes on the grantee the duty to inquire of documents that are referred to by documents in the chain of title.

a. Duty to Inquire

Harper v. Paradise
210 S.E.2d 710 (Ga. 1974).

Facts. In 1922, Susan Harper deeded her farm to her daughter-in-law, Maude Harper, for life with remainder in fee simple to Maude's named children. This deed was lost. In 1957, it was found by

Clyde Harper (one of the named children) and recorded. Maude died in 1972. Susan died sometime during the period 1925–1927. In 1928 all of Susan's heirs but one (John) quitclaimed any interest they might have in the property to Maude. This quitclaim deed mentioned that the 1922 deed had been lost or destroyed. In 1933 Maude executed a security deed to secure a $50 loan to her from Ella Thornton. The loan went into default and Thornton foreclosed, receiving a sheriff's deed in 1936. There was an unbroken chain of title from Thornton to Lincoln and William Paradise (Ps). Ps claimed title through warranty deed executed and recorded in 1955 and by way of adverse possession. Harper and others (Ds) were the remaindermen under the 1922 deed. Ps sued to have title secured in them and won a directed verdict. Ds appeal.

Issue. Must a grantee make inquiry as to the provisions of any deeds referred to in his chain of title?

Held. Yes. Judgment reversed.

♦ Ps contend that since both the 1922 and 1928 deeds emanate from the same source (*i.e.,* Susan), the 1928 deed has priority because it was recorded first. Ps further rely on a statute that protects innocent purchasers without notice who purchased from heirs or legatees (etc.). Such purchasers were protected from unrecorded liens or conveyances created by the deceased person. [Ga. Code § 67–2502]

♦ A subsequent purchaser (Ps) from a life tenant (Maude) cannot defeat the later claim of a remainderman (Ds) who did not join in the conveyance to the purchaser.

♦ The 1928 deed to Maude made reference to the 1922 deed. Thus, Maude is bound to have taken the 1928 deed with knowledge of the 1922 deed. The recitals of the 1928 deed make it clear that Susan's heirs did not have any interest in the property; indeed, the 1928 quitclaim deed actually served as a disclaimer by them of any interest in the land. Thus, since Susan's heirs claimed no interest, the 1928 deed does not come within the purview of Code section 67–2502.

♦ Since the 1928 deed made reference to the 1922 deed, Ps had the duty to inquire as to the contents of the 1922 deed. Having failed to do so, Ps are grantees with notice. A deed in the chain of title gives constructive notice to all other deeds to which it refers. Since Ps have not shown they made inquiry, it is presumed that due inquiry would have disclosed the existing facts.

♦ The time period for obtaining adverse possession from remaindermen begins to run upon the death of the life tenant. (The theory behind this is that the time period for adverse possession does not begin to run until the remaindermen are entitled to possession.) Since Maude, the life tenant, died in 1972, the time period did not begin to run until then. Ps thus have failed to occupy the land for the requisite time period to establish title by adverse possession.

---

b. Inquiry from the Subdivision

A negative reciprocal easement may be implied from the neighborhood. Basically, if from the looks of the neighborhood a buyer could reasonably assume that there is some sort of restriction on lot use, the buyer is put on inquiry notice of the contents of deeds that come from the neighborhood's common grantor.

c. Inquiry from Possession

The majority view is that a buyer is chargeable with the knowledge that would be revealed by physical inspection of the premises. Thus, if it turns out that the person in possession has an unrecorded deed to the property, he cuts off a BFP. The minority view is the opposite.

d. Possession of Condominium

Waldorff Insurance and Bonding, Inc. v. Eglin National Bank
453 So.2d 1383 (Fla. Dist. Ct. App. 1984).

Facts. Waldorff Insurance and Bonding, Inc. (D) entered into a written purchase agreement for condominium unit 111 from Choctaw, one of its clients, in April 1973 for a total of $23,550. At that time, D paid a $1,000 deposit to Choctaw. Shortly thereafter, D began occupancy and paid all monthly maintenance fees, repairs, etc. Choctaw had executed an $850,000 promissory note and mortgage on the entire development in June 1972, which was assigned to Eglin National Bank (P) in January 1975 when the principal balance remaining was $41,562.61. In October 1973 Choctaw executed another note and mortgage for $600,000 in favor of P, which covered D's condo and other units. Again in June 1974 Choctaw executed a note and mortgage for $95,000 in favor of P, covering D's condo and other units. Choctaw fell behind in insurance premiums owed to D and agreed to transfer condo 111 to D in return for cancellation of its debt to D of over $35,000. D agreed and recorded the deed in March 1975. In 1976 P started a foreclosure action against Choctaw, but the status of D's condo was not decided until 1983, when the trial court found that P's liens were superior to D's interest. The trial court found that D's occupancy was equivocal because other occupiers of condos were nonowners and that D did not pay the agreed consideration to Choctaw because D wrote the debt off as a bad debt for tax purposes. D appeals.

Issue. Is actual possession of a condominium constructive notice of the occupant's interest in the property even if other occupiers are not owners?

Held. Yes. Judgment reversed.

♦ When D agreed to buy the condo, equitable title to the condo vested in D even though Choctaw retained legal title. Any subsequent successor to the legal title would have taken the title burdened with D's equitable interest of which it had either actual or constructive notice. If P had actual or constructive notice of D's equitable interest at the time of the October 1973 and June 1974 mortgages, then D's interest has priority.

♦ Generally, actual possession is constructive notice of whatever right the occupants have in the land. D was clearly in open, visible, and exclusive possession of the condo. The trial judge found this possession equivocal because nonowners occupied other condos, but the status of these other possessors could not affect D's rights. The inconvenience to P of checking the various ownership interests in the condos does not remove the constructive notice based on possession.

♦ Even though D wrote off the debt from Choctaw as a bad debt for tax purposes, the consideration to Choctaw was relief from having to pay the debt, which D did provide. Thus, D did provide the agreed consideration and the transfer was valid.

♦ D has priority as to all the mortgages except the 1972 mortgage lien, which predated D's interest.

---

4. Marketable Title Acts

Conceivably, someone can come along and assert that 100 years ago there was a defect in an instrument of title and, as a consequence, they are entitled to the title to Blackacre. Thus, to prevent stale claims, marketable title acts have been passed. These acts forbid the assertion of stale claims. Stale claims are defined as those 30 to 50 years old (depending on the jurisdiction).

5. Title Registration

a. Introduction

With respect to jurisdictions covered by a Torrens Act, once the county sets up a tract index, owners of real property may bring an action (Torrens action) against all the world to vest in the owner absolute title in the land. If the owner succeeds, he is declared absolute owner of the land and all prior interests are forever cut off. The owner's title is then registered and he is issued a certificate of title. The certificate of title is the title of the property. When the owner sells the land, the government cancels the old certificate and issues a new one. If someone, after stealing a certificate and forging the required signatures, sells the land to a BFP, the BFP has title since he has the certificate. The original owner can then seek compensation from a fund established to pay those who are defrauded of their certificates. Since the certificate is conclusive proof of who it is that has title, no one can acquire title by adverse possession.

b. Exception

There is one exception to the rule that he who successfully maintains a Torrens action is the absolute owner. That exception is made only when a party in actual possession of the premises claims an interest in the property.

6. Title Insurance

a. Introduction

Because of the problems with public records, title insurance was developed to insure against any defects in these records. The insurance does not run with the land, but must be purchased by each subsequent purchaser. A mortgagee's policy does not insure the homeowner, who must take out a separate policy if she desires the protection.

b. Title Policy or Title Search

Walker Rogge, Inc. v. Chelsea Title & Guaranty Co.
562 A.2d 208 (N.J. 1989).

Facts. On December 12, 1979, Rogge (P) purchased a tract of land from Kosa. Kosa had purchased the property from Aiello. Before P signed the sale contract, Kosa showed P a 1975 survey that indicated the land was 18.33 acres. The P-Kosa deed described the land by reference to this survey, but did not indicate the acreage and adjusted the price on the basis of $16,000 per acre for deviations from 19 acres. P hired Chelsea Title & Guaranty Co. (D) to handle the title work. D had issued two prior policies on the property. In the Aiello-Kosa deed, the property description was based on a survey done by Shilling, which said the property contained 12.486 acres. D had a copy of this deed in its files. D's title commitment or binder issued before closing, and the title insurance policy described the property by referring to the 1975 survey, and did not indicate acreage. After closing, D issued a policy insuring the title with the exception that it did not insure "Encroachments, overlaps, boundary tine disputes, and other matters which could be disclosed by an accurate survey and inspection of the premises." P paid the mortgage for six years. In 1985, when P sought to acquire adjacent property, he hired a surveyor who discovered the property in question was 12.42 acres. P sued, alleging that the 5.5-acre shortage was an insurable loss and D was liable in negligence for failing to disclose documents in its file revealing the true acreage. The court found for P. The appellate court affirmed but remanded for damages. D appeals.

Issues.

(i) Is the survey exception in the title policy vague and therefore unenforceable?

(ii) Does the issuance of the title commitment and policy place a duty on a title insurance company to search for and disclose to the insured any reasonably discovered information that would affect the insured's decision to close the contract to purchase?

Held. (i) No. (ii) No. Judgment affirmed in part, reversed in part, and case remanded.

♦ In the absence of a recital of acreage, a title company does not insure the quantity of land. To obtain such insurance, P should have provided D with an acceptable survey that recited the quantity of land described or obtained from D an express guaranty of the quantity of land insured in the policy. From a search of relevant public records, a title company cannot ascertain the risks that an accurate survey would disclose.

♦ A title company's liability is limited to the policy and the company is not liable in tort for negligence in searching records. The duty of the title searcher does not depend on negligence but on the agreement between the parties.

♦ D made a title search for its own benefit; P was billed for the search; the real transaction between P and D was a policy of insurance. D did not issue a separate abstract of title for P.

♦ Some out-of-state courts believe that a title company should be liable in tort based on the notion that the insured has the reasonable expectation that the title company will search the title. However, the relationship between the parties is essentially contractual. Notwithstanding this, the company could be subject to a negligence claim if the act complained of was the direct result of duties voluntarily assumed by the insurer in addition to the contract to insure title.

♦ Because it restricted P's claim to the policy, the trial court did not determine whether D knew or should have known of the difference in acreage and of its materiality to the transaction. Therefore, the court did not determine whether D assumed an independent duty to assure the quantity of acreage, whether it breached that duty, or whether the breach caused P damage.

---

c.   Hazardous Substances

Lick Mill Creek Apartments v. Chicago Title Insurance Co.
283 Cal.Rptr. 231 (Cal. Ct. App. 1991).

Facts. In 1979, Kimball Small Investments ("KSI") purchased property that had been toxically contaminated. The California Department of Health Services ("CDHS") ordered KSI to remedy the contamination but KSI did not comply. Lick Mill Creek Apartments and Prometheus Development Company (Ps) acquired Lots 1, 2, and 3 from KSI in two separate transactions and purchased title insurance from two title insurance companies (Ds). In both instances, Ds commissioned a survey and inspection of the property. The surveyor noted tanks, pipes, and other improvements on the property. At the time of the survey, the presence of hazardous substances on the property was a matter of public record. Following purchase of the property, Ps incurred costs for removal and cleanup and sought indemnity from Ds for the sums expended. Ds denied coverage. Ps filed suit; Ds demurred and the court dismissed Ps' complaint. Ps appeal.

Issue. Do the title insurance policies issued by Ds provide coverage for the costs of removing hazardous substances from Ps' property?

Held. No. Judgment affirmed.

♦ The insuring clauses are identical and provide coverage against loss or damage sustained or incurred by the insured by reason of: (i) title being vested otherwise than stated in the relevant schedule; (ii) any defect or lien or encumbrance on such title; (iii) lack of a right of access to and from the land; or (iv) unmarketability of such title.

♦ We do not agree with Ps' contention that marketability encompasses the property's value. One can hold perfect title to land that is valueless; one can have marketable title to land while the land itself is unmarketable.

♦ The presence of hazardous material may affect the market value of Ds' land, but, on the present record, because no lien was recorded, it does not affect title.

♦ We also disagree with Ps' reasoning that because any transfer of contaminated land carries with it the responsibility for cleanup costs, liability for such costs constitutes an encumbrance on title.

♦ Encumbrances are taxes, assessments, and all liens on real property. When an owner of contaminated land may be held fully responsible for cleanup costs, a lien may be imposed to cover such costs; however, there was no such lien here.

———————

Part V
Land Use Controls

A. Nuisance

Nuisances are interferences with a person's right to quiet enjoyment of her land. The interference must come from an invasion of the land. In turn, the invasion can be of particles (including gases), noise, vibration, etc. This all stems from the common law principle that held that one must use her land so as not to injure her neighbors. There are two types of nuisances, public and private.

1. Private Nuisances

There are three elements to private nuisances: (i) there must be a substantial interference with the plaintiff's use and enjoyment of her land caused by the defendant; (ii) the defendant must act intentionally (meaning intending to cause the action that produces the offense), or unintentionally and negligently (including wantonly, recklessly, etc.); and (iii) the plaintiff must be entitled to the use and enjoyment of the land; *i.e.,* she must be in possession, but need not be the owner.

a. Weighing the Harm

From the above rule it is evident that the extent of the harm must be evaluated. This includes looking at the extent and character of the harm, the burden it will cause the defendant to correct the harm, the social value of the land invaded and the suitability of the invaded land to the locality. See the Restatement (Second) of Torts for more details.

b. Nuisances at Law

A nuisance at law (nuisance per se) is one not permitted in the neighborhood in question. Thus, storing highly radioactive atomic wastes in barrels in a residential neighborhood is a nuisance per se.

c. Nuisances in Fact

A nuisance in fact (nuisance per accidens) is one that, due to the location or circumstances, is a nuisance. A business that may lawfully be conducted at the particular location is never a nuisance per se. It can only be a nuisance in fact.

2. Public Nuisances

This is a nuisance that adversely affects the public as a whole. A public nuisance may be a crime and penal sanctions may be available to curb it. Conversely, if the use is permitted by statute or ordinance, it is not a public nuisance. Private individuals can bring public nuisance suits only in limited circumstances. The private plaintiff must show that the nuisance is especially injurious to her and that the harm she suffers is different from the harm to the public generally. Finally, if the plaintiff meets this criteria, she need not have an interest in adversely affected land.

3. Unintentional Act

An unintentional act may be a nuisance. When an unintentional act is involved, the court must take into account not only the gravity of the harm (as in intentional act cases) but also the conduct of the defendant.

4. Compared to Trespass

An invasion of a plaintiff's land may be either a trespass or a nuisance. The chief distinction is that a nuisance involves interference with the quiet enjoyment of the land and trespass involves interference with the right to possess the land.

5. Negligence Is Not an Element if Act Is Intentional

Morgan v. High Penn Oil Co.
77 S.E.2d 682 (N.C. 1953).

Facts. Morgan (P) has lived on nine acres about 1,000 feet from High Penn Oil Co.'s (D's) refinery since 1945. Beginning in 1950, for several hours a week, D dumped large quantities of nauseating gases and odors into the air. These nauseating gases invaded P's land. The gases were highly noticeable for up to two miles away. P sued to recover temporary damages for a private nuisance. P won $2,500 and D appeals.

Issue. Is negligence a necessary element for a private nuisance?

Held. No. Judgment affirmed.

♦ A nuisance per se (nuisance at law) is an act, occupation, or structure that is a nuisance at all times and under any circumstances regardless of location or surroundings. A nuisance per accidens (nuisance in fact) is that which becomes a nuisance by reason of its location or by reason of the manner in which it is constructed.

♦ An oil refinery is a lawful business and hence cannot be a nuisance per se. However, D errs in contending that an oil refinery cannot be a nuisance per accidens, absent it being constructed or operated in a negligent manner.

♦ Negligence and nuisance are two distinct fields of tort liability. While the same act or omission that results in negligence may also result in nuisance liability, such is not always the case.

♦ Basically a private nuisance is (i) any substantial nontrespassory invasion of another's interest in the private use of land, (ii) whether intentional or unintentional:

> If the invasion is unintentional the defendant's conduct must be negligent, reckless, or ultrahazardous (*e.g.,* blasting with dynamite).

> If an intentional invasion is involved, then the defendant's conduct must be unreasonable under the circumstances.

♦ Conduct is "intentional" if the defendant acts with the purpose of causing it or knows that it results from his conduct or knows that it is substantially certain to result from his conduct. Anyone who creates or intentionally creates or maintains a private nuisance is liable regardless of the degree of care or skill exercised by him to avoid such injury.

♦ D intentionally and unreasonably caused noxious gases and odors to escape onto P's land to such a degree as to substantially impair P's use and enjoyment of the land. Thus, D is liable in nuisance. D also intends to operate the refinery in the future in the same manner it has in the past. Thus, P is entitled to an injunction as part of his remedy.

---

6. Remedies

There are basically two types of remedies. One is an injunction forbidding the activity that causes the nuisance. The other is damages. A court may refuse to grant an injunction and instead award damages, as the next case indicates. An aggrieved party is entitled to use reasonable self-help to abate the nuisance. The party can use only reasonable force in doing this. Sometimes a party can bring a summary proceeding to abate the nuisance.

a. Weighing the Value of the Offending Conduct

Courts must weigh the value of the offending conduct. If the offending conduct is of good social value and may suitably be conducted at the particular location, and it is impractical to prevent the invasion, the court may award the plaintiff damages instead of abating the nuisance. [*See* Boomer v. Atlantic Cement Co., *infra*]

b. Rule of Necessity

Estancias Dallas Corp. v. Schultz
500 S.W.2d 217 (Tex. Civ. App. 1973).

Facts. The Schultzes (Ps) owned and lived in a house next to which Estancias Dallas Corp. (D) built a 155-unit apartment building. D's air conditioning equipment made noises described as sounding like a jet plane or helicopter. As a result Ps could not use their backyard, lost sleep, etc. Ps sued D, seeking to abate the nuisance. The trial court found for Ps, awarding a total of $10,000 ($9,000 to the wife and $1,000 to the husband) and granted an injunction. The issue on appeal was not whether the noise was a nuisance but whether the trial court properly balanced the equities.

Issue. When balancing equities in a nuisance action, is the "rule of necessity" to be narrowly construed?

Held. Yes. Judgment affirmed.

♦ Although the injury may be supported by facts sufficient to constitute a nuisance, there should be a balancing of equities to determine if an injunction should be granted.

♦ The doctrine of balancing of equities (also called the doctrine of "comparative injury") considers the injury that may result to the defendant and the public by granting the injunction. If the court finds the injury to the plaintiff slight and the benefit to the public from the nuisance significant, the court will not award an injunction. This leaves the plaintiff to bring an action at law for damages.

♦ We do not find that the trial court abused its discretion in balancing the equities in Ps' favor.

♦ Here it is clear that Ps' enjoyment of their land was substantially impaired. On the other hand, D testified that the apartments were not suitable for renting without air conditioning; that the air conditioning system cost $80,000 new; and that it would now cost $150,000 to $200,000 to change the system. Nevertheless, private financial benefit is not sufficient in this case to justify applying the rule of necessity for D's benefit.

♦ There is no evidence before us that indicates that the necessity of others compels Ps to seek relief by way of an action for damages. The trial court's granting of the injunction is affirmed.

Comment. This court viewed strictly the "rule of necessity" and, although Ps' injury was only $10,000 and D's cost potentially $150,000, it granted an injunction. Also, D had tried unsuccessfully to abate the air conditioning noise.

---

c. Economic Considerations

Boomer v. Atlantic Cement Co.
257 N.E.2d 870 (NY. 1970).

Facts. Atlantic Cement Co. (D) was operating a large cement plant near a large community. Suit was brought by Boomer and others (Ps), as neighboring landowners, for injury to land due to smoke, dirt, and vibration. A nuisance was found at trial, with temporary damages, but the lower courts refused to enjoin continued operation of the plant because of the large disparity in economic consequences between the nuisance and an injunction. This left Ps with the option of bringing successive suits as further damage occurred. The court also found an amount of permanent damages to guide a settlement. Ps appeal.

Issue. Where a nuisance is shown with substantial damages, must an injunction be allowed as a matter of course, regardless of economic consequences?

Held. No. Judgment reversed on other grounds.

♦ The general rule adhered to with great consistency has been that where damages are substantial, an injunction will lie to abate a nuisance. However, to grant an injunction in the instant case would require the court to close down a business that is important to commerce and that cannot at present be operated in a different manner.

♦ The drastic remedy of closing down D's plant can be avoided in various ways. One way would be to grant the injunction but make the effective date far enough in the future to allow technological development sufficient for D to eliminate the nuisance. Another way would be to grant the injunction conditioned on D's payment to Ps of permanent damages.

♦ To grant permanent damages in lieu of injunction would more justly balance the equities in this case. D will be required to pay the damages, or an injunction will lie.

Dissent. We should not change the long-standing rule that an injunction should issue to stop a nuisance that causes substantial continuing damage. This approach licenses a continuing wrong and impairs the incentive for D to eliminate the nuisance.

---

d. Preexisting Lawful Industries

Spur Industries, Inc. v. Del E. Webb Development Co.
494 P.2d 700 (Ariz. 1972).

Facts. Spur Industries, Inc. (D) had owned and operated a cattle feedlot for a number of years prior to the development of the housing subdivisions owned by Del E. Webb Development Co. (P). P began constructing retirement villages and other housing units a couple of miles away from D's cattle feedlot, and as the housing units began to spread in the direction of the feedlot a problem began to develop because of the noxious odor and flies around the feedlot. P began to encounter strong sales resistance to those houses that were closest to the cattle yard. Therefore, P brought suit to enjoin the operation of the feedlot because it constituted a public nuisance. The trial court held that the cattle feedlot was a public nuisance and issued an injunction. D appeals, claiming that it should not be required to close down, and that if it is required to close down it should be indemnified by P.

Issues. When the operation of a lawful business becomes a nuisance by reason of the encroachment of a nearby residential area, may the business operation be enjoined?

Held. Yes. Judgment affirmed in part.

♦ A change in the surrounding area can make a preexisting lawful use into a nuisance. A state statute provides that anything that constitutes a breeding ground for flies and is injurious to the public health is a public nuisance. A business that is not a public nuisance per se may become such by being carried on at a place where the health, comfort, and convenience of a populous neighborhood begins to be affected.

♦ A party that "comes to the nuisance" usually cannot get an injunction against any prior use, on the theory that she knows of the nuisance and accepts the area as it is. But in this case, because the nuisance is injurious to the public health, an injunction is appropriate.

♦ Because P brought people to the nuisance, to the foreseeable detriment of D, P must indemnify D for the reasonable expense of moving or shutting down.

B. Servitudes

A servitude is a burden imposed upon one estate for the benefit of another. Two major types of servitudes are easements and covenants.

1. Easements

An easement is a right afforded a person to make a limited use of another's property. A common example is a right-of-way across the land of another. An easement may endure for years, for life, or in fee. It is more than a mere covenant or promise; it is a nonpossessory interest in land. Although an easement is not a profit, the two are similar. A profit is the right to enter onto the land of another (such entry is implied under an easement) and take something off of the land, be it wild animals, timber, or coal. An easement is also not a license. A license is merely the permission to enter upon or do acts upon the land of another. Most licenses may be revoked at will by the landowner.

a. Various Types of Easements

Leaving aside profits, there are two types of easements. It is important to be able to categorize which type of easement is involved as the rules that apply to them vary. The land subject to an easement is called the "servient" land.

1) Affirmative Easement

This is what most people think of as an easement. It is the right to go onto the land of another and use it, *e.g.,* a right-of-way.

2) Negative Easement

This is the right to make the owner of the servient land not do something that he would otherwise be entitled to do, such as build a swimming pool within 20 feet of the neighbor's yard. These easements are disfavored by the court and, except in the case of easements for light, air, subjacent (and/or lateral) support, and flow of an artificial stream, are not recognized. Instead the courts will construe them to be covenants or servitudes.

b. Easements Appurtenant

An easement that confers a benefit upon a dominant tenement is appurtenant to the dominant estate. The burdened land is called the servient tenement. Assume, for example, A has the right to cross B's land to get to A's farm. This right-of-way is appurtenant to the dominant tenement (A's land). The burdened land (B's land) is the servient tenement.

c. Easements in Gross

Easements that are personal to their owner (easements that are not appurtenant to a dominant tenement) are easements in gross. The servient land is burdened but there is no benefited land. Common examples involve utility rights-of-way and billboards on private land. In case of ambiguity, the courts favor easements appurtenant. Negative easements are always appurtenant to a dominant tenement.

d. Creation of Easements

Easements may be created by written instrument or by implication, necessity, or prescription.

1) Reservation of an Easement

Generally easements are created by grant, that is, party A grants party B an easement across A's land. What happens when A conveys Blackacre to B and reserves in herself an easement across Blackacre? At common law, this was a nullity. An easement could never be reserved. Modern American law recognizes the reservation of an easement.

2) Reservations in Favor of Third Parties

Willard v. First Church of Christ, Scientist
498 P.2d 987 (Cal. 1972).

Facts. McGuigan, a member of the First Church of Christ, Scientist (D), sold a lot adjoining the church building to Petersen. A clause was inserted in the deed giving D an easement on the lot for parking during church hours. Petersen recorded that deed. A few days later Petersen sold the land to Willard (P). The deed to P did not mention the easement for church parking. Upon discovery of that easement, P commenced this action to quiet title in himself on the ground that McGuigan could not reserve an easement for the benefit of a third party (D). The trial court found for P, holding that one could not reserve an interest in property to a stranger to the title, *i.e.*, D.

Issue. May a grantor reserve an easement to the benefit of a stranger to the title?

Held. Yes. Judgment reversed.

♦ At common law a grantor could not, by reservation, vest an interest in land to the benefit of a third party. We reject the common law rule.

♦ The court's primary objective is to construe conveyances to give effect to the intent of the grantor. Here, it was clearly McGuigan's intent to reserve an easement for D's benefit. She even testified that she discounted the price she charged Petersen by one-third because of the easement.

♦ P relies upon a common law rule that courts in other states hold in disdain and have circumvented. P claims that the common law rule should be upheld because grantees and title insurers have relied on it. P has produced no evidence to support this contention. Further, D was using the land for church parking throughout the period when P was purchasing it and after he acquired title; thus, P cannot claim that he was prejudiced by lack of use of the land for an extended period of time.

♦ Finally, we must balance the injustice that would result from refusing to give effect to a grantor's intent versus the injustice, if any, that might result by failing to give effect to reliance on the old rule. Although other cases may warrant application of the common law rule to presently existing deeds, we find no reason to apply the common law in this case.

Comment. The majority of jurisdictions follow the common law. Under the common law, a reservation or exception could not be created in favor of a stranger to a conveyance. However, the same result could be achieved indirectly. Using the above case as an example, McGuigan could have deeded the land to D who in turn deeded it to Petersen, reserving an easement.

---

3) Licenses

Licenses may become irrevocable in certain circumstances. One form of irrevocable license is a license coupled with an interest. For example, if you buy a car and the former owner gives you permission to pick it up anytime, you may enter upon his property to remove the car. The seller cannot revoke the license as long as you have an interest. Many states will estop the grantor of a license from revoking it if the licensee has relied upon the license to his detriment.

a) Licensee's Reliance

Holbrook v. Taylor
532 S.W.2d 763 (Ky. 1976).

Facts. In 1941, D purchased the land over which P claims an easement. From 1944 until 1949, D gave P the right to construct a mining road on D's land for which D was paid a royalty. In 1957, D built a rental house on the land. The mining road was used by both D and the tenants. The rental house burned down in 1961 and was not replaced. In 1964, P purchased a three-acre parcel adjoining D's land, building a residence thereon in 1965. At all times prior to 1965 the road was used with D's permission. Subsequently P brought suit to establish a right to use a roadway, claiming that its right to use the road had been established by either prescription or estoppel. The trial court found that P had acquired a right to use the road by estoppel. D appeals.

Issue. Is a licensor estopped from revoking a license to use a roadway if the licensee has expended money in reliance on the license?

Held. Yes. Judgment affirmed.

♦ An easement may be established by: (i) express agreement; (ii) implication; (iii) prescription; or (iv) estoppel. Only the last two are asserted by P.

♦ To establish an easement by prescription, one must show that he has openly, peaceably, continuously, and under a claim of adverse right to the owner of the soil, and with his knowledge and acquiescence, used a way over the land. Here, P has failed to show his use of the road was either adverse, continuous, or uninterrupted.

♦ One may acquire a license to use a roadway when, with the knowledge of the licensor, he has, in the exercise of the privilege, spent money in improving the way (or for other purposes connected with its use) on the further strength of the license. Here, D acquiesced to P's use of the road. P had constructed a $25,000 house, using the road as ingress and egress. Thus, there were substantial grounds for the trial court to find that D is now estopped from revoking the license. The parties' actions resulted in the creation of an easement by estoppel.

Comment. Evidence showed there was no other location upon which a roadway could reasonably be built to provide an outlet for P.

---

e. Creation by Implication

An easement may be implied when necessary to carry out the intent of the parties or when required by public policy.

1) The Two Types of Implied Easements

Implied easements are one of two types: (i) easements by necessity or (ii) intended easements based on quasi-easement.

a) Easements by Necessity

If, at the time a grantor divides a tract of land and conveys part of it to another (say to B), the only means of ingress and egress is over the remaining land, then an easement will be implied for B's benefit across the remaining land. This form of easement terminates when the necessity terminates.

b) Intended Easement Based on Quasi-Easement

Assume at the time a tract of land is divided into two (or more) parcels there is an existing quasi-easement reasonably necessary for the enjoyment of the property that the court believes was intended by the parties to continue. The court will then hold that there is an implied intended easement based on a quasi-easement. For example, suppose A has two lots, #1 and #2, with lot #1 adjacent to a public road and lot #2 not adjacent to any road. Further suppose a lane leads across lot #1 to lot #2. If A sells lot #1, whoever has lot #2 will have an easement across lot #1. This is different from an easement by necessity in that the quasi-easement already existed at the time of the sale of lot #2 and, in the case of intended easements based on quasi-easement, the easement need only be reasonably necessary. The test for easements by necessity is more strict.

2) Prescription

Just as by adverse possession one may obtain title to property, so by prescription one may obtain an easement. The elements are the same as for adverse possession. Similarly, if the would-be prescription user has the permission of the owner, he cannot obtain a prescriptive easement. For an example of an easement by prescription, *see Othen v. Rosier, infra.*

3) Equity

Van Sandt v. Royster
83 P.2d 698 (Kan. 1938).

Facts. In 1903, common grantor (Bailey) built a sewer that ran under all of her property and tied into a public street line. In 1904, Bailey conveyed by general warranty deed a part of the land to Jones and another part to Murphy, retaining a third part. Jones's parcel was the lowest in elevation. There was no reservation of an easement for the sewer line in the Bailey-Jones deed. Both Bailey and Murphy were tied into the line that ran through the Jones property. In 1920, Jones conveyed part of his parcel to Reynolds, who built a house upon the land, with a basement that was near the underground sewer line; Reynolds did not tie into the line. Reynolds conveyed to Van Sandt (P) in 1924. Royster and Gray (Ds) are successors in interest to Murphy and Bailey, respectively. Their sewage floods P's basement. P sought an injunction against continued use of the sewer that ran under his land. The trial court denied the injunction and P appeals.

Issue. May a court of equity recognize an easement that exists, if at all, only by virtue of an implied reservation?

Held. Yes. Judgment affirmed.

♦ ***Quasi-easement:*** When a landowner uses a portion of her estate to the benefit of the remainder of her estate, a use in the nature of an easement arises, even though the landowner does not specifically "grant" the use to herself.

- ♦ **Necessity:** In circumstances of necessity, such as sewer drainage, a reservation of use may be implied in favor of the prior quasi-dominant estate, even though no reference is made to it in the deed out of a portion of the prior estate (quasi-servient estate).

- ♦ **Notice:** In fairness to the grantee of the quasi-servient estate, the reserved use must be such as to give notice of its existence and necessity. (In this case these requirements were satisfied by the apparent topography and public record information as to the location of the public sewer line.) Here, the court finds that the cost to successors of prior users by necessity to replace the existing sewer with an alternative line exceeds the inconvenience to P of occasional flooding.

Comment. There is a difference between an implied grant and an implied reservation. In the former, the dominant tenement is the parcel conveyed to the grantee, while in the latter it is the parcel retained by the grantor. The requirements for a finding of an implied reservation are the same as those for an implied grant, with the exception that the greater "necessity" is required, even approaching strict necessity. The implied reservation doctrine is recognized in only about half of the jurisdictions.

---

4) Easement of Necessity

Othen v. Rosier
226 S.W.2d 622 (Tex. 1950).

Facts. In 1897, Hill deeded 60 acres, which, after mesne conveyances, came to be owned by Othen (P). In 1899, Hill deeded 53 acres, which, through mesne conveyances, also came to be owned by P in 1913. In 1896, Hill deeded 100 acres and in 1899, 16.3 acres, which through mesne conveyances came to be owned by Rosier (D) in 1924. P's land was not near a highway, so for years he had to travel across both the 16.3-acre and 100-acre plots to get to the road. Erosion was injuring D's land so he constructed a levee to stop it. The impounded water from the levee turned the lane used by P to get to the highway into a muddy mess for weeks at a time. P sued D to enjoin D from interfering with his use of the lane. The trial court found that P had an easement of necessity and enjoined D from interfering with P's use of the lane. The Court of Civil Appeals first affirmed the trial court's determination as to the existence of the easement but found the injunction to be too vague and uncertain to be enforceable. On rehearing, the Court of Civil Appeals found that P had no easement of necessity or prescription and rendered judgment for D. P appeals.

Issue. For there to be an easement of necessity, must the necessity for the easement have existed at the time the original grantor severed the two estates (*i.e.*, the servient and the dominant estates)?

Held. Yes. Judgment affirmed.

- ♦ Before an easement of necessity can be implied it must be shown that: (i) there was a unity of ownership of the alleged dominant and servient estates; (ii) the roadway is a necessity, not a mere convenience; and (iii) the necessity must have existed at the time of severance of the two estates.

- ♦ Hill did not part with his title to the 16.3 acres across which P claims an easement until two years after he sold the acreage (which P now owns). Thus, no easement can exist as to this land. One (Hill) cannot have an easement across land (the 16.3 acres) to which he has the fee simple title.

- ♦ As to the 100 acres, P has failed to prove that the necessity to cross the 100 acres existed in 1896 when Hill deeded the land which P later bought. Thus, no easement of necessity arises on that land. The mere fact that P's land is completely surrounded by the land of another does not, of itself, give P an easement of necessity over D's land since P and D were not in privity of ownership.

♦ P does not have a prescriptive easement across D's land.

An essential element in acquiring a prescriptive right is the adverse use of the easement. Use by express or implied permission, no matter how long continued, cannot ripen into a prescriptive easement. Evidence shows that D consented to P's use of the lane, and hence P does not have a prescriptive easement. It was shown that D's 100 acres had been fenced in 1906 and P had been permitted to use the gates in entering and leaving the land.

P insists that by using the lane for 10 years before the fence was erected (in 1906), he acquired prescriptive rights. P errs. No evidence supports his contention that he used the lane for 10 years, since he moved onto his farm in 1900.

Finally, P did not discharge his burden of proving that his predecessor's adverse possession was in the same place and within the definite lines claimed by him. Thus, he cannot tack the time his predecessor used the lane to the time he used the lane.

---

f. Easements by Prescription

1) Introduction

Unlike adverse possession, an easement by prescription involves the use of land, not its possession. Over time, rights may be acquired through use of land. The time period for prescriptive easements is set by statutes, which generally require open and notorious, continuous, adverse use under a claim of right.

2) Public Trust Doctrine

Matthews v. Bay Head Improvement Association
471 A.2d 355 (N.J. 1984), cert. denied, 469 U.S. 821 (1984).

Facts. The Borough of Bay Head (Bay Head), a narrow strip of land about one and one-quarter miles long, borders the Atlantic Ocean; to its north is the Borough of Point Pleasant Beach, on its south the Borough of Mantoloking, and on the west Barnegat Bay. There are 76 separate parcels of land bordering the beach adjacent to the Atlantic. All except six are owned privately; the six are owned by the Bay Head Improvement Association (Association). The Association's 1932 certificate of incorporation states its purposes are beautifying and improving the Borough, cleaning, policing and otherwise making it safe for the residents, and in doing so, to own property, operate beaches, cleaners, police. . . . " Of the nine Borough streets perpendicular to the beach which end at the dry sand, the Association owns the land beginning at the end of seven streets for the width of each street and extending through the upper dry sand to the mean high water line, the beginning of the wet sand area, or foreshore. The Association also owns the fee in six shore front properties, three of which are contiguous and have a frontage aggregating 310 feet. Many, but not all of the beachfront property owners leased their upper dry sand area to the Association. Some owners have not allowed the Association to use their beaches. Some also have acquired riparian grants from the State extending approximately 1,000 feet east of the high water line. The Association controls and supervises its beach property Between the third week in June and Labor Day, the Association. It engages employees, who serve as life controls and supervises the beach property. One of its actions is to station police at entrances to the beaches where the public streets lead into the beach so that only Association Bay Head property owners; Class B are non-owners. Families of six or more pay $90 per year, and small families pay $60. After applying members or guests enter. Class A Association members are, members are routinely accepted, acquire badges, and local hotels, inns, etc. can get badges for their guests at a cost of $12 per badge. Bay Head firefighters, teachers and Borough employees are provided with badges no matter where they live. Fishermen may walk through the upper dry sand area to the foreshore. Otherwise, only members may use the beach from 10 a.m. to

5:30 p.m. during the season. The public is allowed to use beach from 5:30 p.m. to 10:00 a.m. during the summer and without restriction between Labor Day and mid-June. No attempt has ever been made to stop anyone from occupying the terrain east of the high water mark. During certain parts of the day, when the tide is low, the foreshore could consist of about 50 feet of sand not being flowed by the water. The public could gain access to the foreshore by coming from the Borough of Point Pleasant Beach on the north or from the Borough of Mantoloking on the south. The Borough of Point Pleasant filed this suit against the Borough of Bay Head and the Association (Ds), claiming Ds prevented Point Pleasant residents from gaining access to the Atlantic Ocean and the beachfront in Bay Head. The proceeding was dismissed as to the Borough of Bay Head because it did not own or control the beach. Later, Virginia Matthews, a Point Pleasant resident who wanted to use the Bay Head beach, joined as a party plaintiff, and Stanley Van Ness, as Public Advocate, joined as plaintiff-intervenor. When the Borough of Point Pleasant ceased pursuing the litigation, the Public Advocate became the primary moving party. The Public Advocate asserted that Ds had denied the general public its right of access during the summer bathing season to public trust lands along the beaches in Bay Head and its right to use private property fronting on the ocean incidental to the public's right under the public trust doctrine. The complaint was amended on several occasions, eliminating the Borough of Point Pleasant as plaintiff and adding more than 100 individuals (Ps), who were owners or had interests in properties located on the oceanfront in Bay Head, as defendants. After both parties moved for summary judgment, the trial court entered judgment for Ds. It found that the Association was not a public agency or a public entity and that the action of the private owners through the Association established no general right in the public to the use of the beaches. Ps appealed; the appellate court affirmed. Ps filed a petition for certification which we granted.

Issue. Ancillary to its right to enjoy the tidal lands, does the public have a right to gain access through and to use the dry sand area not owned by a municipality but by a quasi-public body?

Held. Yes. Judgment reversed in part and affirmed in part. Judgment is entered for the plaintiff; judgment of dismissal against the individual property owners is affirmed.

♦ The public trust doctrine acknowledges that the ownership, dominion and sovereignty over land flowed by tidal waters, which extend to the mean high water mark, is vested in the State in trust for the people. The tidal lands and water may be used by the public for navigation, fishing and recreational uses, including bathing, swimming and other shore activities. We have held that the public trust applies to the municipally-owned dry sand beach immediately landward of the high water mark.

♦ The public must have access to municipally-owned dry sand areas as well as the foreshore if it chooses to exercise the rights guaranteed by the public trust doctrine. We have held that from use of dry sand beaches. We have also determined that it is not material whether a municipality has dedicated its beaches to use by the general public. The public must be afforded the right to use and enjoy all dry sand beaches owned by a municipality.

♦ Here, our focus shifts from beaches owned by a municipality to privately-owned dry sand beaches. The public may have an interest in a right to cross privately owned dry sand beaches to gain access to the foreshore. Its right to swim below the mean high water mark may depend on a right to pass across the upland beach. Without a feasible access route, the public's right to swim in the ocean and use the foreshore in connection with that would have no meaning. It would effectively eliminate the rights of the public trust doctrine. There is not an unrestricted right to cross at will over any property bordering on the common property; only a reasonable access to the sea is required.

♦ The public may also have an interest in the right to sunbathe or generally enjoy recreational activities. The bather's right to use the upland sands is not limited to passage; reasonable enjoyment of the foreshore and the ocean implies some enjoyment of the dry sand area. Periods of swimming must be accompanied by periods of rest and relaxation.

- Under the public trust doctrine, we find no reason to limit the use of the upland dry sand area to municipally-owned property. The private owner's interest in the upland dry sand area is not the same as a municipality's; however, where use of the dry sand is essential or reasonably necessary for enjoyment of the ocean, the doctrine warrants the public's use subject to an accommodation of the owner's interests.

- The appropriate level of accommodation is determined on a case-by-case basis (i) location of the dry sand area in relation to the foreshore; (ii) the extent and availability of publicly-owned upland sand area; (iii) the type and scope of public demand; and (iv) the use of upland sand land by the owner.

- We recognize the increased demand for our beaches, and while the public does not enjoy rights in private beaches that they enjoy in municipal beaches, the public must be given both access to and use of privately-owned dry sand areas as reasonably necessary.

- The Association services the recreational needs of all residents of the Borough for swimming and bathing in the public trust property; it owns the street-wide strip of dry sand area at the foot of seven public streets that extends to the mean high water line. It also owns the fee in six other upland sand properties connected or adjacent to the tracts it owns at the end of two streets. In addition, it holds leases to approximately 42 tracts of upland sand area.

- In order for us to address whether the dry sand area that the Association owns or leases should be open to the public to satisfy the public's rights under the public trust doctrine, we must analyze whether the Association may restrict its membership to Bay Head residents, thereby precluding public use of the dry sand area.

- The Association's operation of the beachfront parallels that of a municipality. It makes access to the common tidal property for swimming and bathing and to the upland dry sand area for use incidental thereto available to the Bay Head public. Therefore, membership in the Association must be made available to the public at large. The public will have access to the common beach property during the hours of 10:00 a.m. to 5:30 p.m. between mid-June and September, where they may exercise their right to swim and bathe and to use the Association's dry sand area incidental to those activities.

- We do not find it necessary to open all the privately-owned beachfront property to the public. If changes occur in the Association's leases or its ownership of relevant property, further adjudication of the public's claims in favor of the public trust on part or all of these or other privately-owned upland dry sand lands may be necessary, depending upon the circumstances.

---

g. Assignability of an Easement in Gross

Miller v. Lutheran Conference & Camp Association
200 A. 646 (Pa. 1938).

Facts. Frank Miller (P) obtained the exclusive rights for recreational use of a lake and assigned one-fourth of that interest to his brother Rufus Miller. P and Rufus together operated a recreation area for the public until Rufus's death. P continued to rent boats. Rufus's executors and heirs licensed use of their interest to the Lutheran Conference & Camp Association (D). P sued to enjoin development by D because D wanted to rent boats in competition with P. P won at trial. D appeals.

Issue. Is an easement in gross divisible into jointly held interests?

Held. Yes. Judgment affirmed.

- An easement in gross is similar in nature to a profit in gross. Where it is the intent of the parties to allow assignment of the interest, it will be assignable, especially when it is designed for commercial exploitation. Thus, Rufus's interest was assignable to D.

♦ An easement in gross may be divisible, but it must be exercised jointly. If such joint exercise were not required, it would result in a surcharge on the easement.

♦ P and D are entitled to separate interests but D may not use its interest unilaterally. D cannot use the lake in a manner inconsistent with P's use of the lake without P's consent.

---

h. Scope of Easements

1) Introduction

The scope of an easement depends on what type of easement is involved. An excessive or improper use of an easement normally justifies injunctive relief, as well as provable damages, but does not usually extinguish the easement.

a) Express Easements

The scope of use permitted by an express easement depends first of all on the language used in the easement. Reasonable changes in the dominant estate may support changes in the use permitted. Subdivision of the dominant estate may give each transferee the right to use the easement as long as the burden is not thereby increased. Finally, an easement appurtenant to one parcel cannot be used for the benefit of a separate parcel.

b) Easements by Necessity

The permitted use of an easement created by necessity depends on the extent of the necessity.

c) Other Implied Easements

The scope of use of other easements created by implication depends on the quasi-easement use, as changed by reasonably foreseeable changes in the use of the dominant estate.

d) Prescriptive Easements

The scope of use of a prescriptive easement is normally limited to the original use.

2) Attempt to Expand Scope of Use of Easement to Nondominant Tenement

Brown v. Voss
715 P.2d 514 (Wash. 1986).

Facts. Parcel B, the dominant tenement, was located between parcels A and C. A was the servient tenement because the owner of parcel B had a private road easement across A for ingress to and egress from B. C was an unrelated nondominant tenement. Voss (D) purchased parcel A. Brown (P) subsequently bought parcels B and C from different owners. P intended to remove the house on B and replace it with a house that would extend from B to C. P spent $11,000 in developing the property before D sought to prevent P from using the easement. When D blocked the road, P sued to have the obstructions removed, sought an injunction against further interference, and sought damages. D counterclaimed for damages and an injunction preventing P from using the easement for access to C. The trial court awarded each party $1 in damages and granted P's injunction, limited to use of the easement for access to a single-family residence. The trial court found that P had reasonably developed the property, that the new house involved no increase in traffic over the easement, that without the injunction P could not use parcel C, and that D's counterclaim was filed as leverage. The court of appeals reversed on the ground that the easement could not be used for access to parcel C. P appeals.

Issue. May a court grant an injunction against the owner of a servient tenement that allows the owner of the dominant tenement to use the easement for access to a nondominant tenement?

Held. Yes. Judgment reversed.

♦ The easement was created by express grant and did not give P any rights to access to parcel C. Normally, an easement cannot be extended by the owner of a dominant estate to other parcels owned by him. Thus, by using the easement for access to land to which the easement is not appurtenant, P misused the easement.

♦ The fact that P misused the easement does not necessarily entitle D to injunctive relief. D did not appeal the damages award. When considering equitable relief, the trial court has discretion to act so as to fit the particular facts, circumstances, and equities of the specific case.

♦ The trial court found that P's misuse of the easement did not increase the volume of use of the easement and did not increase the burden on D's estate, that P acted reasonably in developing the property, that D did not act until after P spent $ 11,000, and that D's counterclaim was for leverage. D's injunction would have worked a considerable hardship on P, but its denial would not damage D. P's injunctive relief was limited to access to a single-family residence. Accordingly, the trial court did not abuse its discretion.

Dissent. By extending this easement to nondominant property, P clearly misused the easement. This constitutes a trespass, and if P builds the planned house, P's use of the easement will be a continuing trespass. It does not matter that the extension would not increase the burden on D's estate. Injunctive relief for D is the appropriate remedy. P should acquire access to parcel C and could do so by condemning a private way of necessity in accordance with state law.

---

3) Negative Easements

An owner of the dominant estate may have a right to prevent the owner of the servient estate to refrain from acts on the servient estate. The traditional negative easements are those for (i) light, (ii) air, (iii) subjacent or lateral support, and (iv) the flow of an artificial stream. Hostility to negative easements in England produced the doctrine of equitable servitudes, and American courts generally followed this approach, limiting negative easements to the four traditional types.

i. Termination of Easements

1) Introduction

An easement may be terminated in several ways. If one person acquires title to both the dominant and servient tenements, the easement is extinguished. A subsequent separation of the tenements does not revive the easement. One may release an easement by a written instrument or an oral agreement accompanied by an act done in reliance on the oral agreement. An easement is abandoned if the easement owner indicates clear intent to abandon the easement and acts in a way that indicates that intent (*e.g.*, not using the easement and permitting another to build over it). An easement by necessity terminates when the necessity no longer exists. An easement in a structure will terminate if the structure is destroyed.

2) From Commercial to Recreational Use

Presault v. United States
100 F.3d 1525 (Fed. Cir. 1996).

Facts. The Presaults (Ps) own a fee simple interest in land in Vermont made up of several parcels. An 1899 railroad right-of-way ran across parcels A, B, and C. The railroad acquired Parcels A and B by exercising a power of eminent domain given it by the state. Parcel C was acquired by the railroad via warranty deed appearing to be the standard form used to convey a fee simple. In order to abandon a railroad line, a railroad must have permission of the Interstate Commerce Commission ("ICC"). In 1983, Congress enacted the Rails-to-Trails Act to preserve discontinued railway corridors for future use and to permit public recreational use of discontinued railroad rights-of-way. The Act permits the ICC to authorize abandonment or permit discontinuance. Here, the railroad stopped service in 1970 and removed the tracks going through Ps' parcels in 1975 but did not apply to the ICC for abandonment. In 1985, the ICC, Vermont and Burlington, Vermont, agreed that Burlington would maintain the former track strip as a public trail. The ICC approved the agreement in 1986. Ps sued. The United States Supreme Court held the Act to be constitutional as an appropriate exercise of Congressional power, but held further that Ps may have a Fifth Amendment remedy for the taking of their property as defined by Vermont law. Ps sued the United States (D1) in the Court of Federal Claims; Vermont entered an appearance as codefendant (D2). The court rendered summary judgment against Ps. Ps appeal.

Issue. Does the conversion to a public recreational trail, under the Act and pursuant to the ICC, of a long unused railroad right-of-way constitute a taking of the property of the owners of the underlying fee simple?

Held. Yes. Judgment reversed.

♦ The first question to be determined is whether in 1899 the railroad acquired only easements or a fee simple interest in Ps' property. In Parcels A and B, taken by eminent domain through a Commissioner's Award that fixed damages, it was determined by the trial court judge that the railroad acquired an easement under Vermont law. It is well established Vermont law that a railroad acquiring land for laying track acquires no more than that needed for its purpose, typically an easement, not a fee simple. Parcel C was conveyed by warranty deed, but, again pursuant to Vermont law, the railroad took only so much estate therein as was necessary, *i.e.,* an easement.

♦ The second question to be determined is the scope of the easements, whether they were sufficiently broad in scope to permit use for a public recreational trail—assuming the easements were still in effect in 1986. Vermont follows common law property principles that recognize that the scope of an easement may be adjusted if the change is consistent with the original grant. The parties are presumed to have contemplated such a scope for the created easement as would reasonably serve the purposes of the grant. This presumption often allows an expansion of the use of the easement, but does not permit a change in use not reasonably foreseeable at the time of establishment of the easement. Here, the use as a public recreational trail is clearly different from the original use. The burden on the property as a public trail is greater and is at the whim of many individuals, in contrast to its former burden of having an occasional train crossing the land. Further, the easements in this case are limited by their terms and as a matter of law to railroad purposes.

♦ Even if the original conveyances could permit trail use, the question remains whether the easements were abandoned, and thus extinguished, in 1975, thereby mandating payment of the just compensation required by the Constitution. Something more than nonuse is needed to extinguish an easement. Under Vermont law, "acts by the owner of the dominant tenement conclusively and unequivocally manifesting either a present intent to relinquish the easement or a purpose inconsistent with its future existence" must accompany nonuse. Here, the railroad removed all of its equipment, including switches and tracks, in 1975 and, in the years following the shutting down in 1970 and the removal of equipment in 1975, neither the state nor the railroad made any move to reinstate service or replace the equipment necessary to return the line to service. The railroad had effected an abandonment of the easements in 1975.

♦ Ps are entitled to recover Fifth Amendment compensation if the easements were in existence when the public recreational trail was established because its establishment could not be justified under the terms and within the scope of the original easements for railroad purposes. Alternatively, when the easements were abandoned in 1975, Ps held the property unencumbered in fee simple. The subsequent taking by Burlington pursuant to federal authorization was a physical taking of the right of exclusive possession that belonged to Ps. The federal government put into play a series of events that resulted in a taking of private property through a state agent and requires just compensation be paid.

---

2. Covenants Running with the Land

a. Real Covenants

Real covenants are promises to use or not to use land in a specified way. These covenants run with the land but they are not an interest in land. As in the case of easements, covenants can be affirmative or negative.

1) Benefits and Burdens

"Benefited" land is comparable to "dominant tenement" and "burdened" land is comparable to "servient tenement."

2) Writing Required

The common law required real covenants to be in writing. Real covenants can be contained in a deed; the grantee is bound even if he does not sign the document containing the covenants.

3) Enforceability

These covenants are enforceable by the parties to them. Problems arise when third parties try to enforce them. Their enforceability depends on whether a party is asserting that it is the benefit that runs with the land (and hence to the third party) or the burden that runs with the land.

4) Determining Whether Burdens Run with the Land

A burden runs with the land if (i) it is the intent of the contracting parties that it do so, (ii) there is privity of estate (discussed in detail below), and (iii) the covenant "touches and concerns" the land. If the assignee of the promisor gave valuable consideration, there is an additional requirement that he have notice of the covenant.

5) Privity

Privity of estate between the two parties to the promise is horizontal privity. Privity of estate between the promisor and his successors in interest (those to whom it is asserted the burden ran) is vertical privity. For the burden to run, all courts require vertical privity, and some courts also require horizontal privity.

6) Determining Whether Benefit Runs with the Land

For the benefit to run: (i) the original parties to the promise must intend that it run with the land, (ii) there must be vertical privity of estate, and (iii) the covenant must touch and concern the land.

b. Equitable Servitudes

An equitable servitude is defined as a covenant enforceable at equity against the assignees of the burdened land. It does not matter whether the covenant runs with the land.

1) Writing

Most courts feel that an equitable servitude is an interest in land and for that reason require that it be in writing. However, some courts will, in spite of the lack of a writing, imply an equitable servitude in cases involving restrictions in subdivisions.

2) Reciprocal Negative or Restrictive Equitable Servitudes

If there is a reciprocal scheme in the neighborhood, a court may enforce it. It has to be reciprocal (*i.e.,* other property in the neighborhood must have a similar restriction), it must be either negative or restrictive (it cannot be affirmative), and it must be part of the developer's scheme of development. Not all courts recognize these types of servitudes in residential subdivisions.

3) Equitable Servitudes May Be Enforced by Third Parties

Enforcement is conditioned on the following requirements: (i) there must be an intent that the servitude be binding on assignees; (ii) vertical (not horizontal) privity is required; (iii) the covenant must touch and concern the land; and (iv) a BFP without notice does not take subject to the covenant. Again, notice can be actual, constructive, or inquiry, as will be seen in the next case.

4) The Running of Benefits to Prior Buyers

Because of the nature of equitable servitudes, it is possible for the benefit to be enforceable by prior buyers. In the case of implied equitable servitudes, the prior buyer can only enforce the building scheme that was in effect at the time he made his own purchase. There are two distinct theories used to justify this power of enforcement: first, that the prior purchaser receives an implied reciprocal servitude in the remaining land owned by the common grantor, so that subsequent purchasers take with notice; and second, that the prior purchaser may enforce the restrictions as a third-party beneficiary.

5) Enforceability by and Against Subsequent Assignees

Tulk v. Moxhay
41 Eng.Rep. 1143 (1848).

Facts. P sold land with a covenant that a certain portion of it was to remain open for use of tenants. D received the land through mesne conveyances of P's vendee and now threatens to build on the land. D had notice of the restrictive covenant even though his deed did not speak to it. P brought an action to enjoin D, with judgment for P at trial.

Issue. May D, not being in privity of estate with P, disregard a previous covenant restricting use of land even though he had notice of the covenant?

Held. No. Judgment for P.

♦ Generally a covenant that does not run with the land will not be enforced against a subsequent vendee.

♦ But when a vendee purchases property with notice of a covenant restricting use, it may be enforced against him.

Comment. This was the first case to hold that a written covenant was enforceable against a subsequent purchaser who acquired title to the burdened land *with notice* of the covenant.

---

c. Inquiry Notice

Sanborn v. McLean
206 N.W. 496 (Mich. 1925).

Facts. McLean (D) owned a lot in a strictly residential neighborhood and started to construct a gasoline station on part of the lot behind the residence. Sanborn and other neighbors and occupants of lots and dwelling houses on that street (Ps) sued and obtained an injunction against D, staying the construction. Ps and D obtained title through a common grantor with some of the deeds containing restrictions while others did not. D appeals.

Issue. Will lots conveyed by a common grantor, some conveyed with restrictions and some without, all be impressed with the restrictions?

Held. Yes. Judgment affirmed.

♦ If the owner of two or more lots, situated in such a way as to bear relation to one another, places restrictions on use of one lot for the benefit of the lot retained, a reciprocal negative easement arises on the lot retained and runs with the land to purchasers with notice.

♦ D was put on notice of inquiry as all lots were uniform in use, although there were no restrictions in D's chain of title.

---

d. Affirmative Covenant

Neponsit Property Owners' Association, Inc. v. Emigrant Industrial Savings Bank
15 N.E.2d 793 (N.Y. 1938).

Facts. In 1911, Neponsit Realty Co. filed a residential subdevelopment plan. A 1917 deed of a parcel of the development to Deyer contained covenants that the grantee made for himself and his heirs, successors, and assigns with the intention that they run with the land. The covenants bound the grantee to pay a fixed annual charge for the maintenance of certain common property of the subdivision, which was dedicated to public purposes. The Emigrant Industrial Savings Bank (D) acquired the Deyer interest in a foreclosure sale. D refused to pay the charges under the covenant. The original parties had agreed that the charges were to become "liens" upon the land, to the extent unpaid. Rights to enforcement were expressly created in the covenantee and its successors and assigns. The Neponsit Property Owners' Association (P) is the successor to the original grantor. P brought an action to foreclose on the basis of the liens that arose from nonpayment of the assessments. The trial court denied D's motion for summary judgment on the pleadings, and D appeals.

Issue. Are subsequent purchasers bound by an affirmative covenant to pay money for use in connection with, but not upon, the land that is subject to the burden of the covenant?

Held. Yes. Judgment affirmed.

- A covenant will run with the land if (i) the parties intend the covenant to run with the land; (ii) the covenant "touches" the land it concerns; and (iii) there is privity of estate between the party claiming the benefit and the party burdened with the covenant.

- The test of whether a covenant runs with the land is whether it imposes a burden upon an interest in land that also increases the value a different interest in the same or related land. Because the payment of the maintenance fee is essential to enjoyment of the property, the covenant "touches" the land, and is binding on subsequent purchasers.

- Because P represents all the property owners, the corporate entity is recognized for what it is, a representative form. It succeeds to the estate of the owners and privity of estate is established.

---

e. Servitudes in Gross

1) Introduction

A benefit may be personal to the covenantee yet the burden may touch and concern the covenantor's land. The enforceability of such a servitude in gross depends on which approach is adopted.

a) English Rule

Under the English rule, an easement in gross was not binding on assigns of the burdened land; because an equitable servitude was analogous to a negative easement, the burden of a servitude in gross would not run to assignees of the land. A servitude would run only if there was both a servient and a dominant tenement.

b) American Rule

The American approach to easements in gross permits the burden to run with the land. One would expect that the burden of a servitude in gross would likewise run with the land, and some courts so hold, but many follow the English rule anyway.

2) Restatement View

The Restatement (Third) of Property section 3.2 (2000) looks at a servitude both at its inception and after subsequent events have taken place. The Restatement position has moved from the touch and concern requirement to a rule that assumes the validity of a servitude. The determination that a servitude is invalid often implies that although a servitude was valid at the time of its inception, subsequent events may indicate that it should no longer be enforced. A servitude may not be enforceable at its inception because it violates public policy (*i.e.,* the public's interest in maintaining the privacy of the home, protecting the stability of neighborhoods, preventing the wealthy from foreclosing housing opportunities for others). Subsequently, a servitude may become unenforceable because it imposes an unreasonable direct or indirect restraint on alienation, imposes an unreasonable restraint on trade, or is unconscionable.

3) Modification of a Servitude

The Restatement (Third) of Property section 7.10 (2000) provides that when a change occurs that makes it impossible to accomplish the purpose for which the servitude was created, a court may modify the servitude where practicable. Termination of the servitude is also an option. Beneficiaries may receive compensation for the resulting harm as a condition for modification or termination.

f. Scope of Covenants

1) Judicial Enforcement of Discriminatory Private Agreement

Shelley v. Kraemer
334 U.S. 1 (1948).

Facts. Shelley (D), a black person, purchased residential property that, unknown to D, was encumbered by a restrictive agreement that prevented ownership or occupancy of the property by non-Caucasians. Kraemer (P), a neighbor and owner of the other property subject to the restriction, brought suit to restrain D from possessing the property and to divest title out of D. The trial court denied relief and the Supreme Court of Missouri reversed. D appeals.

Issue. Does the Fourteenth Amendment Equal Protection Clause prohibit judicial enforcement by state courts of restrictive covenants based on race or color?

Held. Yes. Judgment reversed.

♦ Property rights clearly are among those civil rights protected from discriminatory state action by the Fourteenth Amendment. Early decisions invalidated any government restrictions on residency based on race. Here the restrictions are purely private and, standing alone, are not precluded by the Fourteenth Amendment.

♦ Actions of state courts are state actions within the meaning of the Fourteenth Amendment. Judicial enforcement of these private racial restrictions constitutes state discrimination contrary to the Fourteenth Amendment and denies D equal protection.

----

g. Termination of Covenants

1) Introduction

There are several methods by which covenants and servitudes terminate. They can be abandoned, the benefited party can acquiesce to their violation or be estopped from enforcing the covenant, the neighborhood can so change that enforcing the covenant will no longer benefit the neighborhood, and, finally, the hardship on the burdened party may be too great for the court to sanction enforcement of the covenant.

2) Merger

If the benefited estate and the burdened estate come to be held by one owner, the covenant or servitude merges into the estate.

3) Test for Determining if the Covenant Fulfills Its Original Purpose

Western Land Co. v. Truskolaski
495 P.2d 624 (Nev. 1972).

Facts. In 1941 Western (D) subdivided a 40-acre tract. The lots received restrictive covenants that limited the land use to single-family dwellings and prohibited any stores of any kind. In time the area developed and the road bordering the subdivision became a main thoroughfare. In about 1969, D decided to construct a supermarket on the remaining undeveloped 3.5-acre tract. Truskolaski and other homeowners in the subdivision (Ps) sued to enjoin construction on grounds of the restrictive covenant. The trial court found for Ps and D appeals.

Issue. As long as the original purpose of the restrictive covenant can be accomplished to the benefit of the restricted area, will the covenant be enforced?

Held. Yes. Judgment affirmed.

- As long as the original purpose of the covenants can still be accomplished and substantial benefit will inure to the restricted area by their enforcement, the covenants will stand even though the subject property has a greater value if used for other purposes.

- There is ample evidence that shows, in spite of the growing commercial area next to the subdivision, that the restriction substantially benefits the residents of the subdivision. Thus, the trial court will be affirmed.

- Further, the fact that the Reno city council indicated a willingness to change the zoning for the 3.5-acre parcel is not significant. A zoning ordinance cannot override privately placed restrictions.

- Even if this property is more valuable for commercial rather than residential purposes, this does not entitle D to be relieved of the restrictions it created since substantial benefit inures to the restricted area by their enforcement.

- D argues that the restrictive covenants are no longer enforceable due to their abandonment. D showed that some people had built houses on lots less than the required 6,000 sq. ft. minimum; that someone ran a business out of his home in the late 1940s, etc. Even if the alleged occurrences and irregularities could be construed to be violations of the restrictive covenants, they were too distant and sporadic to constitute general consent by the property owners to abandon the restrictive covenants.

---

4) Change of Conditions

Rick v. West
228 N.Y.S.2d 195 (N.Y. App. Div. 1962).

Facts. Chester Rick subdivided 62 acres in 1946 and filed a declaration of covenants, restricting the land to single-family dwellings. In 1956, Rick sold to West (D) a half-acre lot upon which D built a house. Subsequently, Rick contracted for the sale of 45 acres to an industrialist, conditioned on the tract being rezoned. The tract was rezoned, but D would not release the covenant and the sale fell through. In 1961, Rick conveyed to Ps who were likewise prevented by D from selling 15 acres to a hospital. Ps sued, claiming the covenant was no longer enforceable because of change of conditions. The court held for D. Ps appeal.

Issue. Is the covenant nonenforceable due to a substantial change in the general neighborhood?

Held. No. Judgment affirmed.

- Ps' predecessor elected to promote a residential development and in furtherance of his plan imposed residential restrictions where there were previously none.

- D relied on the restrictions and has a right to continue to do so.

- Justice Cardozo in a similar case stated:

  By the settled doctrine of equity, restrictive covenants in respect of land will be enforced by preventive remedies while the violation is still in prospect, unless the attitude of the complaining owner in standing on his covenant is unconscionable or oppressive. Relief is not withheld because the money damage is unsubstantial or even none at all. . . .

  Here, in the case at hand, no process of balancing the equities can make the plaintiff's the greater when compared with the defendant's, or even place the two in equipoise. The defendant, the owner, has done nothing but insist upon adherence to a covenant which is now as valid and binding as at the hour of its making. His neighbors are willing to modify the restriction and forgo a portion of their rights. He refuses to go with them. Rightly or wrongly, he believes that the comfort of his dwelling will be imperiled by the change, and so he chooses to abide by the covenant as framed. The choice is for him only. . . .

♦ Our statute provides no basis for awarding pecuniary damage when the restriction is not outmoded, and when it affords real benefit to the person seeking its enforcement, no consideration can and should be given to any award of pecuniary damages to D in lieu of enforcement of the restrictions.

Comment. Restatement (Third) of Property, Servitudes (2000), section 7.10 provides that a court may modify a servitude to permit the purpose to be accomplished when a change since the creation of the servitude has made it impossible to accomplish the purpose for which the servitude was created.

———————

h. Homeowners' Associations

1) Introduction

Various types of organizations made up of homeowners have been developed to satisfy particular needs. Members subject themselves to certain restrictions and obligations in return for the protection of knowing that the other homeowners also assume the same obligations. Subdivision associations are a common type of homeowner association, made up of individual landowners. Condominiums and cooperatives involve some degree of joint ownership.

a) Condominiums

Condominiums are fairly common in modern society, but they were very rare in the United States until the 1960s. Each individual owner owns in fee simple the living unit, while the land, exterior walls, and common areas are owned by all the unit owners as tenants in common. The unit owners join an association, which has authority to manage the common areas and establish and enforce rules and maintenance charges. This type of ownership is governed by statute as well.

(1) No Cats Allowed

Nahrstedt v. Lakeside Village Condominium Association, Inc.
878 P.2d 1275 (Cal. 1994).

Facts. Nahrstedt (P) sued the Lakeside Village Condominium Association, its officers, and two of its employees (Ds) to obtain a declaration that she is entitled to keep her three cats in her condominium notwithstanding the restrictions imposed by recorded covenants, conditions, and restrictions; P contended that she was not liable for fines assessed against her for her refusal to remove her cats. The trial court sustained, without leave to amend, demurrers to P's five causes of action. The court of appeals reversed and directed the trial court to determine whether P's acts interfered with the peace and quiet enjoyment of other homeowners. Ds appeal to the state supreme court.

Issue. Does enforceability of a pet restriction depend on proof of interference with the right of quiet enjoyment of other homeowners?

Held. No. Judgment reversed and case remanded.

♦ Because recorded use restrictions are essential to a stable and predictable living environment for common interests residential projects, the legislature has provided a presumption of validity to restrictions. The standard applicable to equitable servitudes requires a challenger to demonstrate the unreasonableness of the restriction. Restrictions that are arbitrary, against public policy, or that impose a burden on use that greatly outweighs any benefit will not be enforced.

- Enforcement of a restriction does not depend on an individual owner's conduct, but rather its reasonableness. This is determined by examining the restriction's effect on the common interest of the entire project.

- Some courts afford greater deference to restrictions contained in a master deed in order to promote stability and predictability and to benefit the majority of owners in their expectations. Enforcement also operates to discourage costly legal challenges to restrictions. Our "social fabric" is best preserved by uniform and predictable judicial enforcement of written instruments.

- The recorded pet restriction prohibiting cats and dogs, but allowing some other pets, is not arbitrary. It is rationally related to health, sanitation, and noise concerns. Nor is the burden on P disproportionate to the benefits to the community as a whole.

Dissent. The majority has narrowly interpreted the statutory presumption of validity so as to contribute to the "fraying of our social fabric." The restriction is arbitrary and places a great burden on P by depriving her of the benefits of pet ownership within the confines of her home.

---

b) Cooperatives

A resident in a housing cooperative typically has a long-term renewable lease to the living unit, and owns shares in the corporation that actually holds title to the land and improvements. The resident is a tenant of the corporation in which he has an ownership interest.

(1) Business Judgment Standard

40 West 67th Street Corp. v. Pullman
790 N.E.2d 1174 (NY. 2003).

Facts. Pullman (D) was a shareholder-tenant in a cooperative located at 40 West 67th street (P). Shortly after D moved into his apartment, his behavior became disruptive and, finally, intolerable. Among other things, D complained about his elderly upstairs neighbors, a retired college professor and his wife, who had lived in the building for over 20 years. He wrote numerous angry letters to P, complaining that the couple played their television and stereo loudly late into the night. He also claimed that the couple was carrying on a dangerous and illegal bookbinding business in their apartment and that they stored toxic chemicals there for the business. When P's board investigated, it found that the couple did not have a television or stereo and that there was no evidence of any kind of business in their apartment. Things worsened, resulting in a physical altercation between D and the professor. Afterward, D passed out flyers to other residents, referring to the professor by name, calling him a potential psychopath, and accusing him of cutting D's telephone lines. In another flyer, D claimed that the professor's wife and the board president's wife were having close "intimate personal relations." D also asserted that the previous owners of his apartment had told him the upstairs neighbors had made excessive noise, but the former occupants claimed in an affidavit that this was "completely false." D altered his apartment without board approval and had the work done on weekends in violation of the rules. D filed four lawsuits against the upstairs couple, the president of the cooperative, and the cooperative management, and tried to commence three more.

P's lease provided that a tenancy could be terminated by a two-thirds vote that determined that the lessee's conduct was objectionable and the tenancy of the lessee was undesirable. At a special meeting called by P, the shareholders voted that the board terminate D's proprietary lease and cancel his shares. The board sent D a notice of termination requiring D to vacate his apartment by August 1, 2000. D did not leave, and P brought a suit for possession and ejectment, a declaratory judgment cancelling D's stock, and a money judgment for use and occupancy, along with attorneys' fees and costs.

Instead of applying the business judgment rule to sustain the shareholders' vote and the board's issuance of the notice of termination, the trial court invoked New York statute RPAPL section 711(1) and held that, to terminate a tenancy, a cooperative must prove its claim of objectionable conduct by competent evidence to the satisfaction of the court. A divided appellate division held that under *Levandusky v. One Fifth Ave. Corp.,* 553 N.E.2d 1317 (N.Y. 1990), judicial scrutiny of actions of cooperative boards was prohibited if the actions were "taken in good faith and in the exercise of honest judgment in the lawful and legitimate furtherance of corporate purposes." D appeals.

Issue. Is the business judgment rule the proper standard of review to be applied to P's decision to terminate D's lease?

Held. Yes. Judgment affirmed.

♦ In *Levandusky,* we held that the business judgment rule is the proper standard of judicial review when evaluating decisions made by residential cooperative corporations. The rule is analogous to the corporate business judgment rule, a common law doctrine by which courts exercise restraint and defer to good faith decisions made by boards of directors in business settings. As applied to cooperatives, the business judgment rule provides that a court should defer to a cooperative board's decision as long as the board acts for the purposes of the cooperative, within the scope of its authority and in good faith.

♦ Although we recognized in *Levandusky* that a cooperative board's broad powers could lead to abuse through arbitrary or malicious decisions, we did not want to impair the purposes of a cooperative in protecting the interest of the entire community of residents managed by the board for the common benefit. Also, the limited judicial review provided by the business judgment rule protects the cooperative's decisions against undue court involvement.

♦ D argues that, according to RPAPL section 711(1), a court must make its own evaluation of the board's conduct based on a judicial standard of reasonableness. D also asserts that, when it comes to terminations, the business judgment rule conflicts with RPAPL section 711(1). However, considering the cooperative governance and the lease provision in this case, the cooperative's determination as to D's objectionable behavior stands as the competent evidence needed to sustain P's determination. Otherwise, the contract provision for termination of the lease, to which D agreed, would be meaningless.

♦ P's position that RPAPL section 711(1) is irrelevant to these proceedings is also incorrect. The business judgment rule may be applied consistently with the statute. RPAPL section 711(1) requires competent evidence to show that a tenant is objectionable. The competent evidence that is the basis for the share-holder vote will be reviewed under the business judgment rule; thus, courts will normally defer to that vote and the shareholders' stated findings as the competent evidence under the statute.

♦ Nevertheless, there are cases where courts should review boards' decisions. To trigger further judicial scrutiny, a shareholder-tenant must show that the board acted: (i) outside the scope of its authority, (ii) in a way that did not legitimately further the corporate purpose, or (iii) in bad faith. None of these concerns are indicated here.

C. Zoning

1. Introduction

a. Zoning Power

Only the state has the power to zone. This power has been delegated to cities and counties by statutes called "enabling statutes." Hence, all local zoning activity must abide by the enabling statutes.

b. Goals of Zoning

Zoning has as its goal the orderly development of the community. It promotes economic growth, community health, welfare, and safety.

c. How Zoning Works

One of the fundamental characteristics of zoning is that it segregates uses of land into geographic regions. Thus, highrises may only be permitted downtown rather than in rural areas. It can be used to foster commercial districts as well as residential districts. For health and safety reasons, zoning can regulate the density of human population. This can be achieved by limiting building heights, providing for minimum and maximum yard sizes, yard setbacks, etc.

d. Constitutional Considerations

As with other areas of the law, zoning is affected by the Constitution. For instance, if the zoning in an area is going to be changed, due process requires that the landowners in the area be given a hearing. Zoning restrictions must be for a legitimate governmental objective. The Equal Protection Clause requires that all landowners who are similarly situated be treated equally, unless there is a legitimate reason for not doing so. Of course, as with eminent domain, if zoning regulations amount to a taking, just compensation must be given by the state.

1) Taking

The local government properly exercises its police power when it phases out uses that are inconsistent with newly enacted zoning changes. For example, a city can change the zoning where a cement plant is located and give the plant a couple of years to move before it will be cited for violation of the new zoning. A use that, due to a zoning change, is no longer permitted is a nonconforming use. Most courts say that the landowner must be given a reasonable time to cease his nonconforming use. The length of time for ceasing the nonconformity may be based on the dollar value of the improvements of the land.

2) Leading Case

Village of Euclid v. Ambler Realty Co.
272 U.S. 365 (1926).

Facts. The village of Euclid (D) enacted a comprehensive zoning ordinance restricting uses of property according to areas found on a master plan. Ambler Realty Co.'s (P's) land fell into three different categories, though it consisted of one continuous parcel. P brought suit to enjoin enforcement of the ordinance. At trial P won on the grounds that the statute was unconstitutional. D appeals.

Issue. Is a comprehensive zoning plan restricting uses of properties according to areas designated by a legislative body (where it divides one continuous parcel into three different uses) unconstitutional for violation of Due Process and Equal Protection Clauses of the Constitution?

Held. No. Judgment reversed.

♦ The ordinance under review and all similar ones must find justification under the police power of the state asserted for the public welfare.

♦ If the validity of a legislative classification for zoning purposes is fairly debatable, the legislative judgment must be allowed to control.

♦ It is reasonable for a legislature to regulate building to avoid nuisances and promote safety, and if some harmless type of building is also excluded, this will not invalidate an otherwise good law.

♦ Complete restriction of all industry and apartment buildings from a purely residential district is proper in that fire and health protection is thereby more fairly suited to the task, traffic congestion and street accidents are reduced, and a safer, cleaner, and more enjoyable place for detached housing development is provided. Apartment buildings or industry, taken as a whole, would negate these benefits.

♦ If the provisions of a law are applied to a specific property, they may be found to be arbitrary and unreasonable. The Court will not examine each line of the ordinance and enjoin the enforcement if no injury is shown other than a general allegation that property values were affected.

♦ In the development of constitutional law, the Court will not speculate with general rules beyond the immediate question presented.

Comment. Zoning laws are now presumptively valid.

---

2. Administration of Zoning Ordinances

a. Introduction

Zoning ordinances present numerous opportunities for abuse and for objection by affected landowners. Administration of zoning ordinances thus creates the potential for considerable litigation.

b. Comprehensive Plans

Enabling acts inevitably require the local zoning authority to adopt a comprehensive plan (which can be revised from time to time). The zoning must conform with the plan. The plan serves to limit the local zoning board's whims.

c. Nonconforming Use

PA Northwestern Distributors, Inc. v. Zoning Hearing Board
584 A.2d 1372 (Pa. 1991).

Facts. After PA (D) opened an adult bookstore, the town amended its zoning ordinances to regulate "adult commercial enterprises" and included an amortization provision requiring preexisting uses that conflicted with the amendment to come into compliance within 90 days from the date of the ordinance. P's bookstore cannot meet the ordinance's restrictions because it is not located within an area designated for adult commercial enterprises. After being notified that it was out of compliance, P appealed to D, challenging the validity of the amortization provision. D upheld the validity of the provision, and two lower courts dismissed P's appeals. P appeals.

Issue. Is a zoning ordinance that requires the amortization and discontinuance of a lawful preexisting nonconforming use confiscatory and violative of the state constitution as a taking of property without just compensation?

Held. Yes. Judgment reversed.

♦ The lower court based its dismissal on the opinion in *Sullivan v. Zoning Board of Adjustment*, 478 A.2d 912 (Pa. Commw. Ct. 1984), which is not a correct statement of the law of this commonwealth. *Sullivan* presents a standard whereby the property interests of an individual are balanced with the health, safety, morals, or general welfare of the community at large.

♦ Zoning involves governmental restrictions upon a property owner's constitutionally guaranteed right to use her property, unfettered by governmental restrictions, except where the use violates any law, creates a nuisance, or the owner violates any covenant, restriction, or easement.

♦ A lawful nonconforming use establishes in the property owner a vested property right that cannot be abrogated or destroyed, unless it is a nuisance, it is abandoned, or it is extinguished by eminent domain.

♦ If the effect of a zoning law or regulation is to deprive a property owner of the lawful use of her property, it amounts to a taking for which she must be justly compensated.

Concurrence. A blanket rule against all amortization provisions should be rejected. The instant provision is confiscatory but the *Sullivan* standard should be upheld.

---

d. Variances

Zoning by its nature is general; it does not take into account the particularities of every lot in the zone. For that reason, boards of zoning adjustments have been established locally. They are empowered to grant variances for conditions that are unique to a particular lot or two. If the condition is not unique, a change in zoning should be sought. Suppose, for example, that when a tract of land was changed from a commercial zone to a residential zone, a 20-foot side yard requirement was imposed. If there were a few lots mat, due to their shape, could not be used for housing if the 20-foot side yards were required, the zoning adjustment board could grant a variance.

1) Special Exceptions

A special exception is not the same thing as a variance. Where a particular use is compatible in theory with the surrounding zoning if certain conditions are met, a special exception can be issued to the landowner. Criteria must be established for granting special exceptions.

a) Example

A gas station may be compatible with a residential neighborhood if the gasoline storage tanks are placed under-ground. The ordinance regarding special exceptions would have to set forth the requirements for permitting a gas station in a residential neighborhood.

2) Justification for Refusing Variance Request

Commons v. Westwood Zoning Board of Adjustments
410 A.2d 1138 (N.J. 1980).

Facts. Weingarten and the Commons (Ps) sought a zoning variance for the construction of a single-family home on an undersized lot in Westwood. The Commons owned a vacant lot, and Weingarten, a builder, contracted to purchase the lot on the condition that he could build a one-family home on the lot. The lot had frontage of only 30 feet and a total area of 5,190 square feet but was in a residential zone that required a minimum frontage of 75 feet and a minimum area of 7,500 square feet. Although other nonconforming lots had been in Westwood since before the zoning requirement, many neighbors opposed the variance, and the Westwood Zoning Board of Adjustments (D) refused to grant the variance. D based its denial on the ground that Ps had failed to prove hardship, but D did not specify its reasons. Ps sought judicial review of D's action. Both the trial court and the intermediate appellate court affirmed the denial of the variance request. Ps appeal.

Issue. Must a zoning board specify its reasons for refusing a variance request?

Held. Yes. Judgment reversed and case remanded.

♦ New Jersey law authorizes a board of adjustment to grant a variance if the application of a zoning ordinance would result in undue hardship on the developer of the land. "Undue hardship" involves the notion that no effective use can be made of the property if the variance is denied. An owner is not entitled to have his property zoned to its most profitable use. However, if a regulation renders the property unusable for any purpose, the owner may suffer undue hardship.

♦ Consideration should be given to how the situation came about and the owner's efforts to bring his property into compliance with the zoning requirement. If the owner created the nonconforming condition, the hardship is said to be self-imposed. On the other hand, if the owner tries unsuccessfully to purchase additional land to bring his property into compliance or tries unsuccessfully to sell his property to the adjoining landowners for a reasonable price, undue hardship exists.

♦ Once undue hardship is found to exist, the board of adjustment must be satisfied that the granting of the variance will not substantially impinge upon the public good and the purpose of the zoning ordinance.

♦ In cases such as this, there is the possibility that the denial of a variance will zone the property into inutility so that an exercise of eminent domain is called for and compensation will have to be paid.

♦ Here, D erred in concluding that Ps had failed to demonstrate any hardship. The Commons had tried unsuccessfully to purchase additional property to bring their property into compliance. They also discussed selling the property to a neighbor, but there was a substantial difference in the offering and asking prices.

♦ Although the house would be smaller than others in the neighborhood, the minimum floor requirements in the zone are not per se related to the public health, safety, or morals. On these grounds, D could not refuse the variance request.

♦ The burden of proof is on applicants such as Ps. However, if the applicants comply with the variance ordinance's criteria, the local zoning board must specifically state why the request is denied. Otherwise, a reviewing court cannot determine whether the board acted within its limits.

Comment. This case also illustrates the need for local zoning authorities to comply with the state enabling act's concern for public health, safety, and morals.

----

3) Excessive Discretion Granted to Local Zoning Board

Cope v. Inhabitants of the Town of Brunswick
464 A.2d 223 (Me. 1983).

Facts. The Copes (Ps) sought an exception to the local zoning ordinance so they could construct eight six-unit apartments on land then classified for suburban residential use. The ordinance permitted the Brunswick Zoning Board of Appeals (D) to grant an application for an exception if the applicant proved, inter alia, that (i) the use requested would not adversely affect the health, safety, or general welfare of the public and (ii) that the use requested would not tend to devalue or alter the essential characteristics of the surrounding property. D found that Ps' project complied with the ordinance except for these two factors. D denied Ps' application. The reviewing court upheld the denial and Ps appeal.

Issue. Does a local zoning board have authority to take action based on general statements of policy contained in the zoning ordinance?

Held. No. Judgment reversed.

♦ Local zoning boards and municipalities themselves have no inherent authority to regulate the use of private property. This authority may only be conferred by the state, and only with such a detailed statement of policy that those to whom the law is to be applied may reasonably determine their rights. The determination of rights may not be left to the purely arbitrary discretion of the administrator; the administrator may not have discretion as to whether to grant the permit if the conditions stated in the ordinance exist.

♦ The two factors upon which D rejected Ps' application were so general that they did not limit D's discretion. Instead, they gave D discretionary authority to approve or disapprove applications as D thinks best serves the public interest. The lack of sufficiently detailed standards would permit a discriminatory application of the law, so the ordinance is unconstitutional.

♦ An exception allows the owner to use his property as the ordinance expressly permits. Whether a use would comply with the public health, safety, and welfare and with the essential character of an area is a legislative question. In authorizing exceptions, the legislature makes a determination that the use would not ordinarily be detrimental to the neighborhood within the zone. The delegation to D under this ordinance permits D to decide that same legislative question again.

♦ Because D found that Ps complied with all the requirements of the ordinance except for the two invalid ones, Ps should receive the exception.

----

e. Amending Zoning Ordinances

The local legislative body has power to amend the zoning ordinances. It need not follow the zoning board's recommendations.

1) Spot Zoning

This occurs when the local legislative body amends the zoning ordinance to permit a new zone that is limited in size (although it can be more than one lot) and does not conform to the comprehensive plan.

2) No Spot Zoning Found

State v. City of Rochester
268 N.W.2d 885 (Minn. 1978).

Facts. A group of homeowners (Ps) opposed a zoning change that allowed construction of a 49-unit condominium building on a single 1.18-acre tract in an area zoned for single-family or low-density multiple family dwellings. Across the street from the tract to the east was a 24-unit apartment building and across the street to the north was a 35-unit condominium. The Rochester city council (D) rezoned the tract to high-density residential use. Ps filed suit challenging the rezoning ordinance and seeking a declaratory judgment and injunction. The trial court denied the requested relief. Ps appeal.

Issue. Was the ordinance a valid exercise of the city's delegated legislative police power, reasonably related to the public health, safety, and welfare?

Held. Yes. Judgment affirmed.

♦ When a municipality adopts or amends a zoning ordinance, it acts in a legislative capacity under its delegated police powers. Unless opponents to the rezoning can show no rational basis to support a reclassification or a taking without compensation, the reclassification must be upheld, regardless of the size of the tract of land in question. A legislative body can best determine which zoning classifications best serve the public welfare.

---

f. Contract and Conditional Rezoning

This involves the local zoning authority granting a landowner's request for a variance or change in zoning on the condition that the landowner sign a contract to do certain dungs. For example, the city might require a developer to renovate a traffic intersection adjacent to her property in return for its changing the zoning so that she can build a grocery store.

g. Discretionary Zoning (non-Euclidean Zoning)

The need for some discretion in zoning has become apparent over the years. Hence, things that were formerly forbidden are now permitted. The following are examples:

1) Cluster Zoning

Rather than having 100 families living on 10,000 square-foot lots, some developers wanted to cluster the houses by putting them on smaller lots, leaving the unused land for a park or recreation area. The overall density does not change, only the distribution of the population. This was once forbidden but now is common.

2) Floating Zoning

A city, as an example, can create a new zone but not provide any geographic location for it. A developer can come along and apply to have the zoning for her tract of land changed to the "floating" zone. Once forbidden, this is now a common way of encouraging new types of developments.

3) Planned Unit Developments

This takes cluster zoning one step further and permits several different uses to be clustered on one tract of land. Thus, an apartment building may be next to a single-family home, which may be next to a park area.

3. Nontraditional Zoning Objectives

a. Aesthetic Regulation

The old rule was that cities could not use their police power to accomplish goals that were purely aesthetic. The modern trend is just the opposite. In fact, zoning commissions may have architectural review boards composed of nonelected people who, based on aesthetics, approve or deny building permits.

1) Architectural Style

State ex rel. Stoyanoff v. Berkeley
458 S.W.2d 305 (Mo. 1970).

Facts. P applied for a permit to build on a lot he owned in a very exclusive suburb of St. Louis. Pursuant to city ordinance, the designs for P's house had to be approved by the city architectural board. The houses in the area of P's lot were of traditional architecture. P's planned house was ultramodern. The board found P's planned house to be grotesque and refused to approve the plans. P sued as noted above. The city (D) proved that P's house would cause neighboring houses to decline in value. The trial court found for P and D appeals.

Issue. May a building permit be refused if a proposed house is found to be grotesque by the city architectural board?

Held. Yes. The lower court is reversed.

- The stabilizing of property values is one of the most cogent reasons behind zoning ordinances. It is well within the promotion of the general welfare as stated in the enabling act.

- Property that offends sensibilities and debases property values affects not only adjoining property owners but also the general welfare. Grotesque structures, detrimental to the value and welfare of surrounding property and to the general welfare and happiness of the community, are to be avoided.

- Aesthetic considerations are a matter of general welfare.

- The fact that the ordinance provides for an architectural board, composed of three architects (nonelected officials), is not an impermissible delegation of power. The general standards provided for in the statute are sufficiently specific to guide the board. This is adequate protection against the exercise of arbitrary and uncontrolled discretion of the city council. Further, after an adverse determination, a property owner may appeal to the city council.

---

2) Aesthetic Compatibility and Harmony

Anderson v. City of Issaquah
851 P.2d 744 (Wash. Ct. App. 1993).

Facts. Anderson (P) applied to the city (D) for land use certification to develop property zoned for commercial use. P submitted plans for a commercial building to D's various departments and confronted an obstacle only when he sought approval from the Development Commission, which administers and enforces the city's land use regulations. The Issaquah Municipal Code ("IMC") provides that buildings must be "compatible" with existing buildings; "harmony in texture, lines, and masses [is] encouraged;" "monotony" is to be avoided; the project should be "interesting." On the street where P proposed to build his retail warehouse there were several gas stations, a Victorian-era house used as a visitors' center, a bank, an Elks' hall, an auto repair shop, and a veterinary clinic with a cyclone-fenced dog run. After three appearances before the commission and repeated attempts to comply with the commissioners' interpretation of the IMC, P's application was denied. P appealed to the city council, which affirmed. P filed suit, alleging that IMC building design requirements are unconstitutionally vague. The trial court dismissed P's complaint. P appeals.

Issue. Are the IMC sections at issue here unconstitutionally vague on their face?

Held. Yes. Judgment reversed.

- The purpose of the void for vagueness doctrine is to limit arbitrary and discretionary enforcements of the law.

- The language used in the IMC does not give effective or meaningful guidance to applicants or design professionals. No applicant can determine whether his project is going to be seen by the commission as "monotonous" or "harmonious."

- The commissioners attempted to communicate to P their own individual, subjective feelings and to enforce their own arbitrary concept of IMC provisions. The words employed are not technical words that are commonly understood within the professional building design industry. Nor do these words have a settled common law meaning.

- Aesthetic standards are an appropriate component of land use governance when such standards give clear guidance to all parties concerned.

---

3) Limitation on Residential Signage

City of Ladue v. Gilleo
512 U.S. 43 (1994).

Facts. Gilleo (P) placed a 2- by 3-foot sign on her front lawn printed with the words "Say No to War in the Persian Gulf, Call Congress Now." After the first sign was removed and a replacement knocked down, P went to the police, who informed P such signs were prohibited in Ladue (D). P filed suit alleging that D's ordinance violated her First Amendment right of free speech. The district court issued a preliminary injunction against the enforcement of D's ordinance. P placed an 8.5- by 11-inch sign in a second story window stating, "For Peace in the Gulf." D repealed the original ordinance and enacted a replacement, which prohibited all signs except those that fall into one of 10 exemptions. The exemptions include for sale and other like signs; church, religious institution, and school signs; commercial signs in commercial areas; and onsite advertising. Part of the new ordinance indicated D's concern in enacting the new ordinance: proliferation of signs in a residential area would cause clutter, cause a decline in property values, and may cause safety and traffic hazards to motorists and pedestrians. P amended the complaint to address the new ordinance. The district court held the ordinance unconstitutional and the court of appeals affirmed, holding the ordinance invalid as a "content-based" regulation since D treated commercial speech more favorably than noncommercial speech. D petitioned for certiorari.

Issue. Does D's ordinance violate P's First Amendment right to free speech?

Held. Yes. Judgment affirmed.

- In *Linmark Associates, Inc. v. Willingboro*, 431 U.S. 85 (1977), we found unconstitutional an ordinance prohibiting homeowners from placing "For Sale" or "Sold" signs on their property in that it restrained the free flow of truthful information. *Linmark* is in some respects the mirror image of this case. In *Linmark*, the city's interest was in maintaining a stable, racially integrated neighborhood. D's interest here is minimizing visual clutter. D's interest is no more compelling than those at stake in *Linmark*. Also, Linmark's ordinance applied only to a form of commercial speech; D's ordinance covers "such absolutely pivotal speech as a sign protesting an imminent governmental decision to go to war." The impact of D's ordinance is greater than in *Linmark*. P and others are forbidden to display any sign on their property, foreclosing a complete medium and a unique and important means of communication. Although prohibitions foreclosing entire media may be completely free of content or viewpoint discrimination, the danger they pose to freedom of speech is readily apparent—by eliminating a common means of speaking, such measures can suppress too much speech.

- In *Metromedia, Inc. v. San Diego*, 453 U.S. 490 (1981), we held unconstitutional a San Diego ordinance imposing substantial prohibitions on outdoor advertising displays within the city in the interest of traffic safety and aesthetics. We found that the city treated commercial speech more favorably than noncommercial speech and in effect eliminated the billboard as an effective medium of communication for noncommercial messages.

♦ Regulation of speech may be impermissibly underinclusive. An exemption may represent a government effort to give one side an advantage over another in expressing views in a debatable public issue. Alternatively, through the restriction of general speech and exemptions, the government may attempt to select suitable subjects for public debate, thereby attempting to control "the search for political truth." D claims that its ordinance is content-neutral and triggers neither of these concerns. D argues that the mixture of prohibitions and exemptions in its ordinance "reflects legitimate differences among the side effects of various kinds of signs." The exemptions are not likely to contribute to clutter. Only a few residents at a time display "for sale" and like signs. D has only a few churches, schools, and businesses.

♦ However, D's exemptions demonstrate that D has determined that the interest in permitting some messages to be conveyed through residential signage outweighs D's aesthetic interest in eliminating outdoor signs.

♦ D's ordinance is not a mere regulation of the time, place, or manner of speech simply because P and others remain free to use other means of communication like hand-held signs, telephone calls, and newspaper advertisements. We are not persuaded that what means of communications exist for P and others are adequate substitutes. Signs displayed at one's residence carry a unique message. They identify the speaker, an important component of efforts to persuade. They reach neighbors. They have played an important part in political campaigns. A special respect for individual liberty in the home has long been part of our culture and our law; that principle has special resonance when the government seeks to constrain a person's ability to speak there.

---

b. Protection of Religious Establishment and Uses

Guru Nanak Sikh Society of Yuba City v. County of Sutter
456 F.3d 978 (9th Cir. 2006).

Facts. Guru Nanak (P), a religious organization, attempted to obtain a conditional use permit ("CUP") for the construction of a Sikh temple on its 1.89-acre property on Grove Road in Yuba City. The property was in an area intended mainly for large lot single family residences; churches and temples were only conditionally permitted through issuance of a CUP. The Sutter County planning division issued a report recommending that the planning commission grant a CUP for the Grove Road property. But at a public meeting, the planning commission voted to deny the CUP because of citizens' fears of increased noise and traffic. Subsequently, P acquired a 28.79-acre parcel on George Washington Boulevard in an unincorporated area of the county to build a temple. The site was zoned as a general agricultural district. Again, churches and temples in the district were only conditionally permitted through issuance of a CUP. P applied for a CUP to build a temple limited to approximately 2,850 square feet. County and state departments reviewed P's application and added a variety of conditions.

At a public meeting held by the planning commission. P accepted all of the planning division's proposed conditions on the land's use. Potential neighbors complained that the temple would increase traffic and noise, interfere with the agricultural use of their land, and lower property values. However, the planning commission approved the application, subject to the planning division's conditions. After neighbors filed appeals to the board of supervisors, the board reversed the planning commission's approval and denied P's application. P sued the county and its board of supervisors (Ds), claiming that denial of the CUP violated the Religious Land Use and Institutionalized Persons Act ("RLUIPA") and the Constitution. The district court granted summary judgment in favor of P. Ds appeal.

Issue. Does Ds' denial of P's application for a conditional use permit to construct a temple on the parcel of land zoned "agricultural" constitute a "substantial burden" under RLUIPA?

Held. Yes. Judgment affirmed.

♦ RLUIPA prohibits the government from imposing substantial burdens on religious exercise unless there is a compelling governmental interest and the burden is the least restrictive means of satisfying the governmental interest. RLUIPA, applicable only to regulations regarding land use and prison conditions, applies only if: (i) the state program or activity receives federal financial assistance; (ii) the substantial burden imposed by local law affects or would affect commerce with foreign nations, among the states, or with Indian tribes; or (iii) the substantial burden is imposed in the "implementation" of a land use regulation, under which a government makes, or has procedures or practices in place that permit the government to make, individualized assessments of the proposed uses for the property involved.

♦ The county argues that its denial of P's second CUP application falls outside the legislative scope of RLUIPA because the use permit process is a neutral law of general applicability. However, RLUIPA applies when the government may take into account the particular details of an applicant's proposed use of land when deciding whether to permit that use.

♦ The county's zoning code does not permit churches, as a matter of right, in any of the six types of zoned areas available for church construction in the county; an entity intending to build a church must first apply for a CUP and be approved by the county. The zoning code states that the planning commission, which has original jurisdiction over use applications, may approve or conditionally approve a use permit if it finds that the use will not be detrimental to property in the neighborhood, or to the health, safety, and general welfare of persons residing or working in the neighborhood, or to the general welfare of the county. The zoning code directs the planning commission and the board of supervisors, which reviews the planning commission's conditional use decisions, to implement its system of land use regulations by making individualized assessments of the proposed uses of the land involved.

♦ Although RLUIPA does not apply directly to land use regulations, such as the zoning code here, when the zoning code is applied to grant or deny a certain use to a particular parcel of land, that application is an "implementation" of a land use regulation. Therefore, RLUIPA governs the county's actions.

♦ RLUIPA states, in relevant part, that no government may impose or implement a land use regulation in a manner that imposes a substantial burden on the religious exercise of a person or a religious assembly or institution, unless the government demonstrates that imposition of the burden on that person, assembly, or institution: (i) is in furtherance of a compelling governmental interest; and (ii) is the least restrictive means of furthering that compelling governmental interest. P bears the burden to prove that D's denial of its application imposes a substantial burden on its religious exercise.

♦ The broad reasons that D gave for its denials of P's two CUP applications could easily apply to all future applications by P. Also, D, without explanation, found P's cooperation and agreement to every mitigation measure suggested by the planning division insufficient. Thus, D imposed a substantial burden on P.

♦ After the planning division recommended approval of P's initial CUP application, the planning commission unanimously rejected the application, citing neighbors' complaints regarding increased noise and traffic. P then proposed a smaller temple, with the same 75-person capacity, on a much larger parcel of agricultural land. This would leave more space between the temple and adjacent properties, decreasing the noise and traffic impact on the surrounding area.

♦ Subsequently, the planning commission approved this second application, but the board of supervisors denied it. The board's main reason for denying P's second application was that the temple would contribute to "leapfrog development" (*i.e.*, development not contiguous to areas currently designated for urban or suburban uses). The county could potentially use the leapfrog reason to deny churches access to all such land, but it inconsistently applied its concern with leapfrog development to P. Such inconsistent decisionmaking establishes the uncertainty that P would face if P were to make future CUP applications for a temple on land zoned "agricultural."

♦ When the board of supervisors denied, without explanation, the second CUP application, the board disregarded the planning division's finding that the proposed temple would have an insignificant impact on surrounding land uses due to P's acceptance of use conditions. P agreed to a host of conditions, particularly in regards to its second application, which were proposed to mollify the county's concerns with leapfrog development.

♦ Although the county bears the burden of persuasion, it has presented no argument as to its compelling interest or that the restrictions are narrowly tailored to accomplish such interest. Therefore, we hold that the district court properly invalidated Ds' denial of P's CUP application.

-----

c. Environmental Protection

Fisher v. Giuliani
720 N.Y.S.2d 50 (N.Y. App. Div. 2001).

Facts. The Manhattan Theater District generated approximately $2 billion in economic activity annually and employed about 250,000 people. In response to the destruction of several theaters, New York City amended the Zoning Resolution in 1982. These amendments created a new "Theater subdistrict" that restricted the demolition of certain theaters and attempted to make them more viable by allowing the theater owners to transfer development rights to nearby parcels. Amendments adopted in 1998 authorized the theater owners to transfer development rights from designated theaters to receiving sites anywhere within the subdistrict. A receiving site could increase its floor-to-area ratio to 20% as-of-right, or more through special permit or discretionary authorization. The transfer had to be accompanied by a covenant ensuring that the theater would be kept open.

Before submitting the proposed amendments, the City Planning Commission ("CPC"), through the Environmental Assessment and Review Division of the Department of City Planning ("DCP"), conducted an environmental assessment and prepared an Environmental Assessment Statement as required by the State Environmental Quality Review Act ("SEQRA") and the City Environmental Quality Review ("CEQR"). If it determined that the proposed action could have a significant effect on the environment, the CPC would have to issue a positive declaration, and an Environmental Impact Statement would have to be prepared before the proposed zoning could be adopted. On the other hand, if it determined that the action would have no significant impact, the agency would issue a negative declaration, and no Environmental Impact Statement would have to be prepared.

After the DCP compared the worst-case scenario that could result under the as-of-right amendments with the development that would otherwise have occurred without the amendments, it then considered the potential demand for additional development in the study area over the next 10 years. The DCP found that the existing zoning capacity could accommodate the projected demand. The DCP also determined that the transfer of development rights from theaters did modestly increase the density of particular sites but that this would not affect overall market conditions nor induce development beyond what was already likely to occur. A DCP analysis established that any potential development would not have a significant effect on traffic, transit, and air quality. Finally, the DCP determined that the proposed amendments would not lead to significant displacement of area residents or businesses. The DCP's findings and conclusions resulted in a negative declaration, which was supported by an Environmental Assessment Statement. Subsequently, the CPC adopted the proposed amendments, and the New York City Council approved the amendments.

Residents of a neighboring district (Ps) brought suit, challenging the adequacy of the environmental review and the negative declaration. Ps assert that the underlying analysis supporting the negative declaration was deficient and that an Environmental Impact Statement was warranted. The supreme court annulled the amendments and directed the DCP to prepare an Environmental Impact Statement. The city (D) appeals.

Issues.

(i) Was an Environmental Impact Statement required before the "as-of-right" provisions of the amendments could be adopted?

(ii) Was an Environmental Impact Statement required before the special discretionary permit provisions of the amendments could be adopted?

Held. (i) No. (ii) Yes. Judgment affirmed as modified.

♦ A court reviewing an agency's issuance of a negative declaration is limited to deciding whether the agency identified and examined the relevant areas of environmental concern and reasonably elaborated the basis for its determination.

♦ Ps argue that the DCP: (i) underestimated the projected market demand for development in the Theater Subdistrict; (ii) erroneously determined that the amendments would not stimulate development beyond that which would already have occurred; and (iii) improperly limited its analysis to 10 years into the future and failed to consider that every square inch of buildable space might be developed.

♦ However, the DCP: (i) used a proper forecasting method as to future demand; (ii) rationally determined that market demand and consequent development would remain relatively constant; and (iii) was only required to examine environmental consequences into the foreseeable future, not to examine unsupported theoretical possibilities. Thus, the DCP's detailed analysis was entirely rational regarding the "as-of-right" amendments, and an Environmental Impact Statement was not required.

♦ In the DCP's view, no environmental review of the amendments involving the special permit or discretionary authorization mechanism, which was in addition to the 20% as-of-right transfers, was required because, when an owner applied for a special permit, an assessment would be made at that time. Accordingly, the DCP mistakenly believed that it could defer its analysis.

♦ SEQRA's goal is to promote environmental considerations at the earliest opportunity. Thus, although environmental review may be required when an applicant seeks a special permit, this does not preclude the CPC's obligation to consider potential environmental impact at the time it enacts the zoning changes.

♦ The grant of additional floor-to-area ratio beyond that permitted as-of-right may not have a significant environmental impact. Nevertheless, the DCP was required to consider the matter now, not only in the future. Therefore, because the DCP failed to assess the possible environmental impact that could arise from discretionary grants of floor-to-area ratio, these provisions of the Zoning Resolution are severed and annulled. However, the as-of-right provisions need not be annulled because they were enacted after the DCP carefully examined the relevant environmental concerns and elaborated its determination that there would be no impact.

———————

d. Controls on Household Composition

1) Introduction

Many efforts have been made to restrict land use based on the composition of the household. Usually this is intended to prevent boarding houses, fraternity houses, or overcrowded conditions. Such zoning ordinances do present significant constitutional issues, however.

2) Exclusion of Nonfamilies

Village of Belle Terre v. Boraas
416 U.S. 1 (1974).

Facts. The village of Belle Terre (D) restricted land use to single-family dwellings, excluding lodging houses, boarding houses, fraternity houses, or multiple-dwelling houses. "Family" was defined as one or more persons related by blood, adoption, or marriage, living and cooking together as a single housekeeping unit, exclusive of house-hold servants, or not more than two persons living and cooking together as a single housekeeping unit who were not related by blood, adoption, or marriage. Boraas, the owner of a house in the village, and three of six tenants in the house who were unrelated by blood, adoption, or marriage (Ps), sought an injunction under 42 U.S.C. section 1983 declaring the village ordinance unconstitutional (after they were served with an order to remedy violations of the ordinance). Ps claim that the ordinance interferes with a person's right to travel, that it interferes with the right to migrate to and settle within a state, that it bars people who are uncongenial to the present residents of D, that the ordinance expresses the social preferences of the residents for groups that will be congenial to them, that social homogeneity is not a legitimate interest of government, that the restriction of those whom the neighbors do not like intrudes on the newcomer's rights of privacy, that it is of no rightful concern to villagers whether the residents are married or unmarried, and that the ordinance is antithetical to the nation's experience, ideology, and self-perception as an open, egalitarian, and integrated society. The district court held the ordinance constitutional and the court of appeals affirmed. D appeals to the Supreme Court.

Issue. May a city use household composition as a basis for zoning?

Held. Yes. Judgment reversed.

♦ The ordinance is not aimed at transients, involves no procedural disparity inflicted on some but not on others, and involves no "fundamental" right guaranteed by the constitution (e.g., voting, the right of association, the right of access to the courts, any rights of privacy, etc.).

♦ Police power is not confined to elimination of filth, stench, and unhealthy places, but may be used to lay out zones where "family values, youth values, and the blessings of quiet seclusion and clean air make the area a sanctuary for people." Thus, the ordinance is a reasonable, not arbitrary, exercise of discretion by D.

Dissent (Marshall, J.). The ordinance violates equal protection and unnecessarily burdens Ps' First Amendment rights of freedom of association and their guaranteed rights of privacy. Further, the ordinance limits the density of occupancy of only those homes occupied by unrelated persons, thus reaching beyond control of the use of land or the density of population and instead undertaking to regulate the way people choose to associate with each other within the privacy of their own homes.

Comment. The California Supreme Court has held a similar ordinance to be unconstitutional. The Supreme Court itself held invalid a single-family zoning ordinance that defined "family" as no more than one set of grandchildren. [Moore v. City of East Cleveland, 431 U.S. 494 (1977)] The reason was that the intrusion into the family was too great; the Court could not defer to the legislative findings. *Belle Terre* was distinguished because it affected only unrelated individuals.

---

3) Family Composition Rule

City of Edmonds v. Oxford House, Inc.
514 U.S. 725 (1995).

Facts. The Fair Housing Act ("Act") prohibits housing discrimination against handicapped persons. Section 3607(b)(1) of the Act exempts reasonable governmental restrictions on the maximum number of occupants permitted to occupy a dwelling. Oxford House (D) opened a group home for 10–12 recovering alcoholics in Edmonds (P). P's zoning code prescribes that occupants of single-family dwellings must compose a "family." The code defines a family as "an individual or two or more persons related by genetics, adoption, or marriage, or a group of five or fewer persons who are not related by genetics, adoption, or marriage." P issued a criminal citation to the owner and a resident of the group home. D asked P to make a reasonable accommodation pursuant to the FHA. P declined but passed an ordinance allowing group homes as permitted uses in multifamily and general commercial zones. P sued D in district court seeking a declaration that P's ordinance is exempt from the FHA provisions. D counterclaimed, charging that P failed to make a reasonable accommodation by permitting the home to remain. In response to cross-motions for summary judgment, the trial court found for P. The court of appeals reversed. The Ninth Circuit's decision conflicted with an Eleventh Circuit decision. The Supreme Court granted certiorari to resolve the conflict.

Issue. Does P's family composition rule qualify as a restriction regarding the maximum number of occupants permitted to occupy a dwelling within the meaning of the FHA's absolute exemption?

Held. No. Judgment affirmed.

♦ Reserving land for single-family homes maintains the character of neighborhoods, allowing "zones" where family values, youth values, quiet seclusion, and wholesome air create a sanctuary. To limit land use to accommodate such a zone, a city must define the term "family." Thus, family composition rules are essential to maintain single-family use restrictions.

♦ In contrast, maximum occupancy restrictions cap the number of individuals permitted per dwelling in relation to the available floor space or number and type of rooms. These restrictions are to maintain health and safety by preventing overcrowding.

♦ While maximum occupancy rules clearly fall within the FHA's exemption, rules designed to preserve the family character of a neighborhood, fastening on the composition of households rather than the total number of occupants living quarters can contain, do not.

♦ P's contention that, because its rule caps at five the number of unrelated persons permitted to occupy a single-family dwelling, it falls within the exemption, is erroneous. P's rule does not indicate the maximum number of persons permitted to occupy a house. Unlimited siblings, their parents, and grandparents could live in P's single-family zone without offending the rule.

♦ We decide here only the threshold question. It remains for the lower court to determine whether P's actions against D violate the FHA's provisions against discrimination.

———————

e. Exclusionary Zoning

By regulating various zoning requirements (density, minimum floor space, types of housing), a community can separate the rich, the poor, and the middle class. The old line of cases required that the zoning requirement or regulation bear a rational relationship to a permissible governmental purpose. One of these purposes was to prevent overcrowding.

1) Exclusionary Goal

If the particular zoning ordinance bore no reasonable relationship and had an exclusionary purpose, it was struck down.

2) Modern Trend—The Fair Share Test

Some recent cases have held that any zoning ordinance with an exclusionary impact must be scrutinized in light of the needs of the region. The impact of this is that developing communities must have their share of low and moderate income housing.

3) Exclusion for Fiscal Reasons

Southern Burlington County NAACP v. Township of Mount Laurel
336 A.2d 713 (N.J. 1975).

Facts. The Southern Burlington County NAACP (P) brought suit against the township of Mount Laurel (D), claiming that its zoning ordinance, which permitted only single-family detached dwellings, unlawfully excluded low and moderate income families from the town. The trial court declared the ordinance invalid and ordered D to present a plan of affirmative public action designed to enable and encourage the satisfaction of the indicated needs. D appeals; P, which contended that the relief was not broad enough (*i.e.*, that D should have considered the regional housing needs of low and moderate income families without limitation to those having past, present, and prospective connections with the town), also appeals.

Issue. May a developing municipality, by a system of land use regulation, make it physically and economically impossible to provide low and moderate income housing in the municipality for the various categories of persons who need and want it and thereby exclude such people from living within its confines because of the limited extent of their income and resources?

Held. No. Judgment affirmed.

♦ D's zoning ordinance is presumptively contrary to the general welfare and out-side the intended scope of the zoning power. A facial showing of invalidity is thus established, shifting to the municipality the burden of establishing valid superseding reasons for its action and nonaction.

♦ Considering the basic importance of the opportunity for appropriate housing for all classes, no municipality may exclude or limit categories of housing solely for fiscal reasons.

♦ Every developing municipality must, by its land use regulations, presumptively make realistically possible an appropriate variety and choice of housing.

♦ When land use regulation has a substantial external impact, the welfare of the state's citizens beyond the borders of the municipality cannot be disregarded.

♦ When it is shown that a developing municipality has not made realistically possible a variety and choice of housing, a facial showing of violation of substantive due process or equal protection has been made out and the burden shifts to the municipality to establish a valid basis for its action.

♦ A developing municipality's obligation to afford the opportunity for decent and adequate low and moderate income housing extends at least to that municipality's fair share of the present and prospective regional need therefor.

♦ A municipality should first have full opportunity to itself act without judicial supervision. Therefore, a detailed court order should not be issued.

---

4) *Mount Laurel II*

Eight years after *Mount Laurel, supra,* was decided, the case was consolidated for appeal with five others and came before the court because of noncompliance with the mandate of the original opinion. In *Southern Burlington County NAACP v. Township of Mount Laurel (Mount Laurel II),* 456 A.2d 390 (N.J. 1983), the New Jersey Supreme Court held that courts may take the lead in enforcing fair distribution of all income classes among residential areas. The court reasoned that the constitutional power to zone, as a portion of the police power, must be exercised for the general welfare. Thus, zoning regulations that do not provide the requisite opportunity for a fair share of the region's needs for low and moderate income housing are unconstitutional. To ensure compliance with this rule, the court held that every municipality must provide a realistic opportunity for decent housing for at least some part of its resident poor who now occupy dilapidated housing. Each municipality designated by the State Development Guide Plan ("SDGP") as a growth area must also provide opportunities for a fair share of the region's present and prospective low and moderate income housing needs. It was determined that only judges selected by the Chief Justice would hear all future *Mount Laurel* litigation to insure consistent development of judicial rules and all such litigation should be disposed of in a single trial with one appeal. The court further determined that the builder's remedy, which allows a builder who unsuccessfully proposes a lower income housing project to recover damages, should be granted in most cases unless there are overriding reasons for the denial of the project, and that SDGP designations should normally control the applicability of the *Mount Laurel* obligation to particular municipalities.

f. Regulating Growth

Local communities have become increasingly active in regulating their growth in order to foster a certain type of community ambiance. Sometimes this takes the form of trying to limit the growth of the community.

D. Eminent Domain

1. Introduction

a. Defined

Eminent domain is the power of the government to take privately owned land for public use. Under the Fifth Amendment of the United States Constitution, "just compensation" must be made for the taking.

b. Government "Taking"

If the government uses its eminent domain powers and takes land, it must pay for the land. Whether particular government action constitutes a "taking" is a frequently litigated issue; a taking may be explicit or implicit. If the government takes the property outright, it follows a condemnation proceeding. In some areas, the government must first attempt to purchase from the landowners, but in most jurisdictions, the government petitions the court to condemn the land. Each person having an interest in the subject property is notified, and a trial is held. The government must prove its authority to condemn as well as the value to be paid for compensation. Implicit takings are more troublesome, because the parties may not even agree whether there has been a taking.

2. Public Use

a. Introduction

Condemnation of private property for a private use or purpose is forbidden; the power of eminent domain only extends to condemnation for a public use or purpose. Normally, this means that the government cannot take private property only to turn around and give or sell it to another private party. However, the meaning of the term "public use" depends on what the legislature declares to be the public interest. For the most part, the courts defer to legislative declarations of purpose.

b. Determining Public Use

Kelo v. City of New London
125 S.Ct. 2655 (2005).

Facts. The city of New London (D) was economically distressed; its unemployment rate was almost double that of the state, and its population was at its lowest since 1920. State and local officials targeted D, and its Fort Trumbull area in particular, for economic revitalization. D designated the nonprofit New London Development Corporation ("NLDC") to prepare a plan to revitalize its economy. After the pharmaceutical company Pfizer Inc. announced that it was going to build a $300 million research facility at a location immediately adjacent to Fort Trumbull, NLDC developed a plan to capitalize on the new commerce that the facility was expected to attract. The plan focused on 90 acres of the Fort Trumbull area and sought to create new jobs, increase revenues, and create leisure and recreational opportunities. The plan proposed to develop the area for different uses, including marinas, a conference hotel, new housing, shops and restaurants, research and development office space, and a proposed United States Coast Guard Museum. Not all of the uses were to be opened to the public. The plan was approved, and NLDC was designated to implement the plan and was authorized to acquire the properties slated for redevelopment through purchase or by exercising eminent domain in the city's name. D purchased most of the real estate in the 90-acre area but had to initiate condemnation proceedings to acquire the rest. The nine owners of these parcels (Ps) challenged the takings in the superior court, claiming that D violated the "public use" restriction in the Fifth Amendment. The superior court granted a permanent restraining order prohibiting the taking of some of the properties but found the taking of the other properties to be valid. Ps and Ds appealed to the Connecticut Supreme Court, which upheld all of the takings on the grounds that they were reasonably necessary to achieve the city's intended public use. The Supreme Court granted certiorari.

Issue. Does a city's decision to take property for the purpose of economic development satisfy the "public use" requirement of the Fifth Amendment?

Held. Yes. Judgment affirmed.

♦ The government cannot take the property of a private party for the sole purpose of transferring it to another private party, even with the payment of just compensation. However, the government may transfer property from one private party to another if future use by the public is the reason for the taking (*e.g.*, land for a railroad with common-carrier duties).

♦ Here, although the city's taking is not to benefit specific individuals, the city does not intend to open all of the condemned land to use by the general public. Also, unlike common carriers, the lessees will not be required to make their services available to all. However, to satisfy the "public use" requirement, condemned property need not be put to use for the general public, but it must serve a public purpose. Thus, the disposition of this case rests on a determination of whether the city's plan serves a public purpose.

♦ In previous cases, we have found that community development programs need not be undertaken on a piecemeal basis, individual property by individual property. Broad takings that include properties that are not blighted sometimes occur when a redevelopment area is planned as a whole and the takings are necessary for plans to be successful.

♦ It is the taking's purpose, and not its mechanics, that matters in the determination of public use. We defer to legislative judgments to determine what public needs justify the use of eminent domain. Here, the city invoked a state statute that authorizes the use of eminent domain to advance economic development. The city's determination that the Fort Trumbull area, although not blighted, was sufficiently distressed to justify a plan to revitalize the area is entitled to our deference.

- Ps ask us to adopt a rule that economic development does not qualify as a public use. This position is not supported by precedent or logic. Promoting economic development is a long-accepted governmental function.

- Nothing in our decision prevents the states from restricting the use of eminent domain powers.

Concurrence (Kennedy, J.). While affording legislatures deference in applying the public use test, courts must ensure that a taking does not favor a particular private party and provide only incidental or pretextual public benefits.

Dissent (O'Connor, J., Rehnquist, C.J., Scalia, Thomas, JJ.). In prior cases, three categories of takings have satisfied the public use requirement: transfers of private property to public ownership; transfers of property to private parties, such as common carriers, whose property is available for public use; and transfers of property to private parties as part of a public purpose program. The problem with the third category is that, when the public purpose is economic development, private benefits with incidental public benefits may be justified as long as there is some public advantage. There is usually some incidental benefit to the public when residential property is converted into commercial property. However, the primary beneficiaries of an economic development plan are likely to be those with political power and influence.

Comment. The *Kelo* Court applied its ends test in a very deferential manner, allowing legislatures broad latitude in determining what public needs justify the taking of private property. Some state courts, however, examine the government's justifications with close scrutiny and require the government to show that a project's purposes cannot be achieved by less intrusive means.

---

3. Types of Taking

a. Physical Invasion

Inverse takings were referred to above. If the government invades property substantially enough, it must pay for this de facto taking, even though it has not undertaken a condemnation proceeding. This principle is referred to as inverse condemnation. Physical invasion includes noise, vibration, odors, etc. In this respect it is somewhat similar to nuisance law.

b. Permanent Physical Occupation a Taking

Loretto v. Teleprompter Manhattan CATV Corp.
458 U.S. 419 (1982).

Facts. Loretto (P) bought a New York City apartment building in 1971. The previous owner permitted Teleprompter (D) to install cable on the building and granted D the exclusive privilege of providing cable TV services to the building's tenants. Initially, D's cables did not service P's building but were part of a highway of "crossovers," meaning lines extending from one building to another. D connected a "noncrossover"—a line providing service to a building's own tenants—to P's building two years after she bought it. A 1973 state law prohibited landlords from interfering with the installation of cable TV facilities and from demanding payment from cable companies in excess of an amount deemed reasonable by the state. At that time, reasonable payment was set at $1.00. P sued D, alleging that D trespassed and that the statute allowed taking without just compensation. The trial court held for D and was affirmed on appeal. P appeals.

Issue. Is a minor but permanent physical occupation authorized by government a "taking" of property for which just compensation is due?

Held. Yes. Judgment reversed.

- There is no set formula to determine whether compensation is constitutionally due for a government restriction of property. The degree of interference and economic impact are significant considerations. But when the intrusion is a permanent physical occupation, a taking has occurred, regardless of whether the government's action serves important public interests or has only a slight economic impact on the owner. Moreover, constitutional protection of private property rights does not depend on the size of the area permanently occupied.

- Under this test, D's installation on P's building is a taking. The statute involved here is a valid regulation within the state's police powers. However, it frustrates P's property rights to the extent that compensation is due her.

Dissent (Blackmun, Brennan, White, JJ.). The Court's application of a rigid, per se rule undercuts a carefully considered legislative judgment concerning landlord-tenant relationships. The statute here seeks to carefully balance the interests of all private parties.

---

c. Taking by Regulating

If the government regulates land to the point that it loses all of its value, the injured party can either sue to have the regulation invalidated or seek damages in an inverse condemnation suit. The difficult problems arise when not all the value is lost, but a significant part of the value is.

1) Harm

Some courts hold that the test for determining whether the land has been regulated to the point it has been "taken" involves looking to see if the regulation has as its goal and effect protection of the public from harm. If this is the case, the regulation is a valid exercise of the police power.

2) Loss of Economic Value

Other courts look to see if the regulation deprives the affected land of any practical economic value. The land must have practically no economic value left to it. Sometimes even severe loss is not enough to constitute a taking. [*See* Village of Euclid v. Ambler Realty Co., *supra*] In *Perm Central, infra*, the Supreme Court held that the landowner must be left with some reasonable economic value.

d. The Harm Test

Hadacheck v. Sebastian
239 U.S. 394 (1915).

Facts. Hadacheck (P) was convicted of a misdemeanor for operating a brick kiln in violation of a city ordinance. Sebastian (D) was the chief of police. P operated a brickyard on a parcel of land which, due to the fine quality of its clay, was particularly well adapted to such an operation. Subsequently, the land was annexed by the city of Los Angeles. Later an ordinance was passed prohibiting the operation of brick kilns in the area of town in which P's kiln was located. P continued to run the kiln and was convicted of violating the misdemeanor ordinance and jailed. P sought habeas corpus relief. It was undisputed that on P's land was high quality clay and that the clay could not be transported to some other location. P contended that he was deprived of his property by the ordinance. The state supreme court denied the habeas corpus relief. The Supreme Court granted certiorari.

Issue. Does a city ordinance prohibiting the operation of a heretofore lawful enterprise amount to an implicit taking of the business's property?

Held. No. Judgment affirmed.

- We are dealing with one of the most essential powers of government. To hold that a city cannot change its laws to prohibit existing activities such as P's would preclude development and fix a city forever in its primitive conditions.

- There must be progress and vested private interests must yield to that. This is true even in cases like this where the newly prohibited business is not a nuisance per se. Police powers can be used to regulate a business that is not a nuisance per se.

- Thus, the city can prohibit the operation of brick kilns such as P's. This does not mean, however, that the city can absolutely deprive P of his property. The city, for example, could not prohibit P's removal of clay from his land.

- P contends that the Equal Protection Clause should apply to prevent the city from prohibiting his kiln operation since he has shown that other kilns are permitted in other parts of the city. We reject this contention. Even if brickyards in other localities within the city are not regulated or prohibited, it does not follow that they will not be.

- Further, we reject P's contention that the ordinance fosters a monopoly and suppresses competition.

Comment. The Court held that the city was justified in finding that brickyards, as a class, adversely impacted upon neighboring land. In sum, the Court looked upon the brickyard as a "harmful" or "noxious" use which, like a nuisance, could be abated.

---

e. Total Restriction of Use of Land

Pennsylvania Coal Co. v. Mahon
260 U.S. 393 (1922).

Facts. The Mahons (Ps) purchased the surface rights to certain land from the Pennsylvania Coal Co. (D), which in the deed expressly reserved the right to mine underneath the surface. Ps built a house on the property. Several years later, Pennsylvania enacted the Kohler Act, which forbids mining of coal in such a way as to cause subsidence of human dwellings. Ps sought an injunction against D's mining of coal under their house. The state courts upheld the statute and D appeals.

Issue. May a state regulate use of private property so as to prevent the property owner from using its property?

Held (Holmes, J.). No. Judgment reversed.

- Exercise of the police power necessarily affects some property rights. Government could not act if it had to pay for every diminution of property values caused by the laws it enacts. However, the exercise of the police power is limited by due process.

- One consideration in determining the limits is the extent of the diminution. When it reaches a certain magnitude, there must be an exercise of eminent domain and compensation to sustain the state's action.

- In this case there is a single private house. The source of damage to such house is not a public nuisance; damage is not common or public. In dealing with Ps' position alone, it is clear that the statute does not disclose a public interest sufficient to warrant so extensive a destruction of D's constitutionally protected rights to mine its coal.

- A strong public desire to improve the public condition is not enough to warrant achieving the desire by a shorter route than the constitutional way of paying for the change. Whether compensation is required for taking is a matter of degree. Clearly, it is here so required. The statute is unconstitutional in providing for such a drastic taking without compensation. So far as private persons or communities have seen fit to take the risk of acquiring only surface rights, the fact that their risk has become a danger does not warrant giving to them greater rights than they bought.

Dissent (Brandeis, J.). The right of an owner to use his land to mine coal is not absolute. He may not so use land as to create a public nuisance; and uses, once harmless, may, owing to changed conditions, threaten the public welfare seriously. Whenever they do, the legislature has power to prohibit such uses without paying compensation; and power to prohibit extends alike to manner, character, and purpose of the use. A prohibition of mining that causes subsidence of structures is obviously enacted for a public purpose; and it is likewise clear that mere notice of intention to mine would not in this connection secure public safety. The majority's conclusion that the statute is unconstitutional seems to rest on the assumption that in order to justify such an exercise of the police power there must be "an average reciprocity of advantage" as between the owner of the property restricted and the rest of the community, and that such reciprocity is lacking here. Reciprocity is an important consideration when a state's power is exercised for the purpose of conferring benefits on property of a neighborhood, as in drainage projects, or on adjoining owners, as by party wall provisions. But when police power is exercised, not to confer benefits upon property owners, but to protect the public from danger and detriment, there is no room for considering reciprocity of advantage. There was no reciprocal advantage to the owner prohibited from using his oil tanks, brickyard, billiard hall, oleomargarine factory, etc., unless it be the advantage of living and doing business in a civilized community. That reciprocal advantage is given to the coal operators by the Act.

Comment. There was no fact-finding as to the "commercial practicability" of mining after the state interference by the Kohler Act.

---

f.   Historical Landmarks

Penn Central Transportation Co. v. City of New York
439 U.S. 883 (1978).

Facts. Grand Central Terminal in New York City (D) was designated an historical landmark in 1967 under New York City's Landmark Preservation Law. In 1968, Penn Central Transportation Co. (P), owner of Grand Central Terminal, entered into a renewable 50-year lease with UGP Properties, Inc., under which UGP was to construct a multistory office building above the terminal. A noted architect was hired to design the proposed structure and two different plans (one for construction of a 55-story building and the other for a 53-story building) were submitted to the Landmarks Preservation Commission for approval. Both proposals were rejected and P sued D, claiming that its property had been taken without just compensation. The trial court granted injunctive and declaratory relief to P but referred the question of damages to the appellate division. The appellate division held that the restrictions on development of the terminal were necessary to promote the legitimate public purpose of protecting landmarks, and reversed judgment. The New York Court of Appeals then affirmed and P appeals to the Supreme Court.

Issue. May a city restrict development of individual historic landmarks, beyond applicable zoning regulations, without a "taking" requiring payment of just compensation?

Held. Yes. Judgment affirmed.

♦   The question here revolves around two basic considerations: (i) the nature and extent of the impact on P, and (ii) the character of the governmental action.

♦   The "taking" may not be established by merely showing a government-imposed inability to further develop a property, nor is a diminution in property value determinative. Zoning laws have these effects yet are constitutional because they are part of a comprehensive plan for achieving a significant public purpose, as is D's law.

- P claims the law is discriminatory and arbitrary. Yet numerous other structures are likewise under the landmark regulations. Even if P does not receive benefits to completely offset its burdens, valid zoning laws may have a similar effect. If P finds application of the law to be arbitrary, it may obtain judicial review of any commission decision.

- The government has not taken P's airspace for its own purpose, but for the benefit of the entire public. It has done so pursuant to a legitimate interest in preserving special buildings. The Landmark Preservation Law does not effect a taking of P's property.

- Finally, the impact on P is mitigated by the existence of Transferable Development Rights ("TDRs"), which gives P the opportunity to enhance other properties. P has not been completely prohibited from making improvements. Only the two drastic proposals were rejected by D. Thus P may yet be permitted the use of at least some portion of its airspace.

Dissent (Rehnquist, J., Burger, C.J., Stevens, J.).

- A literal interpretation of the Fifth Amendment would clearly favor P. Even the majority's more relaxed approach would result in a decision for P.

- P's valuable property rights have been destroyed. Destruction of rights is a taking, except in two instances: (i) prohibition of nuisances and (ii) prohibitions covering broad areas that secure an average reciprocity of advantage, such as the zoning laws. Neither exception applies here.

- The people generally, not P individually, ought to pay the cost of the recognized public benefit of having P's property preserved. D contends that the transfer development rights granted to P with respect to other properties was "just compensation" if in fact there was a taking. However, because the lower court found no "taking," the question of whether or not just compensation has already been awarded was never considered.

---

g. Property Value Extinguished

Lucas v. South Carolina Coastal Council
505 U.S. 1003 (1992).

Facts. Lucas (P) purchased two beachfront lots in 1986 on which he planned to build single-family homes. Subsequently, in 1988 the legislature enacted the Beachfront Management Act ("Act"), which barred construction of occupiable improvements in an area that included P's lots. P did not contest the validity of the Act as a lawful exercise of police power, but filed suit, contending that the Act's complete extinguishment of his property's value entitled him to compensation. The trial court found for P; among its factual determinations were that at the time P purchased the lots, they were zoned for single-family residential construction and there were no state or county restrictions imposed on such use of the property. The state supreme court reversed; because P had not contested the validity of the statute, the court felt it was bound to accept the legislature's finding that new construction threatened this public resource, that the statute was designed to prevent serious public harm, and no compensation was due P. P petitioned for certiorari.

Issue. Does the Act's effect of rendering P's property valueless accomplish a taking of private property under the Fifth and Fourteenth Amendments requiring payment of just compensation?

Held. Yes. Judgment reversed and case remanded.

- The state supreme court erred in applying the "harmful or noxious uses" principle to decide this case.

- Regulations that deny the property owner all "economically viable use of his land" constitute one of the discrete categories of regulatory deprivations that require compensation without the usual case-specific inquiry into the public interest advanced in support of the restraint. Although the Court has never set forth the justification for this categorical rule, the practical—

and economic—equivalence of physically appropriating and eliminating all beneficial use of land counsels its preservation.

♦ A review of the relevant decisions demonstrates that the "harmful or noxious use" principle was merely this Court's early formulation of the police power justification necessary to sustain (without compensation) any regulatory diminution in value; that the distinction between regulation that "prevents harmful use" and that which "confers benefits" is difficult, if not impossible, to discern on an objective, value-free basis; and that, therefore, noxious-use logic cannot be the basis for departing from this Court's categorical rule that total regulatory takings must be compensated.

♦ Rather, the question must turn, in accord with this Court's "takings" jurisprudence, on citizens' historic understandings regarding the content of, and the state's power over, the "bundle of rights" that they acquire when they take title to property. Because it is not consistent with the historical compact embodied in the Takings Clause that title to real estate is held subject to the state's subsequent decision to eliminate all economically beneficial use, a regulation having that effect cannot be newly decreed, and sustained, without compensation being paid to the owner. However, no compensation is owed—in this setting as with all takings claims—if the state's affirmative decree simply makes explicit what already inheres in the title itself, in the restrictions that background principles of the state's law of property and nuisance already place upon land ownership.

♦ Although it seems unlikely that common law principles would have prevented the erection of any habitable or productive improvements on P's land, this state law question must be dealt with on remand. To win its case D cannot simply proffer the legislature's declaration that the uses P desires are inconsistent with the public interest, or the conclusory assertion that they violate a common law maxim such as *sic utere tuo ut alienum non laedas*, but must identify back-ground principles of nuisance and property law that prohibit the uses P now intends in the property's present circumstances.

Concurrence (Kennedy, J.). In my view, reasonable expectations must be understood in light of the whole of our legal tradition. The common law of nuisance is too narrow a confine for the exercise of regulatory power in a complex and interdependent society.

Dissent (Blackmun, J.). I find no clear and accepted "historical compact" or "under-standing of our citizens" justifying the Court's new taking doctrine. Instead, the Court seems to treat history as a grab-bag of principles to be adopted when they support the Court's theory, and ignored when they do not.

Dissent (Stevens, J.). The test the Court announces is that the regulation must do no more than duplicate the result that could have been achieved under a state's nuisance law. Under this test the categorical rule will apply unless the regulation merely makes explicit what was otherwise an implicit limitation on the owner's property rights. The Court is doubly in error. The categorical rule the Court establishes is an unsound and unwise addition to the law and the Court's formulation of the exception to that rule is too rigid and too narrow.

———————

h. Post-Enactment Purchase

Palazzolo v. Rhode Island
533 U.S. 606 (2001).

Facts. In 1959, Palazzolo (P) formed a corporation with some associates and purchased a parcel of waterfront property. P later became the sole shareholder. He submitted a subdivision plat and made attempts to develop the property, all of which were rejected by the governing agencies. In 1971, Rhode Island (D) created a Coastal Resources Management Council that promulgated regulations for development of coastal wetlands, including salt marshes such as those on P's property. In 1978, the property passed to P from the corporation. In 1983, P submitted new proposals for development. The applicable regulations required a "special exception" for a landowner wanting to fill a salt marsh, which required that the activity serve a compelling public purpose. P's applications were not approved. P sued for inverse condemnation, claiming he had been deprived of all economically beneficial use of his property. The trial court found for D. The Rhode Island Supreme Court affirmed, holding that P's takings claim was not ripe, that he could not challenge regulations that predated 1978 when he became the owner, and that the fact that one parcel of his property had a development value of $200,000 defeated his claim of deprivation of all economically beneficial use. The court also held that P's *Penn Central, supra*, claim was barred because he obtained the land after the regulation had been in effect. The Supreme Court granted certiorari.

Issue. Is a landowner barred from challenging land use regulations that were adopted prior to the time he acquired the property?

Held (Kennedy J.). No. Judgment affirmed in part and reversed in part and case remanded.

♦ The state courts held that P's post-regulation acquisition of title was fatal to his *Lucas, supra*, (deprivation of all economically beneficial use) and *Penn Central* (taking by defeat of reasonable investment-backed expectation) claims. The rationale is that a purchaser is deemed to have notice of an earlier-enacted restriction and cannot claim that it effects a taking. This approach would allow a state to avoid its obligation to defend its actions restricting land use, no matter how extreme or unreasonable. D could effectively put an expiration date on the Takings Clause. An unreasonable land regulation does not become reasonable through passage of time or title.

♦ The ripeness requirement may take years to satisfy, and D's rule would prevent a successor in interest from asserting a right to compensation even when the claim does become ripe. A newly regulated landowner should not be stripped of the ability to transfer an interest that was possessed prior to the regulation. This is not like direct condemnation, whereby the state pays compensation to the owner and thereby terminates any future right of compensation. A regulation that otherwise would be unconstitutional without compensation does not become a background principle of state law by mere virtue of the passage of title to a new owner.

♦ The court's holding that P was not deprived of all economically beneficial use because the uplands portion of P's property can still be developed is supported in the record. While a state may not evade a compensation duty by leaving a landowner with a token interest, the $200,000 value of P's parcel is substantial enough to defeat P's *Lucas* claim. P's claim that this parcel is distinct from his wetlands parcel was not presented to the lower courts and so cannot be addressed. Because P's claims were ripe and were not barred by his acquisition of the property after the regulation was adopted, on remand, the courts must consider P's *Penn Central* claim.

Concurrence (O'Connor, J.). The Takings Clause demands a careful examination of all of the relevant factors under *Penn Central,* not only the state of regulatory affairs at the time of acquisition.

Concurrence (Scalia, J.). My idea regarding the court's discussion on remand is not Justice O'Connor's. The fact that a restriction existed at the time the purchaser took title should have no bearing on the determination of whether the restriction is so substantial as to constitute a taking.

Concurrence and dissent (Stevens, J.). Where owners have notice of a regulation when they purchase property, but the regulatory event constituting the taking does not happen until after they have title, I would treat the owners' notice as relevant but not necessarily dispositive as to whether the regulation goes "too far."

Dissent (Ginsburg, Souter, Breyer, JJ.). The simple fact that a piece of property has changed hands does not always and automatically bar a takings claim.

---

i. Temporary Moratoriums

Tahoe-Sierra Preservation Council, Inc. v. Tahoe Regional Planning Agency

535 U.S. 302 (2002).

Facts. The clarity of Lake Tahoe was deteriorating due to an increase of development in the area. Because the Lake Tahoe Basin is located in both California and Nevada, those states created the Tahoe Regional Planning Agency (D) to regulate development in the basin and to conserve its natural resources. Between 1981 and 1984, in order to maintain the status quo in the area while studying the impact of development and determining an environmental plan, D issued two moratoria prohibiting development on a substantial portion of the property for 32 months. A class of real estate owners affected by the moratoria and the Tahoe-Sierra Preservation Council, an association representing such owners, (Ps) filed parallel suits, which were later consolidated. Ps claimed that D's actions constituted a taking of their property without just compensation. The district court found that D had not effected a "partial taking" under the analysis adopted in *Penn Central Transportation Co. v. New York City (supra)*. However, the court concluded that the moratoria did constitute a taking under the categorical rule of *Lucas v. South Carolina Coastal Council (supra)*, because D temporarily deprived Ps of all economically viable use of their land. Both parties appealed. The court of appeals held that *Lucas* did not apply because the regulations had only a temporary impact on petitioners' fee interest, and no categorical taking had occurred. The court further found that *Penn Central's* ad hoc balancing approach was appropriate for analyzing whether a taking had occurred. However, Ps had rejected that theory and had not challenged the district court's conclusion that they could not make out a claim under the *Penn Central* factors. The Supreme Court granted certiorari.

Issue. Does a moratorium on development imposed during the process of devising a comprehensive land-use plan constitute a per se taking of property requiring compensation under the Fifth Amendment's Takings Clause?

Held. No. Judgment affirmed.

♦ The Takings Clause of the Fifth Amendment requires the government to pay compensation whenever it acquires private property for a public purpose, even if that use is temporary. However, the distinction between acquisitions of property for public use and regulations prohibiting private uses makes it inappropriate to apply precedent from the physical takings context to regulatory takings claims.

♦ Ps rely on *Lucas*, which is a regulatory takings case, to argue for a categorical rule that whenever the government imposes a deprivation of all economically viable use of property, no matter how brief, it effects a taking. However, *Lucas* applies to cases in which a regulation causes a permanent deprivation of use. It does not apply to temporary takings.

♦ The district court erred when it divided Ps' property into temporal segments corresponding to the regulations and then considered whether Ps were deprived of all productive use during each period. The focus must be on the parcel as a whole, which is defined by its geographic dimensions and also by the term of years that constitutes the temporal aspect of the owner's interest. The court should have determined whether there was a total taking of a whole parcel; if there was not, the court should have applied *Penn Central*.

♦ Ps argue that considerations of fairness and justice and the interest in protecting property owners from bearing public burdens justify the application of a categorical rule. However, fairness and justice will not be better served by a categorical rule that any deprivation of all economic use, even if temporary, constitutes a compensable taking. Such a rule would apply to such normal delays as obtaining building permits and would require changes in practices that have long been considered permissible exercises of the police power. In a regulatory takings case, the concepts of fairness and justice are better served by a *Penn Central* analysis of the particular circumstances of the case.

- Although some Ps may have prevailed under a *Penn Central* ad hoc analysis, Ps failed to appeal from the district court's conclusion that the evidence did not support a *Penn Central* claim.

- A moratorium on development imposed during the formulation of a land-use plan does not constitute a per se taking of property requiring compensation. However, the temporary nature of a land-use restriction does not necessarily mean that there has not been a taking; the duration of the restriction is just one of the factors that must be considered in a regulatory takings case.

---

j. Judicial Takings

Stop the Beach Renourishment, Inc. v. Florida Department of Environmental Protection
560 U.S. 702 (2010).

Facts. Florida owns in trust for the public the land permanently submerged beneath navigable waters, and the foreshore is owned by the state of Florida in trust for the public. The mean high-water line, (the average reach of high tide over the preceding 19 years) is the ordinary boundary between private beachfront, or littoral property, and state-owned land. Littoral owners have, *inter alia,* rights to have access to the water, to use the water for certain purposes, to have an unobstructed view of the water, and to receive accretions and relictions to the littoral property. Central to this case is the right to accretions and relictions. Accretions are additions of alluvion (sand, sediment, or other deposits) to waterfront land; relictions are lands once covered by water that become dry when the water recedes. In order for an addition to dry land to qualify as an accretion, it must have occurred gradually and imperceptibly—that is, so slowly that one could not see the change occurring, though over time the difference became apparent. In contrast, when there is a "sudden or perceptible loss of or addition to land by the action of the water or a sudden change in the bed of a lake or the course of a stream," the change is called an avulsion. The littoral owner automatically takes title to dry land added to his property by accretion. With avulsion, however, the seaward boundary of littoral property remains what it was: the mean high-water line before the event. Thus, when an avulsion has added new land, the littoral owner has no right to subsequent accretions, because the property abutting the water belongs to the owner of the seabed (usually, the State). Florida's Beach and Shore Preservation Act (Act) establishes procedures for depositing sand on eroded beaches (restoration) and maintaining the deposited sand (nourishment).

Once a beach restoration "is determined to be undertaken," the Board of Trustees of the Internal Improvements Trust Fund (Board) sets what is called "an erosion control line." It must be set by reference to the existing mean high-water line, though in theory it can be located seaward or landward of that. Much of the project work occurs seaward of the erosion control line, as sand is dumped on what was once submerged land. The fixed erosion-control line replaces the fluctuating mean high-water line as the boundary between privately owned littoral property and state property. Once the new line is recorded, the common law ceases to apply. Thereafter, when accretion moves the mean high-water line seaward, the littoral property remains bounded by the permanent erosion-control line. Those private landowners "continue to be entitled," however, "to all common-law riparian rights" other than the right to accretions. If the beach erodes back landward of the erosion-control line over a substantial portion of the shoreline covered by the project, the Board may, on its own initiative, or must, if asked by the owners or lessees of a majority of the property affected, direct the agency responsible for maintaining the beach to return the beach to the condition contemplated by the project. If that is not done within a year, the project is canceled and the erosion-control line is null and void. Finally, by regulation, if the use of submerged land would "unreasonably infringe on riparian rights," the project cannot proceed unless the local governments show that they own or have a property interest in the upland property adjacent to the project site.

The city of Destin and Walton County (Ds) sought permits to restore 6.9 miles of beach eroded by several hurricanes, adding about 75 feet of dry sand seaward of the mean high-water line (to be denominated the erosion-control line). The Department of Environmental Protection (Department) issued a notice of intent to award the permits, and the Board approved the erosion-control line. Stop the Beach Renourishment, Inc. (P), a non-profit corporation formed by owners of beachfront property bordering the project area brought an administrative challenge to the proposed project, which was unsuccessful. The permits were approved. P then challenged that action in state court under the Act. The appeals court rescinded the permit, holding that issuance would have resulted in an unconstitutional taking; it concluded that, contrary to the Act's preservation of "all common-law riparian rights," the order had eliminated two of the Ps' littoral rights: (i) the right to receive accretions to their property; and (ii) the right to have the contact of their property with the water remain intact, which would "unreasonably infringe on riparian rights," and therefore require the showing that the local governments owned or had a property interest in the upland property. The state supreme court found that the doctrine of avulsion allowed the state to reclaim the restored beach on the public's behalf. The court described the right to accretions as a future contingent interest, not a vested property right, and held that there is no littoral right to contact with the water independent of the littoral right of access, which the Act does not infringe. P sought rehearing; the request was denied. We granted certiorari.

Issue. By reversing longstanding holdings that littoral rights are constitutionally protected, did the Florida supreme court cause a "judicial taking" proscribed by the Fifth and Fourteenth Amendments?

Held (Scalia, J.). No. Judgment affirmed.

The Takings Clause—"nor shall private property be taken for public use, without just compensation," applies as fully to the taking of a landowner's riparian rights as it does to the taking of an estate in land. Likewise, our doctrine of regulatory takings "aims to identify regulatory actions that are functionally equivalent to the classic taking." *Lingle v. Chevron U.S.A. Inc.*, 544 U.S. 528, 539 (2005). States also can effect a taking if they recharacterize as public property what was previously private property, *i.e.*, the situation before us.

The Takings Clause is concerned with the act, not the actor. The scope of governmental power to expropriate private property without just compensation does not vary according to the branch of government involved.

Our precedents provide no support for the proposition that takings effected by the judicial branch are entitled to special treatment, and in fact suggest the contrary. See *PruneYard Shopping Center v. Robins,* 447 U.S. 74 (1980), and *Webb's Fabulous Pharmacies, Inc. v. Beckwith*, 449 U.S. 155.

In *Webb's Fabulous Pharmacies*, the purchaser of an insolvent corporation had interpleaded the corporation's creditors, placing the purchase price in an interest-bearing account in the registry of the state's county circuit court to be distributed in satisfaction of claims approved by a receiver. The Florida supreme court construed an applicable statute to mean that the interest on the account belonged to the county, because the account was "considered 'public money,' " We determined this to be a taking. We noted that "[t]he usual and general rule is that any interest on an interpleaded and deposited fund follows the principal and is to be allocated to those who are ultimately to be the owners of that principal." "Neither the Florida Legislature by statute, nor the Florida courts by judicial decree," we said, "may accomplish the result the county seeks simply by recharacterizing the principal as 'public money.' " Thus, The Takings Clause bars any instrument of the State from taking private property without paying for it. The manner of state action may matter, however: Condemnation by eminent domain is always a taking, while a legislative, executive, or judicial restriction of property use may or may not be, depending on its nature and extent.

Justice Kennedy concurs in our judgment, but disagrees with our approach. He would have us apply the Due Process Clause, but is not clear which aspect he is applying, the substantive or procedural aspect. His first argument is the courts are not designed to make policy decisions about expropriation and we would be on firm ground were we to rule that a judicial decision that does away with or substantially changes established property rights violates the Due Process Clause.

To be clear, we have held that the separation-of-powers principles that the Constitution imposes upon the Federal Government do not apply against the States. So, to have us avoid the risky step of saying the Takings Clause applies to all government takings, Justice Kennedy would have us use Procedural Due Process to impose judicially crafted separation-of-powers limitations upon the States: courts cannot be used to perform the governmental function of expropriation. The reason given for the due process limitation are that the legislative and executive branches "are accountable in their political capacity" for takings and "[c]ourts . . . are not designed to make policy decisions" about takings. These reasons have nothing to do with the protection of individual rights that is the object of the Due Process Clause.

Justice Kennedy's injection of separation-of-powers principles into the Due Process Clause would, ironically, prevent the assignment of the expropriation function to the branch of government whose procedures are, by far, the *most* protective of individual rights.

Justice Kennedy's other argument pertains to Substantive Due Process, evidenced by his assertion that "[i]t is . . . natural to read the Due Process Clause as limiting the power of courts to eliminate or change established property rights," his endorsement of the proposition that the Due Process Clause imposes "limits on government's ability to diminish property values by regulation," and his contention that "the Due Process Clause would likely prevent a State from doing by judicial decree what the Takings Clause forbids it to do by legislative fiat."

We have held that Substantive Due Process cannot be used to do the work of the Takings Clause. "Where a particular Amendment 'provides an explicit textual source of constitutional protection' against a particular sort of government behavior, 'that Amendment, not the more generalized notion of "substantive due process," must be the guide for analyzing these claims.'" *Albright v. Oliver*, 510 U.S. 266, 273 (1994) (quoting *Graham v. Connor*, 490 U.S. 386, 395 (1989)); *see also* 510 U.S., at 281 (Kennedy, J., concurring in judgment) ("I agree with the plurality that an allegation of arrest without probable cause must be analyzed under the Fourth Amendment without reference to more general considerations of due process").

The second problem is that we have held for many years that the "liberties" protected by Substantive Due Process do not include economic liberties.

There are two other considerations, Justice Kennedy contends we need to address before recognizing judicial takings. One of them is simple and simply answered: the assertion that "it is unclear what remedy a reviewing court could enter after finding a judicial taking." He worries that we may only be able to mandate compensation. In fact, that remedy is even rare for a legislative or executive taking, and there is no reason why it would be the exclusive remedy for a judicial taking. Here, if we were to hold in P's favor, we would simply reverse the Florida court's judgment. The second hurdle Justice Kennedy sees is the determination of when a claim of a judicial taking must be asserted. That and the other "difficulties" Justice Kennedy asserts are either nonexistent or insignificant.

Justice Kennedy places no constraints whatever upon *us*. In his concurrence, he only thinks about applying Substantive Due Process; "but because Substantive Due Process is such a wonderfully malleable concept even a firm commitment to apply it would be a firm commitment to nothing in particular."

Respondents argue that federal courts lack knowledge of state law needed to determine whether a decision that purports to clarify property rights has, instead, taken them. To the contrary, federal courts often decide what property rights exist in nontakings contexts. It is impossible for federal courts to enforce a constitutional provision that forbids uncompensated takings unless they have the power to decide what property rights exist under state law.

Respondents also warn us against the absence of flexibility. We have no need of flexibility here. It is not essential that judges be free to overrule prior cases that establish property entitlements any more than that state legislators be free to revise pre-existing statutes that confer property entitlements, or agency heads pre-existing regulations that do so. And because courts simply clarify and elaborate property entitlements that were previously unclear, they cannot be said to have taken an established property right.

Regarding P's proposition that a judicial taking consists of decision that "constitutes a sudden change in state law, unpredictable in terms of relevant precedents," the focus of this test is misdirected. It is not whether there is a precedent for the alleged confiscatory taking that counts, but whether the property right allegedly taken was established. A judicial property decision need not be predictable, so long as it does not declare that what had been private property under established law no longer is. A decision clarifying property entitlements (or the lack thereof) that were previously unclear might be hard to predict, but it does not eliminate established property rights. A judicial elimination of established private property rights that is foreshadowed by dicta or even by holdings years in advance is nonetheless a taking.

Regarding the decision below, P contends the court took two of P's property rights by holding those rights did not exist. P's theory is because no prior Florida court had held the state's filling of submerged tidal lands could have the effect of depriving a littoral owner of contact with the water and denying him future accretions, the Florida court's judgment in this case took away those two easements to which littoral property owners had been entitled. This puts the burden on the wrong party. There is no taking unless P can show that, before the Florida court's decision, littoral-property owners had rights to future accretions and contact with the water superior to the State's right to fill in its submerged land. Though some may think the question close, we determine the showing cannot be made.

Two basic principles of Florida property law collide here. The State as owner of the submerged land adjacent to littoral property has the right to fill that land, so long as it does not interfere with the rights of the public and the rights of littoral landowners. In addition, if an avulsion exposes land seaward of littoral property that had previously been submerged, that land belongs to the State even if it interrupts the littoral owner's contact with the water.

The issue here is whether there is an exception to this rule when the State is the cause of the avulsion. Prior law suggests there is not. In *Martin v. Busch*, 93 Fla. 535, 112 So. 274 (1927), the Florida supreme court held that when the State drained water from a lakebed belonging to the State, causing land that was formerly below the mean high water line to become dry land, that land continued to belong to the State. " 'The riparian rights doctrine of accretion and reliction,' " the Florida Supreme Court later explained, " 'does not apply to such lands.' " This is not surprising, as there can be no accretions to land that no longer abuts the water.

Thus, Florida law as it stood prior the decision below permitted the State to fill in its own seabed, and the resulting sudden exposure of previously submerged land was treated like an avulsion for purposes of ownership. The right to accretions was therefore subordinate to the State's right to fill.

The Florida supreme court decision before us is consistent with these background principles of state property law. It did not abolish the P's right to future accretions, but merely held that the right was not implicated by the beach-restoration project, because the doctrine of avulsion applied. The opinion describes beach restoration as the reclamation by the State of the public's land, just as *Martin* had described the lake drainage in that case. Although the opinion does not cite *Martin* and is not always clear on this point, it suffices that its characterization of the littoral right to accretion is consistent with *Martin* and the other relevant principles of Florida law we have discussed.

P's property has been deprived of its character and value as oceanfront property by the State's artificial creation of an avulsion. Maybe state-created avulsions should be treated differently from other avulsions insofar as the property right to accretion is concerned. But nothing in prior Florida law makes such a distinction, and *Martin* suggests, if it does not indeed hold, the contrary. Even if there might be different interpretations of *Martin* and other Florida property-law cases that would prevent this arguably odd result, we are not free to adopt them. The Takings Clause only protects property rights as they are established under state law, not as they might have been established or ought to have been established. We cannot say that the decision below eliminated a right of accretion established under Florida law.

Concurrence in part and in the judgment (Kennedy, Sotomayor, JJ.). While the Court's analysis of the principles that control ownership of the land at issue and the P's rights as adjacent owners is correct; however this case does not require the Court to determine whether, or when, a judicial decision determining property owners' rights can violate the Takings Clause. If and when future cases show that the usual principles, including constitutional ones that constrain the judiciary like due process, are inadequate to protect property owners, then the question whether a judicial decision can effect a taking would be properly presented.

Concurrence in part and in the judgment (Breyer, Ginsburg, JJ.). No unconstitutional taking occurred here, but it is unnecessary to decide more than that to resolve this case. Difficult questions of constitutional law—*e.g.,* whether federal courts may review a state court's decision to determine if it unconstitutionally takes private property without compensation, and what the proper test is for evaluating whether a state-court property decision enacts an unconstitutional taking—need not be addressed. Such questions are better left for another day.

----

k. Access to Public Property

Nollan v. California Coastal Commission
483 U.S. 825 (1987).

Facts. The Nollans (Ps) purchased a beachfront lot in southern California on the condition that they replace the existing structure with a new one. Ps applied to the California Coastal Commission (D) for permission to build a home like the others in the neighborhood, but D required Ps to grant a public easement across their property to the ocean. Ps sued and won a judgment. D appealed, but meanwhile Ps built the house. The state court of appeals reversed, and Ps appeal.

Issue. If a state may not require uncompensated conveyance of an easement over private property, may it require the conveyance as a condition to its approval of a land use permit for the property?

Held. No. Judgment reversed.

♦ It is clear that if D had simply required Ps to grant a public easement across their property, there would have been a taking. Such an easement constitutes a permanent physical occupation, and the right to exclude others is an essential stick in the bundle of rights that constitutes property.

♦ A land use regulation is permissible if it substantially advances legitimate state interests and does not deny an owner economically viable use of his land. If a condition is imposed short of an outright ban on construction, it must serve the same governmental purpose as the ban would. Otherwise, the condition is not a valid land use regulation but extortion. If the condition is unrelated to the purported purpose, the true purpose must be evaluated.

♦ In this case, D claims Ps' new house interferes with "visual access" to the beach, which in turn will cause a "psychological barrier" to the public's desire for access. D also claims Ps' house will increase the use of the public beaches. Each of these burdens on "access" would be alleviated by the easement over Ps' property. These arguments are nothing more than a play on words, however. The condition is not the exercise of the land use power for any of the state's purposes. It simply lacks any substantial advancing of a legitimate state interest.

♦ D's final justification is that the easement would serve the public interest, but a mere belief that the public interest would be served is insufficient. D must use its power of eminent domain to acquire the easement if it wants it.

1. Rough Proportionality Standard

Dolan v. City of Tigard

512 U.S. 374 (1994).

Facts. Pursuant to Oregon's land use management program, Tigard developed a Community Development Code ("CDC") that required property owners in the Central Business District to provide 15% of open space and landscaping, limiting structures and paved parking areas to 85% of a parcel; required new development to dedicate land for a bicycle/pedestrian pathway; and required other improvements in the Fanno Creek Basin. Dolan applied to the city for a permit to double the size of her plumbing and electrical supply store and pave the parking lot. The permit was granted, subject to conditions imposed by the CDC. Dolan was required to dedicate a part of her property lying within the 100-year floodplain for improvement of a storm drainage system along Fanno Creek, and to dedicate an additional 15-foot strip of land adjacent to the floodplain as a bicycle/pedestrian pathway. Dolan was unsuccessful in her request for a variance. The city reasoned that the dedicated pathway would be used by additional customers and provide an alternate means of transportation, offsetting traffic; it reasoned that the floodplain dedication was reasonably related to Dolan's request to intensify the use of the site, thereby increasing storm water flow. Dolan appealed unsuccessfully to the Land Use Board of Appeals. The court of appeals affirmed, as did the Oregon Supreme Court. The Supreme Court granted certiorari.

Issues.

(i) Does an essential nexus exist between the legitimate state interest in land use regulation and the permit condition exacted by the city?

(ii) Does the degree of exaction demanded by the city's permit conditions bear the required relationship to the projected impact of Dolan's proposed development?

Held. (i) Yes. (ii) No. Judgment reversed and case remanded.

♦ In *Nollan v. California Coastal Commission (supra)*, we held that the government authority to require a landowner to deed portions of her property to the city was prohibited by the Fifth and Fourteenth Amendments. Under the well-settled doctrine of "unconstitutional conditions," the government may not require a person to give up a constitutional right—here the right to receive just compensation when property is taken for a public use—in exchange for a discretionary benefit conferred by the government where the benefit sought has little or no relationship to the property.

♦ The city's interest in prevention of flooding along Fanno Creek and the reduction of traffic congestion are legitimate public purposes, and a nexus exists between preventing flooding and limiting development within the creek's 100-year floodplain. Similarly, a pathway for bicycles/pedestrians provides a useful alternative to reduce traffic congestion.

♦ In *Nollan, supra*, we said, "[A] use restriction may constitute a taking if not reasonably necessary to the effectuation of a substantial government purpose."

♦ Here, the city required that Dolan dedicate to the city all of her property that fell within the floodplain and the property 15 feet above the floodplain boundary; it required that Dolan's store not intrude on the greenway area. The city relied on tentative findings that storm water flow from Dolan's property "can only add to the public need to manage the [floodplain] for drainage purposes" to conclude that the required dedication was related to Dolan's development plan. In regard to the pathway, the city found it "*could* offset some of the traffic demand...." (Emphasis added.)

- The standard required by the Fifth Amendment is "rough proportionality," no precise mathematical calculation, but some sort of individualized determination that the required dedication is related both in nature and extent to the impact of the proposed development.

- Here, the city not only wanted Dolan not to build on the floodplain, but it demanded her property along the Creek. The city has never said why a public greenway, as opposed to a private one, was required in the interest of flood control, or why a recreational easement was required for flood control.

- For Dolan, it means loss of the ability to exclude others, one of the most essential property rights. Even though Dolan is enlarging a retail establishment to attract more customers, she also wants to control the time and manner in which they enter. With the permanent recreational easement the city plans, Dolan would lose these rights along with the right to exclude.

- The findings on which the city relies do not show the required reasonable relationship between the floodplain easement and Dolan's new building.

---

m. Inverse Condemnation

Koontz v. St. Johns River Water Management District
133 S.Ct. 2586 (2013).

Facts. In 1972, Koontz (P) purchased an undeveloped 14.9-acre tract of land in the St. Johns River Water Management District (D).

Although largely classified as wetlands by the State, the northern section drains well; the most significant standing water forms in ruts in an unpaved road. The natural topography of the property's southern section is diverse, with a small creek, forested uplands, and wetlands that sometimes have water as much as a foot deep.

Also in 1972, Florida enacted the Water Resources Act (Act), which divided the State into five water management districts and authorized each district to regulate "construction that connects to, draws water from, drains water into, or is placed in or across the waters in the state." Under the Act, a landowner wishing to undertake such construction must obtain from the relevant district a Management and Storage of Surface Water (MSSW) permit, which may impose "such reasonable conditions" on the permit as are "necessary to assure" that construction will "not be harmful to the water resources of the district."

In 1984, the Florida Legislature passed the Henderson Wetlands Protection Act, which made it illegal for anyone to "dredge or fill in, on, or over surface waters" without a Wetlands Resource Management (WRM) permit. Under the Henderson Act, permit applicants are required to provide "reasonable assurance" that proposed construction on wetlands is "not contrary to the public interest," as defined by an enumerated list of criteria. D requires that permit applicants wishing to build on wetlands offset the resulting environmental damage by creating, enhancing, or preserving wetlands elsewhere. When P decided to develop his land, he applied for the necessary permits and proposed raising the elevation of the northernmost section of his land to make it suitable for a building, grading the land, and installing a dry-bed pond for retaining and gradually releasing storm water runoff from the building and its parking lot. To mitigate the environmental effects of his proposal, P offered to foreclose any possible future development of the approximately 11-acre southern section of his land by deeding to the District a conservation easement on that portion of his property. D found the easement inadequate, and told P it would approve construction only if he either reduced the size of his development to 1 acre, deeded to D a conservation easement on the remaining 13.9 acres, and eliminated the dry-bed pond and instead installed a more costly subsurface storm water management system beneath the building site; or, if P built only on 3.7 acres and deeded a conservation easement to the government on the remainder of the property, and if he also agreed to hire contractors to make improvements to D-owned land several miles away. Either choice would improve approximately 50 acres of D-owned wetlands. As is its practice when it asks permit applicants to fund offsite mitigation work, D never requires any particular offsite project, and it did not do so here. Instead, D said that it "would also favorably consider" alternatives to its suggested offsite mitigation projects if petitioner proposed something "equivalent." P found D's demands to be excessive and filed suit in state court. P argued he was entitled to relief under a Florida statute that allows owners to recover "monetary damages" if a state agency's action is "an unreasonable exercise of the state's police power constituting a taking without just compensation." The trial court found the District's actions unlawful because they failed the requirements of *Nollan v. California Coastal Comm'n*, 483 U.S. 825 (1987), and *Dolan v. City of Tigard*, 512 U.S. 374 (1994). The appeal court affirmed, but the supreme court reversed on two grounds: (i) it held that P's claim failed because, unlike in *Nollan* or *Dolan*, the District denied the application; and, (ii) the State Supreme Court held that a demand for money cannot give rise to a claim under *Nollan* and *Dolan*. We granted certiorari.

Issue.

(i)   Must the government's demand for property from a land-use permit applicant satisfy the *Nollan/Dolan* requirements even when it denies the permit?

(ii) Must the government's demand for property from a land-use permit applicant satisfy the *Nollan/Dolan* requirements even when its demand is for money?

Held (Alito, J.). (i) Yes. (ii) Yes. Judgment reversed and case remanded.

Nollan and *Dolan* protect against the misuse of the power of land-use regulation. In those cases, we held that a unit of government may not condition the approval of a land-use permit on the owner's relinquishment of a portion of his property unless there is a "nexus" and "rough proportionality" between the government's demand and the effects of the proposed land use.

Here, D believes that its actions circumvent *Nollan/Dolan* because it did not approve P's application on the condition that he surrender an interest in his land, but instead, after suggesting that P could obtain approval by signing over such an interest, denied his application because he refused to yield. We disagree.

The Florida supreme court distinguished *Nollan* and *Dolan* on two grounds. First, the majority thought it significant that in this case, unlike *Nollan* or *Dolan*, the D did not approve P's application on the condition that he accede to D's demands; instead, D denied his application because P refused to make concessions. Second, the majority drew a distinction between a demand for an interest in real property (what happened in *Nollan* and *Dolan*) and a demand for money.

The unconstitutional conditions doctrine confirms the Constitution's enumerated rights by preventing the government from coercing people into giving them up by overreaching. For example, in *Memorial Hospital v. Maricopa County*, 415 U.S. 250 (1974), we concluded that a county impermissibly burdened the right to travel by extending healthcare benefits only to those indigent sick who had been residents of the county for at least one year.

Nollan and *Dolan* represent a special application of this doctrine that protects the Fifth Amendment right to just compensation for property the government takes when owners apply for land-use permits. The standard set out in *Nollan* and *Dolan* reflects the danger of governmental coercion in this context while accommodating the government's legitimate need to offset the public costs of development through land use exactions.

Land-use permit applicants are especially vulnerable to the type of coercion that the unconstitutional conditions doctrine prohibits because the government often has broad discretion to deny a permit that is worth far more than property it would like to take. By imposing a condition of granting the permit on the owner's deeding over a portion of the land, for example, the government can pressure an owner into voluntarily giving up property for which the Fifth Amendment would otherwise require just compensation. On the other hand, another reality of the process is that permitting various projects threatens to impose costs on the public that dedications of property can offset. Approval of a proposal that would increase traffic congestion, for example, might condition permit approval on the owner's agreement to deed over the land needed to widen a public road. *Nollan* and *Dolan* accommodate both realities by allowing the government to condition approval of a permit on the dedication of property to the public so long as there is a "nexus" and "rough proportionality" between the property that the government demands and the social costs of the applicant's proposal.

The principles that support *Nollan* and *Dolan* do not change depending on whether the government *approves* a permit on the condition that the applicant turn over property or *denies* a permit because the applicant refuses to do so. This distinction would allow the government to avoid the *Nollan/Dolan* limitations just by phrasing its demands for property as conditions precedent to permit approval.

It makes no difference that no property was actually taken. Extortionate demands for property in the land-use permitting context run afoul of the Takings Clause not because they take property but because they impermissibly burden the right not to have property taken without just compensation. Neither does it matter that D might have been able to deny P's application outright. It is settled that the unconstitutional conditions doctrine applies even when the government threatens to withhold a gratuitous benefit.

D concedes that the denial of a permit could give rise to a valid *Nollan/Dolan* claim, but urges that this Court should not review this particular denial because Koontz sued in the wrong court, for the wrong remedy, and at the wrong time. Most of its arguments raise questions of state law. But to the extent that D alleges a federal obstacle to adjudication of P's claim, the Florida courts can consider D's arguments in the first instance on remand. Finally, D errs in arguing that because it gave P another avenue to obtain permit approval, we need not decide whether its demand for offsite improvements satisfied *Nollan* and *Dolan*. Had P been offered at least one alternative that satisfied *Nollan* and *Dolan*, he would not have been subjected to an unconstitutional condition. But D's offer to approve a less ambitious project does not obviate the need to apply *Nollan* and *Dolan* to the conditions it imposed on its approval of the project P actually proposed.

We turn next to the Florida supreme court's alternative holding that P's claim fails because D asked him to spend money rather than give up an easement on his land. D and the dissent take the same position, citing the concurring and dissenting opinions in *Eastern Enterprises v. Apfel*, 524 U.S. 498 (1998), for the proposition that an obligation to spend money can never provide the basis for a takings claim.

In *Eastern Enterprises*, the United States retroactively imposed on a former mining company an obligation to pay for the medical benefits of retired miners and their families. A four-Justice plurality concluded that the statute's imposition of retroactive financial liability was so arbitrary that it violated the Takings Clause. Justice Kennedy concurred in the result, but joined the dissenting Justices in arguing that the Takings Clause does not apply to government-imposed financial obligations that "d[o] not operate upon or alter an identified property interest." Justice Breyer, dissenting, wrote: "The 'private property' upon which the [Takings] Clause traditionally has focused is a specific interest in physical or intellectual property").

D's argument rests on a mistaken premise. Unlike the financial obligation in *Eastern Enterprises*, the demand for money at issue here did "operate upon . . . an identified property interest." It directed P, the property owner, to make a monetary payment. This obligation burdened P's ownership of a specific property. In that regard, this case is similar to cases where we have held that the government must pay just compensation when it takes a lien—a right to receive money that is secured by a particular piece of property. There is a direct link between the government's demand and a specific piece of property. Because of that, this case intersects with the central concern of *Nollan* and *Dolan*: the risk that the government may use its substantial power and discretion in land-use permitting to pursue governmental ends that lack an essential nexus and rough proportionality to the effects of the proposed new use of the specific property at issue, thereby diminishing without justification the value of the property.

P's claim rests on the limited proposition that when the government commands the relinquishment of funds linked to a specific, identifiable property interest such as a bank account or parcel of real property, a "*per se* [takings] approach" is the proper mode of analysis under the Court's precedent.

If we were to accept D's argument, it would open the door to land-use officials evading the limitations of *Nollan* and *Dolan*. Because the government need only provide a permit applicant with one alternative that satisfies the nexus and rough proportionality standards, a permitting authority wishing to exact an easement could simply give the owner a choice of either surrendering an easement or making a payment equal to the easement's value. These "in lieu of" fees are common and identical to other types of land use exactions. For this and the reasons above, we reject D's argument and hold that so-called "monetary exactions" must satisfy the nexus and rough proportionality requirements of *Nollan* and *Dolan*.

R's argument that if money extractions are subject to *Nollan/Dolan* scrutiny, there will be no principled way of distinguishing impermissible land-use exactions from property taxes exaggerates the degree to which that problem is unique to the land-use permitting context and the practical difficulty of distinguishing between the power to tax and the power to take by eminent domain. Taxes and user fees are not takings.

We have repeatedly rejected the dissent's argument that other constitutional doctrines leave no room for the nexus and rough proportionality requirements of *Nollan* and *Dolan*. Mindful of the special vulnerability of land use permit applicants to extortionate demands for money, we do so again today.

We hold that the government's demand for property from a land-use permit applicant must satisfy the requirements of *Nollan* and *Dolan* even when the government denies the permit and even when its demand is for money. The Court expresses no view on the merits of P's claim that R's actions here failed to comply with the principles set forth in this opinion and those two cases. The Florida supreme court's judgment is reversed, and this case is remanded for further proceedings not inconsistent with this opinion.

Dissent (Kagan, Ginsburg, Breyer, Sotomayor, JJ.). My basic disagreement concerns the majority extending *Nollan* and *Dolan* to cases in which the government conditions a permit not on the transfer of real property, but instead on the payment or expenditure of money. *Eastern Enterprises* held that the government may impose ordinary financial obligations without triggering the Takings Clause's protections. With today's ruling running roughshod over that holding, the boundaries of the majority's new rule are uncertain. Its threat is to subject a vast array of land-use regulations, applied daily in States and localities throughout the country, to heightened constitutional scrutiny. That is unwise. Another reason I would affirm is that D never demanded anything in exchange for the permit. The *Nollan-Dolan* standard therefore does not come into play (even assuming that test applies to demands for money). Also, no taking occurred in this case because P never acceded to a demand (even had there been one), and so no property changed hands; as just noted, Koontz therefore cannot claim just compensation under the Fifth Amendment.

Comment. The Court did not rule on the merits that D's actions violated the *Nollan-Dolan* tests. It remanded the case to the Florida court to make this determination.

Table of Cases